D0337564

AGNOSTICISM AND CHRISTIANITY

AND OTHER ESSAYS

Agnosticism and Christianity

AND OTHER ESSAYS

THOMAS HENRY HUXLEY

GREAT MINDS SERIES

PROMETHEUS BOOKS
Buffalo, New York

Published 1992 by Prometheus Books

Editorial offices located at 700 East Amherst Street, Buffalo, New York 14215, and distribution facilities at 59 John Glenn Drive, Amherst, New York 14228.

Library of Congress Cataloging-in-Publication Data

Huxley, Thomas Henry, 1825–1895.
    [Selections. 1992]
    Agnosticism and Christianity, and other essays / Thomas Henry Huxley.
        p.   cm. — (Great minds series)
    Originally published: Lectures and essays. London : C. A. Watt for the Rationalist Press Association, 1931.
    Contents: Autobiography—Lectures on evolution—On the physical basis of life—Naturalism and supernaturalism—The value of witness to the miraculous—Agnosticism—The Christian tradition in relation to Judaic Christianity—Agnosticism and Christianity.
    ISBN 0-87975-749-3 (pbk. : alk. paper)
    1. Religion—Philosophy. 2. Christianity—Controversial literature.
3. Science—Philosophy. 4. Jesus Christ—Rationalistic interpretations.
I. Title. II. Series.
BL51.H9815   1992
210—dc20   92–9345
                                                     CIP

Printed on acid-free paper in the United States of America

Also Available in Prometheus's Great Minds Paperback Series

Charles Darwin
The Origin of Species

Galileo Galilei
Dialogues Concerning Two New Sciences

Edward Gibbon
On Christianity

Ernst Haeckel
The Riddle of the Universe

Ernest Renan
The Life of Jesus

Adam Smith
Wealth of Nations

For a complete list of titles in Prometheus's Great Books in Philosophy and Great Minds Series, see the order form at the back of this volume.

THOMAS HENRY HUXLEY was born on May 4, 1825, in Ealing, England. Although the son of a schoolmaster, Huxley had no formal education as a child; he read voraciously, however, and at a young age began to study medicine. Later, he entered Charing Cross Hospital medical school, taking his degree in 1845.

After passing the Royal College of Surgeons examination in 1846, Huxley was appointed assistant surgeon aboard the H.M.S. *Rattlesnake* on its four-year scientific exploration of the southern seas around Australia. During that time, Huxley made extensive studies of the local marine life, which were later published to great acclaim. These marine studies, as well as Huxley's detailed investigations into comparative anatomy, paleontology, and evolution confirmed forever his reputation as one of England's foremost scientists and controversialists.

Huxley met Charles Darwin in 1851; after the publication of *The Origin of Species* in 1859, Huxley became Darwin's principal defender against the anti-evolutionists, including the Duke of Argyll, William Gladstone, and Bishop Samuel Wilberforce, whom Huxley engaged in a fierce debate over evolution in 1860. In 1863, Huxley published his *Evidence as to Man's Place in Nature,* which argued that human beings were closely related to anthropoid apes. Unorthodox both in science and religion, Huxley attacked what he called "that clericalism, which in England, as everywhere else, and to whatever denomination it may belong, is the deadly enemy of science." In a series of spirited essays and lectures on philosophy, religion, and science delivered in England and abroad, Huxley denounced ortho-

viii THOMAS HENRY HUXLEY

doxy and biblical infallibility; in light of the fact that no irrefutable evidence of the unseen world of religion could be adduced, Huxley espoused a healthy agnosticism concerning the supernatural.

For his work in science, Huxley held several academic positions concurrently and reaped many honors: from 1854 until 1885, he was Lecturer at the Royal School of Mines; Hunterian Professor at the Royal College of Surgeons (1863–1869); and Fullerian Professor at the Royal Institution (1863–1867). In 1883, Huxley was elected president of the Royal Society, a post he held for two years. A tireless popularizer of science as well as a specialist, Huxley served from 1870 to 1872 on the first London school board, and did much to promote educational techniques and the study of biology. Thomas Henry Huxley died on June 29, 1895, in Eastbourne, England.

Huxley's other major works include *Introduction to the Classification of Animals* (1869), *Lay Sermons* (1870), *Manual of the Comparative Anatomy of Vertebrated Animals* (1871), and *Evolution and Ethics* (1893).

CONTENTS

LIST OF ILLUSTRATIONS

LECTURES ON EVOLUTION

[NEW YORK; 1876]

I

THE THREE HYPOTHESES RESPECTING THE HISTORY OF NATURE

WE live in and form part of a system of things of immense diversity and perplexity, which we call Nature; and it is a matter of the deepest interest to all of us that we should form just conceptions of the constitution of that system and of its past history. With relation to this universe, man is, in extent, little more than a mathematical point; in duration but a fleeting shadow; he is a mere reed shaken in the winds of force. But as Pascal long ago remarked, although a mere reed, he is a thinking reed; and in virtue of that wonderful capacity of thought, he has the power of framing for himself a symbolic conception of the universe which, although doubtless highly imperfect and inadequate as a picture of the great whole, is yet sufficient to serve him as a chart for the guidance of his practical affairs. It has taken long ages of toilsome and often fruitless labour to enable man to look steadily at the shifting scenes of the phantasmagoria of Nature, to notice what is fixed among her fluctuations, and what is regular among her apparent irregularities; and it is only comparatively lately, within the last few centuries, that the conception of a universal order and of a definite course of things, which we term the course of Nature, has emerged.

But, once originated, the conception of the constancy of the order of Nature has become the dominant idea of modern thought. To any person who is familiar with the facts upon which that conception is based, and is competent to estimate their significance, it has ceased to be conceivable that chance should have any place in the universe, or that events should depend upon any but the natural sequence of cause and effect. We have come to look upon the present as the child of the past and as the parent of the future; and, as we have excluded chance from a place in the universe, so we ignore, even as a possibility, the notion of any interference with the order of Nature. Whatever may be men's speculative doctrines, it is quite certain that every intelligent person guides his life and risks his fortune upon the belief that the order of Nature is constant, and that the chain of natural causation is never broken.

In fact, no belief which we entertain has so complete a logical basis as that to which I have just referred. It tacitly underlies every process of reasoning; it is the foundation of every act of the will. It is based upon the broadest induction, and it is verified by the most constant, regular, and universal of deductive processes. But we must recollect that any human belief, however broad its basis, however defensible it may seem, is, after all, only a probable belief, and that our widest and safest generalisations are simply statements of the highest degree of probability. Though we are quite clear about the constancy of the order of Nature at the present time, and in the present state of things, it by no means necessarily follows that we are justified in expanding this generalisation into the infinite past, and in denying, absolutely, that there may have been a time when Nature did not follow a fixed order, when the relations of cause and effect were not definite, and when extra-natural agencies interfered with the general course of Nature. Cautious men will allow that a universe so different from that which we know may have existed; just as a very candid thinker may admit that a world in which two and two do not make four, and in which two straight lines do inclose a space, may exist. But the same caution which forces the admission of such possibilities demands a great deal of evidence before it recognises them to be anything more substantial. And when it is asserted that, so many thousand years ago, events occurred in a manner utterly foreign to and inconsistent with the existing laws of Nature, men who, without being particularly cautious, are simply honest thinkers, unwilling to deceive themselves or delude others, ask for trustworthy evidence of the fact.

Did things so happen or did they not? This is a historical question, and one the answer to which must be sought in the same way as the solution of any other historical problem.

So far as I know, there are only three hypotheses which ever have been entertained, or which well can be entertained, respecting the past history of Nature. I will, in the first place, state the hypotheses, and then I will consider what evidence bearing upon them is in our possession, and by what light of criticism that evidence is to be interpreted.

Upon the first hypothesis, the assumption is that phenomena of Nature similar to those exhibited by the present world have always existed; in other words, that the universe has existed from all eternity in what may be broadly termed its present condition.

The second hypothesis is that the present state of things has had only a limited duration; and that at some period in the past a condition of the world essentially similar to that which we now know came into existence, without any precedent condition from which it could have naturally proceeded. The assumption that successive states of Nature have arisen, each without any relation of natural causation to an antecedent state, is a mere modification of this second hypothesis.

The third hypothesis also assumes that the present state of things has had but a limited duration; but it supposes that this state has been evolved by a natural process from an antecedent state, and that from another, and so on; and, on this hypothesis, the attempt to assign any limit to the series of past changes is usually given up.

It is so needful to form clear and distinct notions of what is really meant by each of these hypotheses that I will ask you to imagine what, according to each, would have been visible to a spectator of the events which constitute the history of the earth. On the first hypothesis, however far back in time that spectator might be placed, he would see a world essentially, though perhaps not in all its details, similar to that which now exists. The animals which existed would be the ancestors of those which now live, and similar to them; the plants, in like manner, would be such as we know; and the mountains, plains, and waters would foreshadow the salient features of our present land and water. This view was held more or less distinctly, sometimes combined with the notion of recurrent cycles of change, in ancient times; and its influence has been felt down to the present day. It is worthy of remark that it is a hypothesis which is not inconsistent with the doctrine of Uniformitarianism, with which geologists are familiar. That doctrine was held by Hutton, and in his earlier days by Lyell. Hutton was struck by the demonstration of astronomers that the perturbations of the planetary bodies, however great they may be, yet sooner or later right themselves; and that the solar system possesses a self-adjusting power by which these aberrations are all brought back to a mean condition. Hutton imagined that the like might be true of terrestrial changes; although no one recognised more clearly than he the fact that the dry land is being constantly washed down by rain and rivers and deposited in the sea; and that thus, in a longer or shorter time, the inequalities of the earth's surface must be levelled, and its high lands brought down to the ocean. But, taking into account the internal forces of the earth, which, upheaving the sea-bottom, give rise to new land, he thought that these operations of degradation and elevation might compensate each other; and that thus, for any assignable time, the general features of our planet might remain what they are. And inasmuch as, under these circumstances, there need be no limit to the propagation of animals and plants, it is clear that the consistent working-out of the uniformitarian idea might lead to the conception of the eternity of the world. Not that I mean to say that either Hutton or Lyell held this conception—assuredly not; they would have been the first to repudiate it. Nevertheless, the logical development of some of their arguments tends directly towards this hypothesis.

The second hypothesis supposes that the present order of things, at some no very remote time, had a sudden origin, and that the world, such as it now is, had chaos for its phenomenal antecedent. That is the doctrine which you will find stated most fully and clearly in the immortal poem of John Milton— the English *Divina Commedia*—" Paradise Lost." I believe it is largely to the influence of that remarkable work, combined with the daily teachings to which we have all listened in our childhood, that this hypothesis owes its general wide diffusion as one of the current beliefs of English-speaking people. If you turn to the seventh book of " Paradise Lost," you will find there stated the hypothesis to which I refer, which is briefly this : That this visible universe of ours came into existence at no great distance of time from the present; and that the parts of which it is composed made their appearance, in a certain definite order, in the space of six natural days, in such a manner that on the first of these days light appeared; that on the second the firmament, or sky, separated the waters above, from the waters beneath, the firmament; that on the third day the waters drew away from the dry land, and upon it a varied vegetable life, similar to that which now exists, made its appearance; that the fourth day was signalised by the apparition of the sun, the stars, the moon, and the planets; that on the fifth day aquatic animals originated within the waters; that on the sixth day the earth gave rise to our four-footed terrestrial creatures, and to all varieties of terrestrial animals except birds, which had appeared on the preceding day; and, finally, that man appeared upon the earth, and the emergence of the universe from chaos was finished.   Milton tells us, without the least ambiguity, what a spectator of these marvellous occurrences would have witnessed.   I doubt not that his poem is familiar to all of you, but I should like to recall one passage to your minds, in order that I may be justified in what I have said regarding the perfectly concrete, definite, picture of the origin of the animal world which Milton draws.   He says :—

" The sixth, and of creation last, arose
    With evening harps and matin, when God said,
    ' Let the earth bring forth soul living in her kind,
    Cattle and creeping things, and beast of the earth,
    Each in their kind ! '   The earth obeyed, and, straight
    Opening her fertile womb, teemed at a birth
    Innumerous living creatures, perfect forms,
    Limbed and full-grown.   Out of the ground uprose,
    As from his lair, the wild beast, where he wons
    In forest wild, in thicket, brake, or den;
    Among the trees in pairs they rose, they walked;
    The cattle in the fields and meadows green;
    Those rare and solitary; these in flocks
    Pasturing at once, and in broad herds upsprung.
    The grassy clods now calved; now half appears
    The tawny lion, pawing to get free
    His hinder parts—then springs, as broke from bonds,
    And rampant shakes his brinded mane; the ounce,
    The libbard, and the tiger, as the mole
    Rising, the crumbled earth above them threw
    In hillocks; the swift stag from underground
    Bore up his branching head; scarce from his mould
    Behemoth, biggest born of earth, upheaved
    His vastness; fleeced the flocks and bleating rose
    As plants; ambiguous between sea and land,
    The river-horse and scaly crocodile.
    At once came forth whatever creeps the ground,
    Insect or worm.''

There is no doubt as to the meaning of this statement, nor as to what a man of Milton's genius expected
would have been actually visible to an eye-witness
of this mode of origination of living things.

The third hypothesis, or the hypothesis of evolution, supposes that at any comparatively late period
of past time our imaginary spectator would meet
with a state of things very similar to that which now
obtains; but that the likeness of the past to the
present would gradually become less and less, in
proportion to the remoteness of his period of observation from the present day; that the existing distribution of mountains and plains, of rivers and seas,
would show itself to be the product of a slow process
of natural change operating upon more and more
widely different antecedent conditions of the mineral
framework of the earth; until, at length, in place of
that framework, he would behold only a vast nebulous
mass, representing the constituents of the sun and
of the planetary bodies. Preceding the forms of life
which now exist, our observer would see animals and
plants, not identical with them, but like them,
increasing their differences with their antiquity and,
at the same time, becoming simpler and simpler;
until, finally, the world of life would present nothing
but that undifferentiated protoplasmic matter which,
so far as our present knowledge goes, is the common
foundation of all vital activity.

The hypothesis of evolution supposes that in all
this vast progression there would be no breach of
continuity, no point at which we could say " This is a
natural process," and " This is not a natural process "; but that the whole might be compared to that
wonderful operation of development which may be
seen going on every day under our eyes, in virtue of
which there arises, out of the semi-fluid, comparatively
homogeneous, substance which we call an egg, the
complicated organisation of one of the higher animals.
That, in a few words, is what is meant by the hypothesis of evolution.

I have already suggested that, in dealing with these three hypotheses, in endeavouring to form a judgment as to which of them is the more worthy of belief, or whether none is worthy of belief—in which case our condition of mind should be that suspension of judgment which is so difficult to all but trained intellects—we should be indifferent to all *a priori* considerations. The question is a question of historical fact. The universe has come into existence somehow or other, and the problem is whether it came into existence in one fashion, or whether it came into existence in another; and, as an essential preliminary to further discussion, permit me to say two or three words as to the nature and the kinds of historical evidence.

The evidence as to the occurrence of any event in past time may be ranged under two heads, which, for convenience' sake, I will speak of as testimonial evidence and as circumstantial evidence. By testimonial evidence I mean human testimony; and by circumstantial evidence I mean evidence which is not human testimony. Let me illustrate by a familiar example what I understand by these two kinds of evidence, and what is to be said respecting their value.

Suppose that a man tells you that he saw a person strike another and kill him; that is testimonial evidence of the fact of murder. But it is possible to have circumstantial evidence of the fact of murder; that is to say, you may find a man dying with a wound upon his head having exactly the form and character of the wound which is made by an axe, and, with due care in taking surrounding circumstances into account, you may conclude with the utmost certainty that the man has been murdered; that his death is the consequence of a blow inflicted by another man with that implement. We are very much in the habit of considering circumstantial evidence as of less value than testimonial evidence, and it may be that, where the circumstances are not perfectly clear and intelligible, it is a dangerous and unsafe kind of evidence; but it must not be forgotten that, in many cases, circumstantial is quite as conclusive as testimonial evidence, and that not unfrequently it is a great deal weightier than testimonial evidence. For example, take the case to which I referred just now. The circumstantial evidence may be better and more convincing than the testimonial evidence; for it may be impossible, under the conditions that I have defined, to suppose that the man met his death from any cause but the violent blow of an axe wielded by another man. The circumstantial evidence in favour of a murder having been committed, in that case, is as complete and as convincing as evidence can be. It is evidence which is open to no doubt and to no falsification. But the testimony of a witness is open to multitudinous doubts. He may have been mistaken. He may have been actuated by malice. It has constantly happened that even an accurate man has declared that a thing has happened in this, that, or the other way, when a careful analysis of the circumstantial evidence has shown that it did not happen in that way, but in some other way.

We may now consider the evidence in favour of or against the three hypotheses. Let me first direct your attention to what is to be said about the hypothesis of the eternity of the state of things in which we now live. What will first strike you is that it is a hypothesis which, whether true or false, is not capable of verification by any evidence. For, in order to obtain either circumstantial or testimonial evidence sufficient to prove the eternity of duration of the present state of nature, you must have an eternity of witnesses or an infinity of circumstances, and neither of these is attainable. It is utterly impossible that such evidence should be carried beyond a certain point of time; and all that could be said, at most, would be that, so far as the evidence could be traced, there was nothing to contradict the hypothesis. But when you look, not to the testimonial evidence—

which, considering the relative insignificance of the
antiquity of human records, might not be good for
much in this case—but to the circumstantial evidence, then you find that this hypothesis is absolutely incompatible with such evidence as we have;
which is of so plain and so simple a character that it
is impossible in any way to escape from the conclusions
which it forces upon us.

You are, doubtless, all aware that the outer substance of the earth, which alone is accessible to direct
observation, is not of a homogeneous character, but
that it is made up of a number of layers or strata,
the titles of the principal groups of which are placed
upon the accompanying diagram. Each of these
groups represents a number of beds of sand, of
stone, of clay, of slate, and of various other materials.

On careful examination, it is found that the
materials of which each of these layers of more or
less hard rock are composed are, for the most part,
of the same nature as those which are at present
being formed under known conditions on the surface
of the earth. For example, the chalk, which constitutes a great part of the Cretaceous formation in
some parts of the world, is practically identical in its
physical and chemical characters with a substance
which is now being formed at the bottom of the
Atlantic Ocean, and covers an enormous area; other
beds of rock are comparable with the sands which
are being formed upon sea-shores, packed together,
and so on. Thus, omitting rocks of igneous origin,
it is demonstrable that all these beds of stone, of
which a total of not less than seventy thousand feet
is known, have been formed by natural agencies,
either out of the waste and washing of the dry land,
or else by the accumulation of the exuviæ of plants and
animals. Many of these strata are full of such exuviæ
—the so-called " fossils." Remains of thousands of
species of animals and plants, as perfectly recognisable
as those of existing forms of life which you meet with
in museums, or as the shells which you pick up upon

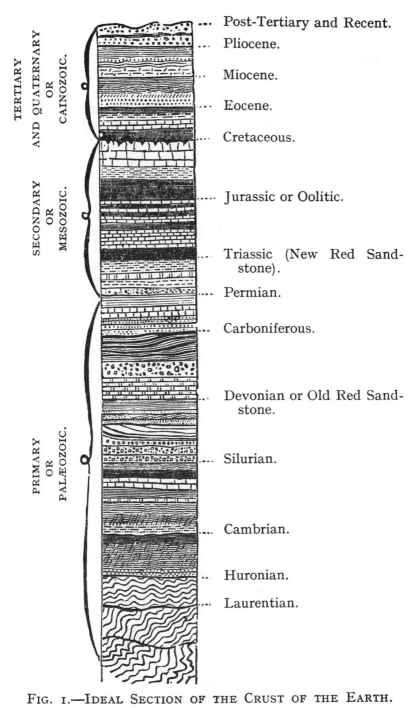

FIG. 1.—IDEAL SECTION OF THE CRUST OF THE EARTH.

the sea-beach, have been imbedded in the ancient sands, or muds, or limestones, just as they are being imbedded now in sandy, or clayey, or calcareous sub-aqueous deposits. They furnish us with a record, the general nature of which cannot be misinterpreted, of the kinds of things that have lived upon the surface of the earth during the time that is registered by this great thickness of stratified rocks. But even a superficial study of these fossils shows us that the animals and plants which live at the present time have had only a temporary duration; for the remains of such modern forms of life are met with, for the most part, only in the uppermost or latest tertiaries, and their number rapidly diminishes in the lower deposits of that epoch. In the older tertiaries, the places of existing animals and plants are taken by other forms, as numerous and diversified as those which live now in the same localities, but more or less different from them; in the mesozoic rocks these are replaced by others yet more divergent from modern types; and in the palæozoic formations the contrast is still more marked. Thus the circumstantial evidence absolutely negatives the conception of the eternity of the present condition of things. We can say, with certainty, that the present condition of things has existed for a comparatively short period; and that, so far as animal and vegetable nature are concerned, it has been preceded by a different condition. We can pursue this evidence until we reach the lowest of the stratified rocks, in which we lose the indications of life altogether. The hypothesis of the eternity of the present state of Nature may therefore be put out of court.

We now come to what I will term Milton's hypothesis—the hypothesis that the present condition of things has endured for a comparatively short time; and, at the commencement of that time, came into existence within the course of six days. I doubt not that it may have excited some surprise in your minds that I should have spoken of this as Milton's hypothesis, rather than that I should have chosen the terms which are more customary, such as " the doctrine of creation," or " the Biblical doctrine," or " the doctrine of Moses," all of which denominations, as applied to the hypothesis to which I have just referred, are certainly much more familiar to you than the title of the Miltonic hypothesis. But I have had what I cannot but think are very weighty reasons for taking the course which I have pursued. In the first place, I have discarded the title of the " doctrine of creation," because my present business is not with the question why the objects which constitute Nature came into existence, but when they came into existence, and in what order. This is as strictly a historical question as the question when the Angles and the Jutes invaded England, and whether they preceded or followed the Romans. But the question about creation is a philosophical problem, and one which cannot be solved, or even approached, by the historical method. What we want to learn is, whether the facts, so far as they are known, afford evidence that things arose in the way described by Milton, or whether they do not; and when that question is settled it will be time enough to inquire into the causes of their origination.

In the second place, I have not spoken of this doctrine as the Biblical doctrine. It is quite true that persons as diverse in their general views as Milton the Protestant and the celebrated Jesuit Father Suarez, each put upon the first chapter of Genesis the interpretation embodied in Milton's poem. It is quite true that this interpretation is that which has been instilled into every one of us in our childhood; but I do not for one moment venture to say that it can properly be called the Biblical doctrine. It is not my business, and does not lie within my competency, to say what the Hebrew text does, and what it does not, signify; moreover, were I to affirm that this is the Biblical doctrine, I should be met by the authority of many eminent scholars, to say nothing of men of science, who, at various times, have absolutely denied that any such doctrine is to be found in Genesis. If we are to listen to many expositors of no mean authority, we must believe that what seems so clearly defined in Genesis— as if very great pains had been taken that there should be no possibility of mistake—is not the meaning of the text at all. The account is divided into periods that we may make just as long or as short as convenience requires. We are also to understand that it is consistent with the original text to believe that the most complex plants and animals may have been evolved by natural processes, lasting for millions of years, out of structureless rudiments. A person who is not a Hebrew scholar can only stand aside and admire the marvellous flexibility of a language which admits of such diverse interpretations. But assuredly, in the face of such contradictions of authority upon matters respecting which he is incompetent to form any judgment, he will abstain, as I do, from giving any opinion.

In the third place, I have carefully abstained from speaking of this as the Mosaic doctrine, because we are now assured upon the authority of the highest critics, and even of dignitaries of the Church, that there is no evidence that Moses wrote the Book of Genesis, or knew anything about it. You will understand that I give no judgment—it would be an impertinence upon my part to volunteer even a suggestion—upon such a subject. But, that being the state of opinion among the scholars and the clergy, it is well for the unlearned in Hebrew lore, and for the laity, to avoid entangling themselves in such a vexed question. Happily, Milton leaves us no excuse for doubting what he means, and I shall therefore be safe in speaking of the opinion in question as the Miltonic hypothesis.

Now we have to test that hypothesis. For my part, I have no prejudice one way or the other. If there is evidence in favour of this view, I am burdened by no theoretical difficulties in the way of accepting it; but there must be evidence. Scientific men get an awkward habit—no, I won't call it that, for it is a valuable habit—of believing nothing unless there is evidence for it; and they have a way of looking upon belief which is not based upon evidence, not only as illogical, but as immoral. We will, if you please, test this view by the circumstantial evidence alone; for, from what I have said, you will understand that I do not propose to discuss the question of what testimonial evidence is to be adduced in favour of it. If those whose business it is to judge are not at one as to the authenticity of the only evidence of that kind which is offered, nor as to the facts to which it bears witness, the discussion of such evidence is superfluous.

But I may be permitted to regret this necessity of rejecting the testimonial evidence the less, because the examination of the circumstantial evidence leads to the conclusion, not only that it is incompetent to justify the hypothesis, but that, so far as it goes, it is contrary to the hypothesis.

The considerations upon which I base this conclusion are of the simplest possible character. The Miltonic hypothesis contains assertions of a very definite character relating to the succession of living forms. It is stated that plants, for example, made their appearance upon the third day, and not before. And you will understand that what the poet means by plants are such plants as now live, the ancestors, in the ordinary way of propagation of like by like, of the trees and shrubs which flourish in the present world. It must needs be so; for, if they were different, either the existing plants have been the result of a separate origination since that described by Milton, of which we have no record, nor any ground for supposition that such an occurrence has taken place; or else they have arisen by a process of evolution from the original stocks.

In the second place, it is clear that there was no

animal life before the fifth day, and that on the fifth day aquatic animals and birds appeared. And it is further clear that terrestrial living things, other than birds, made their appearance upon the sixth day and not before. Hence, it follows that if, in the large mass of circumstantial evidence as to what really has happened in the past history of the globe, we find indications of the existence of terrestrial animals other than birds at a certain period, it is perfectly certain that all that has taken place since that time must be referred to the sixth day.

In the great Carboniferous formation, whence America derives so vast a proportion of her actual and potential wealth, in the beds of coal which have been formed from the vegetation of that period, we find abundant evidence of the existence of terrestrial animals. They have been described, not only by European, but by your own, naturalists. There are to be found numerous insects allied to our cock-roaches. There are to be found spiders and scorpions of large size, the latter so similar to existing scorpions that it requires the practised eye of the naturalist to distinguish them. Inasmuch as these animals can be proved to have been alive in the Carboniferous epoch, it is perfectly clear that, if the Miltonic account is to be accepted, the huge mass of rocks extending from the middle of the Palæozoic formations to the uppermost members of the series must belong to the day which is termed by Milton the sixth. But, further, it is expressly stated that aquatic animals took their origin on the fifth day, and not before; hence, all formations in which remains of aquatic animals can be proved to exist, and which therefore testify that such animals lived at the time when these formations were in course of deposition, must have been deposited during or since the period which Milton speaks of as the fifth day. But there is absolutely no fossiliferous formation in which the remains of aquatic animals are absent. The oldest fossils in the Silurian rocks are exuviæ of marine animals; and if the view which is entertained by Principal Dawson and Dr. Carpenter respecting the nature of the *Eozoön* be well founded, aquatic animals existed at a period as far antecedent to the deposition of the coal as the coal is from us; inasmuch as the *Eozoön* is met with in those Laurentian strata which lie at the bottom of the series of stratified rocks. Hence it follows, plainly enough, that the whole series of stratified rocks, if they are to be brought into harmony with Milton, must be referred to the fifth and sixth days, and that we cannot hope to find the slightest trace of the products of the earlier days in the geological record. When we consider these simple facts, we see how absolutely futile are the attempts that have been made to draw a parallel between the story told by so much of the crust of the earth as is known to us and the story which Milton tells. The whole series of fossiliferous stratified rocks must be referred to the last two days; and neither the Carboniferous nor any other formation can afford evidence of the work of the third day.

Not only is there this objection to any attempt to establish a harmony between the Miltonic account and the facts recorded in the fossiliferous rocks, but there is a further difficulty. According to the Miltonic account, the order in which animals should have made their appearance in the stratified rocks would be this : Fishes, including the great whales, and birds; after them, all varieties of terrestrial animals except birds. Nothing could be further from the facts as we find them : we know of not the slightest evidence of the existence of birds before the Jurassic, or perhaps the Triassic, formation; while terrestrial animals, as we have just seen, occur in the Carboniferous rocks.

If there were any harmony between the Miltonic account and the circumstantial evidence, we ought to have abundant evidence of the existence of birds in the Carboniferous, the Devonian, and the Silurian rocks. I need hardly say that this is not the case and that not a trace of birds makes its appearance until the far later period which I have mentioned.

And again, if it be true that all varieties of fishes and the great whales, and the like, made their appearance on the fifth day, we ought to find the remains of these animals in the older rocks—in those which were deposited before the Carboniferous epoch. Fishes we do find, in considerable number and variety; but the great whales are absent, and the fishes are not such as now live. Not one solitary species of fish now in existence is to be found in the Devonian or Silurian formations. Hence we are introduced afresh to the dilemma which I have already placed before you : either the animals which came into existence on the fifth day were not such as those which are found at present, are not the direct and immediate ancestors of those which now exist; in which case, either fresh creations of which nothing is said, or a process of evolution, must have occurred; or else the whole story must be given up, as not only devoid of any circumstantial evidence, but contrary to such evidence as exists.

I placed before you in a few words, some little time ago, a statement of the sum and substance of Milton's hypothesis. Let me now try to state, as briefly, the effect of the circumstantial evidence bearing upon the past history of the earth which is furnished, without the possibility of mistake, with no chance of error as to its chief features, by the stratified rocks. What we find is that the great series of formations represents a period of time of which our human chronologies hardly afford us a unit of measure. I will not pretend to say how we ought to estimate this time, in millions or in billions of years. For my purpose, the determination of its absolute duration is wholly unessential. But that the time was enormous there can be no question.

It results from the simplest methods of interpretation that, leaving out of view certain patches of metamorphosed rocks and certain volcanic products, all that is now dry land has once been at the bottom of the waters. It is perfectly certain that, at a comparatively recent period of the world's history—the Cretaceous epoch—none of the great physical features which at present mark the surface of the globe existed. It is certain that the Rocky Mountains were not. It is certain that the Himalaya Mountains were not. It is certain that the Alps and the Pyrenees had no existence. The evidence is of the plainest possible character, and is simply this : We find raised up on the flanks of these mountains, elevated by the forces of upheaval which have given rise to them, masses of Cretaceous rock which formed the bottom of the sea before those mountains existed. It is therefore clear that the elevatory forces which gave rise to the mountains operated subsequently to the Cretaceous epoch ; and that the mountains themselves are largely made up of the materials deposited in the sea which once occupied their place. As we go back in time, we meet with constant alternations of sea and land, of estuary and open ocean ; and, in correspondence with these alternations, we observe the changes in the fauna and flora to which I have referred.

But the inspection of these changes gives us no right to believe that there has been any discontinuity in natural processes. There is no trace of general cataclysms, of universal deluges, or sudden destructions of a whole fauna or flora. The appearances which were formerly interpreted in that way have all been shown to be delusive, as our knowledge has increased and as the blanks which formerly appeared to exist between the different formations have been filled up. That there is no absolute break between formation and formation, that there has been no sudden disappearance of all the forms of life and replacement of them by others, but that changes have gone on slowly and gradually, that one type has died out and another has taken its place, and that thus, by insensible degrees, one fauna has been replaced by another, are conclusions strengthened by constantly increasing evidence. So that within the whole of the immense period indicated by the fossiliferous stratified rocks, there is assuredly not the slightest proof of any break in the uniformity of Nature's operations, no indication that events have followed other than a clear and orderly sequence.

That, I say, is the natural and obvious teaching of the circumstantial evidence contained in the stratified rocks. I leave you to consider how far, by any ingenuity of interpretation, by any stretching of the meaning of language, it can be brought into harmony with the Miltonic hypothesis.

There remains the third hypothesis, that of which I have spoken as the hypothesis of evolution; and I purpose that, in lectures to come, we should discuss it as carefully as we have considered the other two hypotheses. I need not say that it is quite hopeless to look for testimonial evidence of evolution. The very nature of the case precludes the possibility of such evidence, for the human race can no more be expected to testify to its own origin than a child can be tendered as a witness of its own birth. Our sole inquiry is, what foundation circumstantial evidence lends to the hypothesis, or whether it lends none, or whether it controverts the hypothesis. I shall deal with the matter entirely as a question of history. I shall not indulge in the discussion of any speculative probabilities. I shall not attempt to show that Nature is unintelligible unless we adopt some such hypothesis. For anything I know about the matter, it may be the way of Nature to be un-intelligible; she is often puzzling, and I have no reason to suppose that she is bound to fit herself to our notions.

I shall place before you three kinds of evidence entirely based upon what is known of the forms of animal life which are contained in the series of stratified rocks. I shall endeavour to show you that there is one kind of evidence which is neutral, which neither helps evolution nor is inconsistent with it. I shall then bring forward a second kind of evidence which indicates a strong probability in favour of evolution, but does not prove it; and, lastly, I shall adduce a third kind of evidence which, being as complete as any evidence which we can hope to obtain upon such a subject and being wholly and strikingly in favour of evolution, may fairly be called demonstrative evidence of its occurrence.

II

THE HYPOTHESIS OF EVOLUTION. THE NEUTRAL AND THE FAVOURABLE EVIDENCE

In the preceding lecture I pointed out that there are three hypotheses which may be entertained, and which have been entertained, respecting the past history of life upon the globe. According to the first of these hypotheses, living beings, such as now exist, have existed from all eternity upon this earth. We tested that hypothesis by the circumstantial evidence, as I called it, which is furnished by the fossil remains contained in the earth's crust, and we found that it was obviously untenable. I then proceeded to consider the second hypothesis, which I termed the Miltonic hypothesis, not because it is of any particular consequence whether John Milton seriously entertained it or not, but because it is stated in a clear and unmistakable manner in his great poem. I pointed out to you that the evidence at our command as completely and fully negatives that hypothesis as it did the preceding one. And I confess that I had too much respect for your intelligence to think it necessary to add that the negation was equally clear and equally valid whatever the source from which that hypothesis might be derived, or whatever the authority by which it might be supported. I further stated that, according to the third hypothesis, or that of evolution, the existing state of things is the last term of a long series of states, which, when traced back, would be found to show no interruption and no breach in the continuity of natural causation. I propose, in the present and the following lecture, to test this hypothesis rigorously by the evidence at command, and to inquire how far that evidence can be said to be indifferent to it, how far it can be said to be favourable to it, and, finally, how far it can be said to be demonstrative.

From almost the origin of the discussions about the existing condition of the animal and vegetable worlds and the causes which have determined that condition, an argument has been put forward as an objection to evolution, which we shall have to consider very seriously. It is an argument which was first clearly stated by Cuvier in his criticism of the doctrines propounded by his great contemporary, Lamarck. The French expedition to Egypt had called the attention of learned men to the wonderful store of antiquities in that country, and there had been brought back to France numerous mummified corpses of the animals which the ancient Egyptians revered and preserved, and which, at a reasonable computation, must have lived not less than three or four thousand years before the time at which they were thus brought to light. Cuvier endeavoured to test the hypothesis that animals have undergone gradual and progressive modifications of structure, by comparing the skeletons and such other parts of the mummies as were in a fitting state of preservation with the corresponding parts of the representatives of the same species now living in Egypt. He arrived at the conviction that no appreciable change had taken place in these animals in the course of this considerable lapse of time, and the justice of his conclusion is not disputed.

It is obvious that, if it can be proved that animals have endured, without undergoing any demonstrable change of structure, for so long a period as four thousand years, no form of the hypothesis of evolution which assumes that animals undergo a constant and necessary progressive change can be tenable; unless, indeed, it be further assumed that four thousand years is too short a time for the production of a change sufficiently great to be detected.

But it is no less plain that if the process of evolution of animals is not independent of surrounding conditions; if it may be indefinitely hastened or retarded by variations in these conditions; or if evolution is simply a process of accommodation to varying conditions; the argument against the hypothesis of evolution based on the unchanged character of the Egyptian fauna is worthless. For the monuments which are coeval with the mummies testify as strongly to the absence of change in the physical geography and the general conditions of the land of Egypt, for the time in question, as the mummies do to the unvarying characters of its living population.

The progress of research since Cuvier's time has supplied far more striking examples of the long duration of specific forms of life than those which are furnished by the mummified Ibises and Crocodiles of Egypt. A remarkable case is to be found in your own country, in the neighbourhood of the falls of Niagara. In the immediate vicinity of the whirlpool, and again upon Goat Island, in the superficial deposits which cover the surface of the rocky subsoil in those regions, there are found remains of animals in perfect preservation, and among them shells belonging to exactly the same species as those which at present inhabit the still waters of Lake Erie. It is evident, from the structure of the country, that these animal remains were deposited in the beds in which they occur at a time when the lake extended over the region in which they are found. This involves the conclusion that they lived and died before the falls had cut their way back through the gorge of Niagara; and, indeed, it has been determined that when these animals lived the falls of Niagara must have been at least six miles further down the river than they are at present. Many computations have been made of the rate at which the falls are thus cutting their way back. Those computations have varied greatly, but I believe

I am speaking within the bounds of prudence if I assume that the falls of Niagara have not retreated at a greater pace than about a foot a year. Six miles, speaking roughly, are thirty thousand feet; thirty thousand feet, at a foot a year, gives thirty thousand years; and thus we are fairly justified in concluding that no less a period than this has passed since the shell-fish whose remains are left in the beds to which I have referred were living creatures.

But there is still stronger evidence of the long duration of certain types. I have already stated that, as we work our way through the great series of the Tertiary formations, we find many species of animals identical with those which live at the present day, diminishing in numbers, it is true, but still existing, in a certain proportion, in the oldest of the Tertiary rocks. Furthermore, when we examine the rocks of the Cretaceous epoch, we find the remains of some animals which the closest scrutiny cannot show to be, in any important respect, different from those which live at the present time. That is the case with one of the cretaceous lamp-shells (*Terebratula*) which has continued to exist unchanged, or with insignificant variations, down to the present day. Such is the case with the *Globigerinæ*, the skeletons of which, aggregated together, form a large proportion of our English chalk. Those *Globigerinæ* can be traced down to the *Globigerinæ* which live at the surface of the present great oceans, and the remains of which, falling to the bottom of the sea, give rise to a chalky mud. Hence it must be admitted that certain existing species of animals show no distinct sign of modification, or transformation, in the course of a lapse of time as great as that which carries us back to the Cretaceous period; and which, whatever its absolute measure, is certainly vastly greater than thirty thousand years.

There are groups of species so closely allied together, that it needs the eye of a naturalist to distinguish them one from another. If we disregard the small differences which separate these forms, and consider all the species of such groups as modifications of one type, we shall find that, even among the higher animals, some types have had a marvellous duration.   In the chalk, for example, there is found a fish belonging to the highest and the most differentiated group of osseous fishes, which goes by the name of *Beryx*.   The remains of that fish are among the most beautiful and well-preserved of the fossils found in our English chalk. It can be studied anatomically, so far as the hard parts are concerned, almost as well as if it were a recent fish.   But the genus *Beryx* is represented, at the present day, by very closely allied species which are living in the Pacific and Atlantic Oceans.   We may go still farther back.   I have already referred to the fact that the Carboniferous formations, in Europe and in America, contain the remains of scorpions in an admirable state of preservation, and that those scorpions are hardly distinguishable from such as now live.   I do not mean to say that they are not different, but close scrutiny is needed in order to distinguish them from modern scorpions.

More than this.   At the very bottom of the Silurian series, in beds which are by some authorities referred to the Cambrian formation, where the signs of life begin to fail us—even there, among the few and scanty animal remains which are discoverable, we find species of molluscous animals which are so closely allied to existing forms that at one time they were grouped under the same generic name.   I refer to the well-known *Lingula* of the *Lingula* flags, lately, in consequence of some slight differences, placed in the new genus *Lingulella*.   Practically, it belongs to the same great generic group as the *Lingula*, which is to be found at the present day upon your own shores and those of many other parts of the world.

The same truth is exemplified if we turn to certain great periods of the earth's history—as, for example, the Mesozoic epoch.   There are groups of reptiles, such as the *Ichthyosauria* and the *Plesiosauria*, which appear shortly after the commencement of this epoch, and they occur in vast numbers. They disappear with the chalk, and throughout the whole of the great series of Mesozoic rocks they present no such modifications as can safely be considered evidence of progressive modification.

Facts of this kind are undoubtedly fatal to any form of the doctrine of evolution which postulates the supposition that there is an intrinsic necessity, on the part of animal forms which have once come into existence, to undergo continual modification; and they are as distinctly opposed to any view which involves the belief that such modification as may occur must take place, at the same rate, in all the different types of animal or vegetable life. The facts, as I have placed them before you, obviously directly contradict any form of the hypothesis of evolution which stands in need of these two postulates.

But one great service that has been rendered by Mr. Darwin to the doctrine of evolution in general is this: he has shown that there are two chief factors in the process of evolution: one of them is the tendency to vary, the existence of which in all living forms may be proved by observation; the other is the influence of surrounding conditions upon what I may call the parent form and the variations which are thus evolved from it. The cause of the production of variations is a matter not at all properly understood at present. Whether variation depends upon some intricate machinery—if I may use the phrase—of the living organism itself, or whether it arises through the influence of conditions upon that form, is not certain, and the question may, for the present, be left open. But the important point is that, granting the existence of the tendency to the production of variations, then, whether the variations which are produced shall survive and supplant the parent, or whether the parent form shall survive and supplant the variations, is a matter which depends entirely on those conditions which give rise to the struggle for existence. If the surrounding conditions are such that the parent form is more competent to deal with them, and flourish in them than the derived forms, then, in the struggle for existence, the parent form will maintain itself, and the derived forms will be exterminated.   But if, on the contrary, the conditions are such as to be more favourable to a derived than to the parent form, the parent form will be extirpated, and the derived form will take its place.   In the first case there will be no progression, no change of structure, through any imaginable series of ages; in the second place there will be modification of change and form.

Thus the existence of these persistent types, as I have termed them, is no real obstacle in the way of the theory of evolution.   Take the case of the scorpions to which I have just referred.   No doubt, since the Carboniferous epoch, conditions have always obtained such as existed when the scorpions of that epoch flourished : conditions in which scorpions find themselves better off, more competent to deal with the difficulties in their way, than any variation from the scorpion type which they may have produced; and, for that reason, the scorpion type has persisted, and has not been supplanted by any other form.   And there is no reason, in the nature of things, why, as long as this world exists, if there be conditions more favourable to scorpions than to any variation which may arise from them, these forms of life should not persist.

Therefore, the stock objection to the hypothesis of evolution, based on the long duration of certain animal and vegetable types, is no objection at all.   The facts of this character—and they are numerous—belong to that class of evidence which I have called indifferent.   That is to say, they may afford no direct support to the doctrine of evolution, but they are capable of being interpreted in perfect consistency with it.

There is another order of facts belonging to the class of negative or indifferent evidence.   The great group of Lizards, which abound in the present world, extends through the whole series of formations as far back as the Permian, or latest Palæozoic, epoch. These Permian lizards differ astonishingly little from the lizards which exist at the present day.   Comparing the amount of the differences between them and modern lizards, with the prodigious lapse of time between the Permian epoch and the present age, it may be said that the amount of change is insignificant. But, when we carry our researches farther back in time, we find no trace of lizards, nor of any true reptile whatever, in the whole mass of formations beneath the Permian.

Now, it is perfectly clear that if our palæontological collections are to be taken, even approximately, as an adequate representation of all the forms of animals and plants that have ever lived; and if the record furnished by the known series of beds of stratified rock covers the whole series of events which constitute the history of life on the globe, such a fact as this directly contravenes the hypothesis of evolution; because this hypothesis postulates that the existence of every form must have been preceded by that of some form little different from it.   Here, however, we have to take into consideration that important truth so well insisted upon by Lyell and by Darwin— the imperfection of the geological record.   It can be demonstrated that the geological record must be incomplete; that it can only preserve remains found in certain favourable localities and under particular conditions; that it must be destroyed by processes of denudation, and obliterated by processes of metamorphosis.   Beds of rock of any thickness, crammed full of organic remains, may yet, either by the percolation of water through them or by the influence of subterranean heat, lose all trace of these remains, and present the appearance of beds of rock formed under conditions in which living forms were absent.   Such metamorphic rocks occur in formations of all ages; and in various cases there are very good grounds for the belief that they have contained organic remains, and that those remains have been absolutely obliterated.

I insist upon the defects of the geological record the more because those who have not attended to these matters are apt to say, " It is all very well, but when you get into a difficulty with your theory of evolution you appeal to the incompleteness and the imperfection of the geological record ; " and I want to make it perfectly clear to you that this imperfection is a great fact, which must be taken into account in all our speculations, or we shall constantly be going wrong.

You see the singular series of footmarks, drawn of its natural size, in the large diagram hanging up here

FIG. 2.—TRACKS OF BRONTOZOUM.

(Fig. 2), which I owe to the kindness of my friend Professor Marsh, with whom I had the opportunity recently of visiting the precise locality in Massachusetts in which these tracks occur. I am, therefore, able to give you my own testimony, if needed, that the diagram accurately represents what we saw. The valley of the Connecticut is classical ground for the geologist. It contains great beds of sandstone, covering many square miles, which have evidently formed a part of an ancient sea-shore, or, it may be, lake-shore. For a certain period of time after their deposition, these beds have remained sufficiently soft to receive the impressions of the feet of whatever animals walked over them, and to preserve them afterwards, in exactly the same way as such impressions are at this hour preserved on the shores of the Bay of Fundy and elsewhere. The diagram represents the track of some gigantic animal, which walked on its hind legs. You see the series of marks made alternately by the right and by the left foot; so that from one impression to the other of the three-toed foot on the same side is one stride, and that stride, as we measured it, is six feet nine inches. I leave you, therefore, to form an impression of the magnitude of the creature which, as it walked along the ancient shore, made these impressions.

Of such impressions there are untold thousands upon these sandstones. Fifty or sixty different kinds have been discovered, and they cover vast areas. But, up to this present time, not a bone, not a fragment, of any one of the animals which left these great footmarks has been found; in fact, the only animal remains which have been met with in all these deposits, from the time of their discovery to the present day— though they have been carefully hunted over—is a fragmentary skeleton of one of the smaller forms. What has become of the bones of all these animals? You see, we are not dealing with little creatures, but with animals that make a step of six feet nine inches; and their remains must have been left somewhere. The probability is that they have been dissolved away and completely lost.

I have had occasion to work out the nature of fossil remains of which there was nothing left except casts of the bones, the solid material of the skeleton having been dissolved out by percolating water. It was a chance, in this case, that the sandstone happened to be of such a constitution as to set, and to allow the bones to be afterwards dissolved out, leaving cavities of the exact shape of the bones. Had that constitution been other than what it was, the bones would have been dissolved, the layers of sandstone would have fallen together into one mass, and not the slightest indication that the animal had existed would have been discoverable.

I know of no more striking evidence than these facts afford, of the caution which should be used in drawing the conclusion, from the absence of organic remains in a deposit, that animals or plants did not exist at the time it was formed. I believe that, with a right understanding of the doctrine of evolution on the one hand, and a just estimation of the importance of the imperfection of the geological record on the other, all difficulty is removed from the kind of evidence to which I have adverted; and that we are justified in believing that all such cases are examples of what I have designated negative or indifferent evidence—that is to say, they in no way directly advance the hypothesis of evolution, but they are not to be regarded as obstacles in the way of our belief in that doctrine.

I now pass on to the consideration of those cases which, for reasons which I will point out to you by and by, are not to be regarded as demonstrative of the truth of evolution, but which are such as must exist if evolution be true, and which therefore are, upon the whole, evidence in favour of the doctrine. If the doctrine of evolution be true, it follows that, however diverse the different groups of animals and of plants may be, they must all, at one time or other, have been connected by gradational forms; so that, from the highest animals, whatever they may be, down to the lowest speck of protoplasmic matter in which life can be manifested, a series of gradations, leading from one end of the series to the other, either exists or has existed. Undoubtedly that is a necessary postulate of the doctrine of evolution. But when we look upon living Nature as it is, we find a totally different state of things. We find that animals and plants fall into groups, the different members of which are pretty closely allied together, but which are separated by definite, larger or smaller, breaks, from other groups. In other words, no intermediate forms which bridge over these gaps or intervals are, at present, to be met with.

To illustrate what I mean : Let me call your attention to those vertebrate animals which are most familiar to you, such as mammals, birds, and reptiles.

At the present day, these groups of animals are perfectly well defined from one another. We know of no animal now living which, in any sense, is intermediate between the mammal and the bird, or between the bird and the reptile; but, on the contrary, there are many very distinct anatomical peculiarities, well-defined marks, by which the mammal is separated from the bird, and the bird from the reptile. The distinctions are obvious and striking if you compare the definitions of these great groups as they now exist.

The same may be said of many of the subordinate groups, or orders, into which these great classes are divided. At the present time, for example, there are numerous forms of non-ruminant pachyderms, or what we may call, broadly, the pig tribe, and many varieties of ruminants. These latter have their definite characteristics, and the former have their distinguishing peculiarities. But there is nothing that fills up the gap between the ruminants and the pig tribe. The two are distinct. Such also is the case in respect of the minor groups of the class of reptiles. The existing fauna shows us crocodiles, lizards, snakes, and tortoises; but no connecting link between the crocodile and lizard, nor between the lizard and snake, nor between the snake and the crocodile, nor between any two of these groups. They are separated by absolute breaks. If, then, it could be shown that this state of things had always existed, the fact would be fatal to the doctrine of evolution. If the intermediate gradations, which the doctrine of evolution requires to have existed between these groups, are not to be found anywhere in the records of the past history of the globe, their absence is a strong and weighty negative argument against evolution; while, on the other hand, if such intermediate forms are to be found, that is so much to the good of evolution; although, for reasons which I will lay before you by and by, we must be cautious in our estimate of the evidential cogency of facts of this kind.

It is a very remarkable circumstance that, from the commencement of the serious study of fossil remains, in fact from the time when Cuvier began his brilliant researches upon those found in the quarries of Montmartre, palæontology has shown what she was going to do in this matter, and what kind of evidence it lay in her power to produce.

I said just now that in the existing Fauna the group of pig-like animals and the group of ruminants are entirely distinct; but one of the first of Cuvier's discoveries was an animal which he called the *Anoplotherium*, and which proved to be, in a great many important respects, intermediate in character between the pigs on the one hand and the ruminants on the other. Thus, research into the history of the past did, to a certain extent, tend to fill up the breach between the group of ruminants and the group of pigs. Another remarkable animal restored by the great French palæontologist, the *Palæotherium*, similarly tended to connect together animals to all appearance so different as the rhinoceros, the horse, and the tapir. Subsequent research has brought to light multitudes of facts of the same order; and, at the present day, the investigations of such anatomists as Rütimeyer and Gaudry have tended to fill up, more and more, the gaps in our existing series of mammals, and to connect groups formerly thought to be distinct.

But I think it may have an especial interest if, instead of dealing with these examples, which would require a great deal of tedious osteological detail, I take the case of birds and reptiles; groups which, at the present day, are so clearly distinguished from one another that there are perhaps no classes of animals which, in popular apprehension, are more completely separated. Existing birds, as you are aware, are covered with feathers; their anterior extremities, specially and peculiarly modified, are converted into wings, by the aid of which most of them are able to fly; they walk upright upon two legs; and these limbs, when they are considered anatomically, present a great number of exceedingly remarkable peculiarities, to which I may have occasion to advert incidentally as I go on, and which are not met with, even approximately, in any existing forms of reptiles. On the other hand, existing reptiles have no feathers. They may have naked skins, or be covered with horny scales, or bony plates, or with both. They possess no wings; they neither fly by means of their fore-limbs, nor habitually walk upright upon their hind-limbs; and the bones of their legs present no such modifications as we find in birds. It is impossible to imagine any two groups more definitely and distinctly separated, notwithstanding certain characters which they possess in common.

As we trace the history of birds back in time, we find their remains, sometimes in great abundance, throughout the whole extent of the tertiary rocks; but, so far as our present knowledge goes, the birds of the tertiary rocks retain the same essential characters as the birds of the present day. In other words, the tertiary birds come within the definition of the class constituted by existing birds, and are as much separated from reptiles as existing birds are. Not very long ago no remains of birds had been found below the tertiary rocks, and I am not sure but that some persons were prepared to demonstrate that they could not have existed at an earlier period. But in the course of the last few years such remains have been discovered in England; though, unfortunately, in so imperfect and fragmentary a condition that it is impossible to say whether they differed from existing birds in any essential character or not. In your country the development of the cretaceous series of rocks is enormous; the conditions under which the later cretaceous strata have been deposited are highly favourable to the preservation of organic remains; and the researches, full of labour and risk, which have been carried on by Professor Marsh in these cretaceous rocks of Western America, have rewarded him with the discovery of forms of birds of which we had hitherto no conception.   By his kindness, I am enabled to place before you a restoration of one of these extraordinary birds, every part of which can be

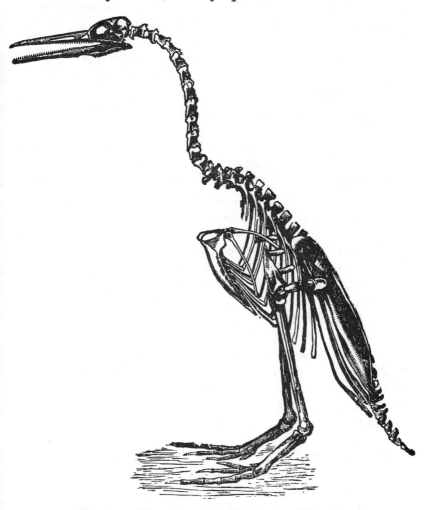

FIG. 3.—HESPERORNIS REGALIS (Marsh).

thoroughly justified by the more or less complete skeletons, in a very perfect state of preservation, which he has discovered.   This *Hesperornis* (Fig. 3), which measured between five and six feet in length, is astonishingly like our existing divers or grebes in a

great many respects; so like them, indeed, that, had
the skeleton of *Hesperornis* been found in a museum
without its skull, it probably would have been placed
in the same group of birds as the divers and grebes
of the present day.[1]   But *Hesperornis* differs from all
existing birds, and so far resembles reptiles, in one
important particular—it is provided with teeth.   The
long jaws are armed with teeth which have curved
crowns and thick roots (Fig. 4), and are not set in
distinct sockets, but are lodged in a groove.   In
possessing true teeth, the *Hesperornis* differs from every
existing bird, and from every bird yet discovered in
the tertiary formations, the tooth-like serrations of the
jaws in the *Odontopteryx* of the London clay being
mere processes of the bony substance of the jaws, and
not teeth in the proper sense of the word.   In view
of the characteristics of this bird we are therefore
obliged to modify the definitions of the classes of
birds and reptiles.   Before the discovery of *Hesperornis*, the definition of the class Aves based upon
our knowledge of existing birds might have been
extended to all birds; it might have been said that
the absence of teeth was characteristic of the class of
birds; but the discovery of an animal which, in every
part of its skeleton, closely agrees with existing birds,
and yet possesses teeth, shows that there were ancient
birds which, in respect of possessing teeth, approached
reptiles more nearly than any existing bird does, and
to that extent, diminishes the *hiatus* between the two
classes.

The same formation has yielded another bird,
Ichthyornis (Fig. 5), which also possesses teeth; but
the teeth are situated in distinct sockets, while those
of *Hesperornis* are not so lodged.   The latter also has
such very small, almost rudimentary, wings that it

[1] The absence of any keel on the breast-bone and some
other osteological peculiarities, observed by Professor Marsh,
however, suggest that *Hesperornis* may be a modification of a
less specialised group of birds than that to which these
existing aquatic birds belong.

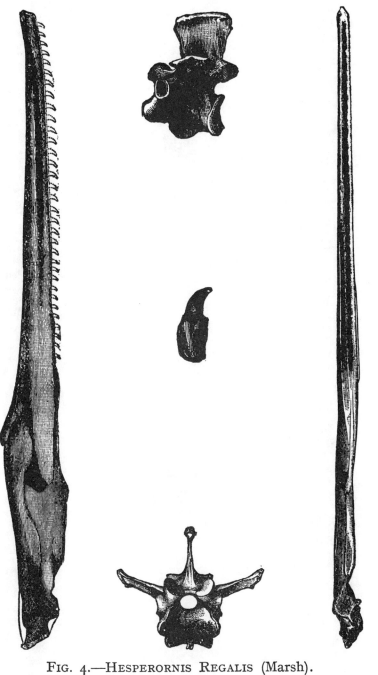

FIG. 4.—HESPERORNIS REGALIS (Marsh).

(Side and upper views of half the lower jaw; side and end views of a vertebra
and a separate tooth.)

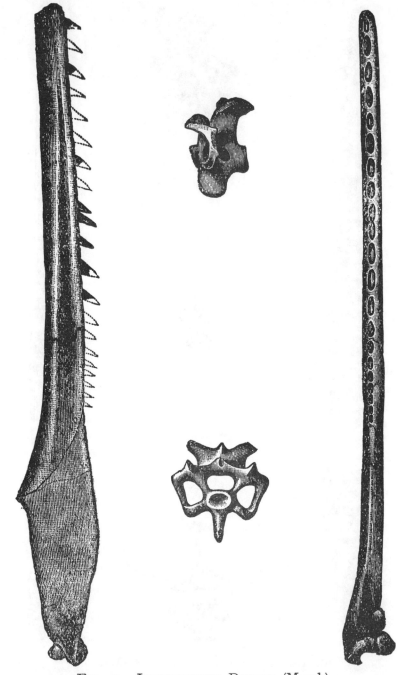

FIG. 5.—ICHTHYORNIS DISPAR (Marsh).

(Side and upper views of half the lower jaw; and side and end views of a vertebra.)

must have been chiefly a swimmer and a diver like a Penguin; while *Ichthyornis* has strong wings, and no doubt possessed corresponding powers of flight. *Ichthyornis* also differed in the fact that its vertebræ have not the peculiar characters of the vertebræ of existing and of all known tertiary birds, but were concave at each end. This discovery leads us to make a further modification in the definition of the group of birds, and to part with another of the characters by which almost all existing birds are distinguished from reptiles.

Apart from the few fragmentary remains from the English greensand, to which I have referred, the Mesozoic rocks, older than those in which *Hesperornis* and *Ichthyornis* have been discovered, have afforded no certain evidence of birds, with the remarkable exception of the Solenhofen slates. These so-called slates are composed of a fine-grained calcareous mud which has hardened into lithographic stone, and in which organic remains are almost as well preserved as they would be if they had been imbedded in so much plaster of Paris. They have yielded the *Archæopteryx*, the existence of which was first made known by the finding of a fossil feather, or rather of the impression of one. It is wonderful enough that such a perishable thing as a feather, and nothing more, should be discovered; yet for a long time, nothing was known of this bird except its feather. But by and by a solitary skeleton was discovered which is now in the British Museum. The skull of this solitary specimen is unfortunately wanting, and it is therefore uncertain whether the *Archæopteryx* possessed teeth or not.[1] But the remainder of the skeleton is so well preserved as to leave no doubt respecting the main features of the animal, which are very singular. The feet are not only altogether bird-

[1] A second specimen, discovered in 1877, and at present in the Berlin Museum, shows an excellently preserved skull with teeth : and three digits, all terminated by claws, in the fore-limb. 1893.

like, but have the special characters of the feet of
perching birds, while the body had a clothing of true
feathers. Nevertheless, in some other respects,
Archæopteryx is unlike a bird and like a reptile. There
is a long tail composed of many vertebræ. The
structure of the wing differs in some very remarkable
respects from that which it presents in a true bird.
In the latter, the end of the wing answers to the thumb
and two fingers of my hand; but the metacarpal
bones, or those which answer to the bones of the
fingers which lie in the palm of the hand, are fused
together into one mass; and the whole apparatus,
except the last joints of the thumb, is bound up in a
sheath of integument, while the edge of the hand
carries the principal quill feathers. In the *Archæopteryx*, the upper-arm bone is like that of a bird;
and the two bones of the forearm are more or less
like those of a bird, but the fingers are not bound
together—they are free. What their number may
have been is uncertain; but several, if not all, of
them were terminated by strong curved claws, not
like such as are sometimes found in birds, but such
as reptiles possess; so that in the *Archæopteryx* we
have an animal which, to a certain extent, occupies
a midway place between a bird and a reptile. It is a
bird so far as its foot and sundry other parts of its
skeleton are concerned; it is essentially and thoroughly
a bird by its feathers; but it is much more properly
a reptile in the fact that the region which represents
the hand has separate bones, with claws resembling
those which terminate the fore-limb of a reptile.
Moreover, it had a long, reptile-like tail with a fringe
of feathers on each side; while in all true birds
hitherto known the tail is relatively short, and the
vertebræ which constitute its skeleton are generally
peculiarly modified.

Like the *Anoplotherium* and the *Palæotherium*,
therefore, *Archæopteryx* tends to fill up the interval
between groups which, in the existing world, are
widely separated, and to destroy the value of the

definitions of zoological groups based upon our knowledge of existing forms. And such cases as these constitute evidence in favour of evolution, in so far as they prove that, in former periods of the world's history, there were animals which overstepped the bounds of existing groups, and tended to merge them into larger assemblages. They show that animal organisation is more flexible than our knowledge of recent forms might have led us to believe; and that many structural permutations and combinations, of which the present world gives us no indication, may nevertheless have existed.

But it by no means follows, because the *Palæotherium* has much in common with the horse on the one hand, and with the rhinoceros on the other, that it is the intermediate form through which rhinoceroses have passed to become horses, or *vice versa;* on the contrary, any such supposition would certainly be erroneous. Nor do I think it likely that the transition from the reptile to the bird has been effected by such a form as *Archæopteryx.* And it is convenient to distinguish these intermediate forms between two groups, which do not represent the actual passage from the one group to the other, as *intercalary* types, from those *linear* types which, more or less approximately, indicate the nature of the steps by which the transition from one group to the other was effected.

I conceive that such linear forms, constituting a series of natural gradations between the reptile and the bird, and enabling us to understand the manner in which the reptilian has been metamorphosed into the bird type, are really to be found among a group of ancient and extinct terrestrial reptiles known as the *Ornithoscelida.* The remains of these animals occur throughout the series of Mesozoic formations, from the Trias to the Chalk, and there are indications of their existence even in the later Palæozoic strata.

Most of these reptiles at present known are of great size, some having attained a length of forty feet, or perhaps more. The majority resembled lizards and crocodiles in their general form, and many of them were, like crocodiles, protected by an armour of heavy bony plates. But in others the hind-limbs elongate and the fore-limbs shorten, until their relative proportions approach those which are observed in the short-winged, flightless, ostrich tribe among birds.

The skull is relatively light, and in some cases the jaws, though bearing teeth, are beak-like at their extremities, and appear to have been enveloped in a horny sheath. In the part of the vertebral column which lies between the haunch bones, and is called the sacrum, a number of vertebræ may unite together into one whole, and in this respect, as in some details of its structure, the sacrum of these reptiles approaches that of birds.

But it is in the structure of the pelvis and of the hind-limb that some of these ancient reptiles present the most remarkable approximation to birds, and clearly indicate the way by which the most specialised and characteristic features of the bird may have been evolved from the corresponding parts in the reptile.

In Fig. 6, the pelvis and hind-limbs of a crocodile, a three-toed bird, and an ornithoscelidan, are represented side by side; and, for facility of comparison, in corresponding positions; but it must be recollected that while the position of the bird's limb is natural, that of the crocodile is not so. In the bird the thigh-bone lies close to the body, and the metatarsal bones of the foot (ii., iii., iv., Fig. 6) are, ordinarily, raised into a more or less vertical position; in the crocodile the thigh-bone stands out at an angle from the body, and the metatarsal bones (i., ii., iii., iv., Fig. 6) lie flat on the ground. Hence, in the crocodile the body usually lies squat between the legs, while in the bird it is raised upon the hind legs, as upon pillars.

In the crocodile the pelvis is obviously composed of three bones on each side : the ilium (*Il.*), the pubis (*Pb.*), and the ischium (*Is.*). In the adult bird there appears to be but one bone on each side. The examination of the pelvis of a chick, however, shows

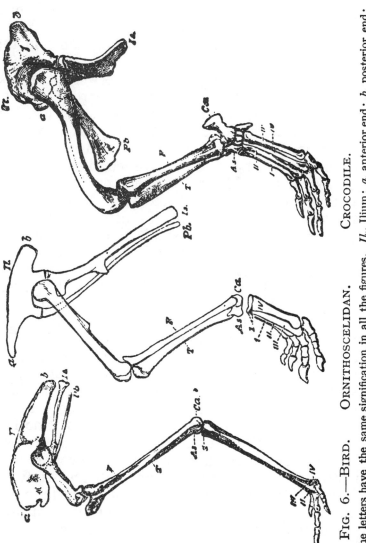

FIG. 6.—BIRD.   ORNITHOSCELIDAN.   CROCODILE.

(The letters have the same signification in all the figures. *Il*, Iliun; *a*, anterior end; *b*, posterior end; *Is.*, ischium; *Pb*,, pubis; *T*, tibia; *F*, fibula; *As.*, astragalus; *Ca.*, calcaneum; I, distal portion of the tarsus ; i., ii., iii., iv., metatarsal bones.)

that each half is made up of three bones, which answer to those which remain distinct throughout life in the crocodile. There is, therefore, a fundamental identity of plan in the construction of the pelvis of both bird and reptile; though the differences in form, relative size, and direction of the corresponding bones in the two cases are very great.

But the most striking contrast between the two lies in the bones of the leg and of that part of the foot termed the tarsus, which follows upon the leg. In the crocodile the fibula (*F*) is relatively large, and its lower end is complete. The tibia (*T*) has no marked crest at its upper end, and its lower end is narrow and not pulley-shaped. There are two rows of separate tarsal bones (*As.*, *Ca.*, &c.) and four distinct meta-tarsal bones, with a rudiment of a fifth.

In the bird the fibula is small, and its lower end diminishes to a point. The tibia has a strong crest at its upper end, and its lower extremity passes into a broad pulley. There seem at first to be no tarsal bones; and only one bone, divided at the end into three heads for the three toes which are attached to it, appears in the place of the metatarsus.

In a young bird, however, the pulley-shaped apparent end of the tibia is a distinct bone, which represents the bones marked *As.*, *Ca.*, in the crocodile; while the apparently single metatarsal bone consists of three bones, which early unite with one another and with an additional bone, which represents the lower row of bones in the tarsus of the crocodile.

In other words, it can be shown by the study of development that the bird's pelvis and hind limb are simply extreme modifications of the same fundamental plan as that upon which these parts are modelled in reptiles.

On comparing the pelvis and hind limb of the ornithoscelidan with that of the crocodile on the one side and that of the bird on the other (Fig. 6), it is obvious that it represents a middle term between the two. The pelvic bones approach the form of those of the birds, and the direction of the pubis and ischium is nearly that which is characteristic of birds; the thigh-bone, from the direction of its head, must have lain close to the body; the tibia has a great crest; and immovably fitted on to its lower end there is a pulley-shaped bone, like that of the bird, but remaining distinct. The lower end of the fibula is much more slender, proportionally, than in the crocodile. The metatarsal bones have such a form

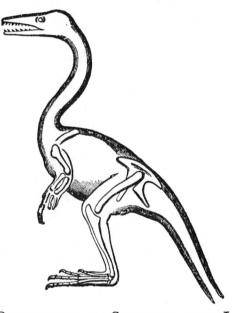

FIG. 7.—RESTORATION OF COMPSOGNATHUS LONGIPES.

that they fit together immovably, though they do not enter into bony union; the third toe is, as in the bird, longest and strongest. In fact, the ornithoscelidan limb is comparable to that of an unhatched chick.

Taking all these facts together, it is obvious that the view which was entertained by Mantell, and the probability of which was demonstrated by your own distinguished anatomist, Leidy, while much additional evidence in the same direction has been furnished by Professor Cope, that some of these animals may have walked upon their hind legs, as birds do, acquires great weight. In fact, there can be no reasonable doubt that one of the smaller forms of the *Ornithoscelida, Compsognathus*, the almost entire skeleton of which has been discovered in the Solenhofen slates, was a bipedal animal. The parts of this skeleton are somewhat twisted out of their natural relations, but the accompanying figure gives a just view of the general form of *Compsognathus* and of the proportions of its limbs; which, in some respects, are more completely bird-like than those of other *Ornithoscelida*.

We have had to stretch the definition of the class of birds so as to include birds with teeth and birds with paw-like fore-limbs and long tails. There is no evidence that *Compsognathus* possessed feathers; but, if it did, it would be hard indeed to say whether it should be called a reptilian bird or an avian reptile.

As *Compsognathus* walked upon its hind legs, it must have made tracks like those of birds. And as the structure of the limbs of several of the gigantic *Ornithoscelida*, such as *Iguanodon*, leads to the conclusion that they also may have constantly, or occasionally, assumed the same attitude, a peculiar interest attaches to the fact that in the Wealden strata of England there are to be found gigantic footsteps, arranged in order like those of the *Brontozoum*, and which there can be no reasonable doubt were made by some of the *Ornithoscelida*, the remains of which are found in the same rocks. And, knowing that reptiles that walked upon their hind-legs and shared many of the anatomical characters of birds did once exist, it becomes a very important question whether the tracks in the Trias of Massachusetts, to which I referred some time ago, and which formerly used to be unhesitatingly ascribed to birds, may not all have been made by Ornithoscelidan reptiles; and whether, if we could obtain the skeletons of the animals which made these tracks, we should not find in them the actual steps of the evolutional process by which reptiles gave rise to birds.

The evidential value of the facts I have brought

forward in this lecture must be neither over- nor under-estimated. It is not historical proof of the occurrence of the evolution of birds from reptiles, for we have no safe ground for assuming that true birds had not made their appearance at the commencement of the Mesozoic epoch. It is, in fact, quite possible that all these more or less aviform reptiles of the Mesozoic epoch are not terms in the series of progression from birds to reptiles at all, but simply the more or less modified descendants of Palæozoic forms through which that transition was actually effected.

We are not in a position to say that the known *Ornithoscelida* are intermediate in the order of their appearance on the earth between reptiles and birds. All that can be said is that, if independent evidence of the actual occurrence of evolution is producible, then these intercalary forms remove every difficulty in the way of understanding what the actual steps of the process, in the case of birds, may have been.

That intercalary forms should have existed in ancient times is a necessary consequence of the truth of the hypothesis of evolution; and, hence, the evidence I have laid before you in proof of the existence of such forms, is, so far as it goes, in favour of that hypothesis.

There is another series of extinct reptiles which may be said to be intercalary between reptiles and birds, in so far as they combine some of the characters of both these groups; and which, as they possessed the power of flight, may seem, at first sight, to be nearer representatives of the forms by which the transition from the reptile to the bird was effected, than the *Ornithoscelida*.

These are the *Pterosauria*, or Pterodactyles, the remains of which are met with throughout the series of Mesozoic rocks, from the lias to the chalk, and some of which attain a great size, their wings having a span of eighteen or twenty feet. These animals, in the form and proportions of the head and neck relatively to the body, and in the fact that the ends of the jaws

were often, if not always, more or less extensively
ensheathed in horny beaks, remind us of birds.
Moreover, their bones contained air cavities, rendering

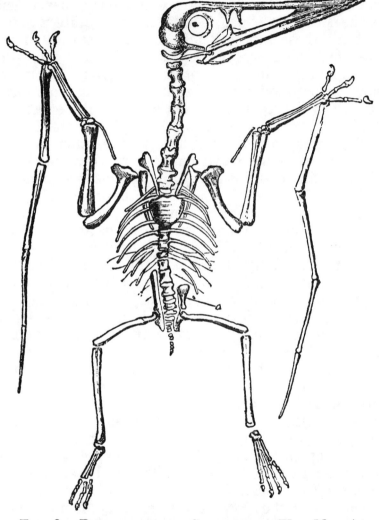

Fig. 8.—Pterodactylus Spectabilis (Von Meyer).

them specifically lighter, as is the case in most birds.
The breast-bone was large and keeled, as in most
birds and in bats, and the shoulder-girdle is strikingly
similar to that of ordinary birds.   But it seems to me

that the special resemblance of pterodactyles to birds ends here, unless I may add the entire absence of teeth which characterises the great pterodactyles (*Pteranodon*) discovered by Professor Marsh. All other known pterodactyles have teeth lodged in sockets. In the vertebral column and the hind-limbs there are no special resemblances to birds, and when we turn to the wings, they are found to be constructed on a totally different principle from those of birds.

There are four fingers. These four fingers are large, and three of them—those which answer to the thumb and two following fingers in my hand—are terminated by claws, while the fourth is enormously prolonged and converted into a great jointed style. You see at once, from what I have stated about a bird's wing, that there could be nothing less like a bird's wing than this is. It was concluded by general reasoning that this finger had the office of supporting a web which extended between it and the body. An existing specimen proves that such was really the case, and that the pterodactyles were devoid of feathers, but that the fingers supported a vast web like that of a bat's wing; in fact, there can be no doubt that this ancient reptile flew after the fashion of a bat.

Thus, though the pterodactyle is a reptile which has become modified in such a manner as to enable it to fly, and therefore, as might be expected, presents some points of semblance to other animals which fly, it has, so to speak, gone off the line which leads directly from reptiles to birds, and has become disqualified for the changes which lead to the characteristic organisation of the latter class. Therefore, viewed in relation to the classes of reptiles and birds, the pterodactyles appear to me to be, in a limited sense, intercalary forms; but they are not even approximately linear, in the sense of exemplifying those modifications of structure through which the passage from the reptile to the bird took place.

III

THE DEMONSTRATIVE EVIDENCE OF EVOLUTION

THE occurrence of historical facts is said to be demonstrated when the evidence that they happened is of such a character as to render the assumption that they did not happen in the highest degree improbable; and the question I now have to deal with is, whether evidence in favour of the evolution of animals of this degree of cogency is, or is not, obtainable from the record of the succession of living forms which is presented to us by fossil remains.

Those who have attended to the progress of palæontology are aware that evidence of the character which I have defined has been produced in considerable and continually-increasing quantity during the last few years. Indeed, the amount and the satisfactory nature of that evidence are somewhat surprising, when we consider the conditions under which alone we can hope to obtain it.

It is obviously useless to seek for such evidence except in localities in which the physical conditions have been such as to permit of the deposit of an unbroken, or but rarely interrupted, series of strata through a long period of time; in which the group of animals to be investigated has existed in such abundance as to furnish the requisite supply of remains; and in which, finally, the materials composing the strata are such as to ensure the preservation of these remains in a tolerably perfect and undisturbed state.

It so happens that the case which, at present, most nearly fulfils all these conditions is that of the series of extinct animals which culminates in the horses; by which term I mean to denote not merely the domestic animals with which we are all so well acquainted, but their allies, the ass, zebra, quagga, and the like. In short, I use "horses" as the equivalent of the technical name *Equidæ*, which is applied to the whole group of existing equine animals.

The horse is in many ways a remarkable animal; not least so in the fact that it presents us with an example of one of the most perfect pieces of machinery in the living world. In truth, among the works of human ingenuity it cannot be said that there is any locomotive so perfectly adapted to its purposes, doing so much work with so small a quantity of fuel, as this machine of Nature's manufacture—the horse. And, as a necessary consequence of any sort of perfection, of mechanical perfection as of others, you find that the horse is a beautiful creature, one of the most beautiful of all land animals. Look at the perfect balance of its form, and the rhythm and force of its action. The locomotive machinery is, as you are aware, resident in its slender fore- and hind-limbs; they are flexible and elastic levers, capable of being moved by very powerful muscles; and, in order to supply the engines which work these levers with the force which they expend, the horse is provided with a very perfect apparatus for grinding its food and extracting therefrom the requisite fuel.

Without attempting to take you very far into the region of osteological detail, I must nevertheless trouble you with some statements respecting the anatomical structure of the horse; and more especially will it be needful to obtain a general conception of the structure of its fore- and hind-limbs, and of its teeth. But I shall only touch upon those points which are absolutely essential to our inquiry.

Let us turn in the first place to the fore-limb. In most quadrupeds, as in ourselves, the fore-arm contains distinct bones called the radius and the ulna. The corresponding region in the horse seems at first to possess but one bone. Careful observation, however, enables us to distinguish in this bone a part which clearly answers to the upper end of the ulna. This is closely united with the chief mass of the bone which represents the radius, and runs out into a slender shaft which may be traced for some distance downwards upon the back of the radius, and then in most cases thins out and vanishes. It takes still more trouble to make sure of what is nevertheless the fact—that a small part of the lower end of the bone of the horse's fore-arm, which is only distinct in a very young foal, is really the lower extremity of the ulna.

What is commonly called the knee of a horse is its wrist. The " cannon bone " answers to the middle bone of the five metacarpal bones, which support the palm of the hand in ourselves. The " pastern," " coronary," and " coffin " bones of veterinarians answer to the joints of our middle fingers, while the hoof is simply a greatly enlarged and thickened nail. But if what lies below the horse's " knee " thus corresponds to the middle finger in ourselves, what has become of the four other fingers or digits? We find in the places of the second and fourth digits only two slender splint-like bones, about two-thirds as long as the cannon-bone, which gradually taper to their lower ends and bear no finger joints, or, as they are termed, phalanges. Sometimes, small bony or gristly nodules are to be found at the bases of these two metacarpal splints, and it is probable that these represent rudiments of the first and fifth toes. Thus, the part of the horse's skeleton which corresponds with that of the human hand contains one overgrown middle digit, and at least two imperfect lateral digits; and these answer, respectively, to the third, the second, and the fourth fingers in man.

Corresponding modifications are found in the hindlimb. In ourselves, and in most quadrupeds, the leg contains two distinct bones, a large bone, the tibia, and a smaller and more slender bone, the fibula. But, in the horse, the fibula seems, at first, to be reduced to its upper end; a short slender bone united with the tibia, and ending in a point below, occupying its place. Examination of the lower end of a young foal's shin-bone, however, shows a distinct portion of osseous matter, which is the lower end of the fibula; so that the apparently single lower end of the shinbone is really made up of the coalesced ends of the tibia and fibula, just as the apparently single lower end of the fore-arm bone is composed of the coalesced radius and ulna.

The heel of the horse is the part commonly known as the hock. The hinder cannon-bone answers to the middle metatarsal bone of the human foot, the pastern, coronary, and coffin bones to the middle toe bones; the hind hoof to the nail, as in the fore-foot. And, as in the fore-foot, there are merely two splints to represent the second and the fourth toes. Sometimes a rudiment of a fifth toe appears to be traceable.

The teeth of a horse are not less peculiar than its limbs. The living engine, like all others, must be well stoked if it is to do its work; and the horse, if it is to make good its wear and tear, and to exert the enormous amount of force required for its propulsion, must be well and rapidly fed. To this end, good cutting instruments and powerful and lasting crushers are needful. Accordingly, the twelve cutting teeth of a horse are close-set, and concentrated in the fore-part of its mouth, like so many adzes or chisels. The grinders or molars are large, and have an extremely complicated structure, being composed of a number of different substances of unequal hardness. The consequence of this is that they wear away at different rates; and, hence, the surface of each grinder is always as uneven as that of a good millstone.

I have said that the structure of the grinding teeth is very complicated, the harder and the softer parts being, as it were, interlaced with one another. The result of this is that, as the tooth wears, the crown presents a peculiar pattern, the nature of which is not very easily deciphered at first, but which it is important we should understand clearly. Each grinding tooth of the upper jaw has an *outer wall* so shaped that, on the worn crown, it exhibits the form of two crescents, one in front and one behind, with their concave sides turned outwards. From the inner side of the front crescent a crescentic *front ridge* passes inwards and backwards, and its inner face enlarges into a strong longitudinal fold or *pillar*. From the front part of the hinder crescent a *back ridge* takes a like direction, and also has its *pillar*.

The deep interspaces or *valleys* between these ridges and the outer wall are filled by bony substance, which is called *cement*, and coats the whole tooth.

The pattern of the worn face of each grinding tooth of the lower jaw is quite different. It appears to be formed of two crescent-shaped ridges, the convexities of which are turned outwards. The free extremity of each crescent has a *pillar*, and there is a large double *pillar* where the two crescents meet. The whole structure is, as it were, imbedded in cement, which fills up the valleys, as in the upper grinders.

If the grinding faces of an upper and of a lower molar of the same side are applied together, it will be seen that the apposed ridges are nowhere parallel, but that they frequently cross; and that thus, in the act of mastication, a hard surface in the one is constantly applied to a soft surface in the other, and *vice versa*. They thus constitute a grinding apparatus of great efficiency, and one which is repaired as fast as it wears, owing to the long-continued growth of the teeth.

Some other peculiarities of the dentition of the horse must be noticed, as they bear upon what I shall have to say by and by. Thus the crowns of the cutting teeth have a peculiar deep pit, which gives rise to the well-known " mark " of the horse. There is a large space between the outer incisors and the front grinder. In this space the adult male horse presents, near the incisors on each side, above and below, a canine or " tush," which is commonly absent in mares. In a young horse, moreover, there is not unfrequently to be seen in front of the first grinder a very small tooth, which soon falls out. If this small tooth be counted as one, it will be found that there are seven teeth behind the canine on each side; namely, the small tooth in question, and the six great grinders, among which, by an unusual peculiarity, the foremost tooth is rather larger than those which follow it.

I have now enumerated those characteristic structures of the horse which are of most importance for the purpose we have in view.

To any one who is acquainted with the morphology of vertebrated animals, they show that the horse deviates widely from the general structure of mammals; and that the horse type is, in many respects, an extreme modification of the general mammalian plan. The least modified mammals, in fact, have the radius and ulna, the tibia and fibula, distinct and separate. They have five distinct and complete digits on each foot, and no one of these digits is very much larger than the rest. Moreover, in the least modified mammals the total number of the teeth is very generally forty-four, while in horses the usual number is forty, and in the absence of the canines, it may be reduced to thirty-six; the incisor teeth are devoid of the fold seen in those of the horse: the grinders regularly diminish in size from the middle of the series to its front end; while their crowns are short, early attain their full length, and exhibit simple ridges or tubercles in place of the complex foldings of the horse's grinders.

Hence the general principles of the hypothesis of evolution lead to the conclusion that the horse must have been derived from some quadruped which possessed five complete digits on each foot; which had the bones of the fore-arm and of the leg complete and separate; and which possessed forty-four teeth, among which the crowns of the incisors and grinders had a simple structure; while the latter gradually increased in size from before backwards, at any rate in the anterior part of the series, and had short crowns.

And if the horse has been thus evolved, and the remains of the different stages of its evolution have been preserved, they ought to present us with a series of forms in which the number of the digits becomes reduced; the bones of the fore-arm and leg gradually take on the equine condition; and the form and arrangement of the teeth successively approximate to those which obtain in existing horses.

Let us turn to the facts, and see how far they fulfil these requirements of the doctrine of evolution.

In Europe abundant remains of horses are found in the Quaternary and later Tertiary strata as far as the Pliocene formation. But these horses, which are so common in the cave-deposits and in the gravels of Europe, are in all essential respects like existing horses. And that is true of all the horses of the latter part of the Pliocene epoch. But in deposits which belong to the earlier Pliocene and later Miocene epochs, and which occur in Britain, in France, in Germany, in Greece, in India, we find animals which are extremely like horses—which, in fact, are so similar to horses that you may follow descriptions given in works upon the anatomy of the horse upon the skeletons of these animals—but which differ in some important particulars. For example, the structure of their fore- and hind-limbs is somewhat different. The bones which in the horse are represented by two splints, imperfect below, are as long as the middle metacarpal and metatarsal bones; and attached to the extremity of each is a digit with three joints of the same general character as those of the middle digit, only very much smaller. These small digits are so disposed that they could have had but very little functional importance, and they must have been rather of the nature of the dew-claws, such as are to be found in many ruminant animals. The *Hipparion*, as the extinct European three-toed horse is called, in fact, presents a foot similar to that of the American *Protohippus* (Fig. 9), except that in the *Hipparion* the smaller digits are situated farther back, and are of smaller proportional size, than in the *Protohippus*.

The ulna is slightly more distinct than in the horse; and the whole length of it, as a very slender shaft intimately united with the radius, is completely traceable. The fibula appears to be in the same condition as in the horse. The teeth of the *Hipparion* are essentially similar to those of the horse, but the pattern of the grinders is in some respects a little more complex, and there is a depression on the face of the skull in front of the orbit, which is not seen in existing horses.

In the earlier Miocene, and perhaps the later Eocene deposits of some parts of Europe, another extinct animal has been discovered, which Cuvier, who first described some fragments of it, considered to be a *Palæotherium*. But as further discoveries threw new light upon its structure, it was recognised as a distinct genus, under the name of *Anchitherium*.

In its general characters, the skeleton of *Anchitherium* is very similar to that of the horse. In fact, Lartet and De Blainville called it *Palæotherium equinum* or *hippoides ;* and De Christol, in 1847, said that it differed from *Hipparion* in little more than the characters of its teeth, and gave it the name of *Hipparitherium*. Each foot possesses three complete toes; while the lateral toes are much larger in proportion to the middle toe than in *Hipparion*, and doubtless rested on the ground in ordinary locomotion.

The ulna is complete and quite distinct from the radius, though firmly united with the latter. The fibula seems also to have been complete. Its lower end, though intimately united with that of the tibia, is clearly marked off from the latter bone.

There are forty-four teeth. The incisors have no strong pit. The canines seem to have been well developed in both sexes. The first of the seven grinders, which, as I have said, is frequently absent, and, when it does exist, is small in the horse, is a good-sized and permanent tooth, while the grinder which follows it is but little larger than the hinder ones. The crowns of the grinders are short, and though the fundamental pattern of the horse-tooth is discernible, the front and back ridges are less curved, the accessory pillars are wanting, and the valleys, much shallower, are not filled up with cement.

Seven years ago, when I happened to be looking critically into the bearing of palæontological facts upon the doctrine of evolution, it appeared to me that the *Anchitherium*, the *Hipparion*, and the modern horses constitute a series in which the modifications of structure coincide with the order of chronological occurrence, in the manner in which they must coincide if the modern horses really are the result of the gradual metamorphosis, in the course of the Tertiary epoch, of a less specialised ancestral form. And I found by correspondence with the late eminent French anatomist and palæontologist, M. Lartet, that he had arrived at the same conclusion from the same data.

That the *Anchitherium* type had become metamorphosed into the *Hipparion* type, and the latter into the *Equine* type, in the course of that period of time which is represented by the latter half of the Tertiary deposits, seemed to me to be the only explanation of the facts for which there was even a shadow of probability.[1]

And, hence, I have ever since held that these facts afford evidence of the occurrence of evolution, which, in the sense already defined, may be termed demonstrative.

All who have occupied themselves with the structure of *Anchitherium*, from Cuvier onwards, have acknowledged its many points of likeness to a well-known genus of extinct Eocene mammals, *Palæotherium*. Indeed, as we have seen, Cuvier regarded his remains of *Anchitherium* as those of a species of *Palæotherium*. Hence, in attempting to trace the

---

[1] I use the word " type " because it is highly probable that many forms of *Anchitherium*-like and *Hipparion*-like animals existed in the Miocene and Pliocene epochs, just as many species of the horse tribe exist now; and it is highly improbable that the particular species of *Anchitherium* or *Hipparion* which happen to have been discovered should be precisely those which have formed part of the direct line of the horse's pedigree.

pedigree of the horse beyond the Miocene epoch and the Anchitheroid form, I naturally sought among the various species of Palæotheroid animals for its nearest ally, and I was led to conclude that the *Palæotherium minus* (*Plagiolophus*) represented the next step more nearly than any form then known.

I think that this opinion was fully justifiable; but the progress of investigation has thrown an unexpected light on the question, and has brought us much nearer than could have been anticipated to a knowledge of the true series of the progenitors of the horse.

You are all aware that when your country was first discovered by Europeans there were no traces of the existence of the horse in any part of the American continent. The accounts of the conquest of Mexico dwell upon the astonishment of the natives of that country when they first became acquainted with that astounding phenomenon—a man seated upon a horse. Nevertheless, the investigations of American geologists have proved that the remains of horses occur in the most superficial deposits of both North and South America, just as they do in Europe. Therefore, for some reason or other—no feasible suggestion on that subject, so far as I know, has been made—the horse must have died out on this continent at some period preceding the discovery of America. Of late years there has been discovered in your Western Territories that marvellous accumulation of deposits, admirably adapted for the preservation of organic remains, to which I referred the other evening, and which furnishes us with a consecutive series of records of the fauna of the older half of the Tertiary epoch, for which we have no parallel in Europe. They have yielded fossils in an excellent state of conservation and in unexampled number and variety. The researches of Leidy and others have shown that forms allied to the *Hipparion* and the *Anchitherium* are to be found among these remains. But it is only recently that the admirably conceived and most

thoroughly and patiently worked-out investigations
of Professor Marsh have given us a just idea of the
vast fossil wealth, and of the scientific importance,
of these deposits. I have had the advantage of
glancing over the collections in Yale Museum; and
I can truly say that, so far as my knowledge extends,
there is no collection from any one region and series
of strata comparable for extent, or for the care with
which the remains have been got together, or for
their scientific importance, to the series of fossils
which he has deposited there. This vast collection
has yielded evidence bearing upon the question of
the pedigree of the horse of the most striking character. It tends to show that we must look to
America, rather than to Europe, for the original
seat of the equine series; and that the archaic forms
and successive modifications of the horse's ancestry
are far better preserved here than in Europe.

Professor Marsh's kindness has enabled me to put
before you a diagram, every figure in which is an
actual representation of some specimen which is to
be seen at Yale at this present time (Fig. 9).

The succession of forms which he has brought
together carries us from the top to the bottom of
the Tertiaries. Firstly, there is the true horse.
Next we have the American Pliocene form of the
horse (*Pliohippus*); in the conformation of its limbs
it presents some very slight deviations from the
ordinary horse, and the crowns of the grinding teeth
are shorter. Then comes the *Protohippus*, which
represents the European *Hipparion*, having one large
digit and two small ones on each foot, and the general
characters of the fore-arm and leg to which I have
referred. But it is more valuable than the European
Hipparion, for the reason that it is devoid of some
of the peculiarities of that form—peculiarities which
tend to show that the European *Hipparion* is rather
a member of a collateral branch, than a form in the
direct line of succession. Next, in the backward
order in time, is the *Miohippus*, which corresponds

Fore Foot. Hind Foot. Fore-arm. Leg.   Upper Molar.   Lower Molar.

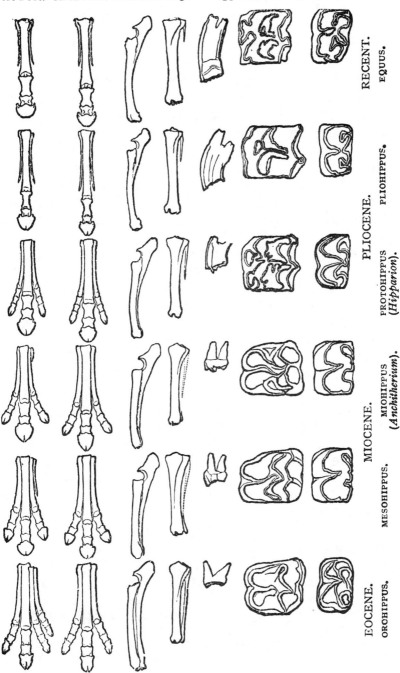

FIG. 9.

pretty nearly with the *Anchitherium* of Europe. It presents three complete toes—one large median and two smaller lateral ones; and there is a rudiment of that digit which answers to the little finger of the human hand.

The European record of the pedigree of the horse stops here; in the American Tertiaries, on the contrary, the series of ancestral equine forms is continued into the Eocene formations. An older Miocene form, termed *Mesohippus*, has three toes in front, with a large splint-like rudiment representing the little finger, and three toes behind. The radius and ulna, the tibia and the fibula, are distinct, and the short crowned molar teeth are anchitheroid in pattern.

But the most important discovery of all is the *Orohippus*, which comes from the Eocene formation, and is the oldest member of the equine series as yet known. Here we find four complete toes on the front limb, three toes on the hind-limb, a well-developed ulna, a well-developed fibula, and short-crowned grinders of simple pattern.

Thus, thanks to these important researches, it has become evident that, so far as our present knowledge extends, the history of the horse-type is exactly and precisely that which could have been predicted from a knowledge of the principles of evolution. And the knowledge we now possess justifies us completely in the anticipation that when the still lower Eocene deposits, and those which belong to the cretaceous epoch, have yielded up their remains of ancestral equine animals, we shall find, first, a form with four complete toes and a rudiment of the innermost or first digit in front, with probably a rudiment of the fifth digit in the hind foot; [1] while in still

[1] Since this lecture was delivered, Professor Marsh has discovered a new genus of equine mammals (*Eohippus*) from the lowest Eocene deposits of the West, which corresponds very nearly to this description.—*American Journal of Science*, November, 1876.

older forms the series of the digits will be more and more complete, until we come to the five-toed animals, in which, if the doctrine of evolution is well founded, the whole series must have taken its origin.

That is what I mean by demonstrative evidence of evolution. An inductive hypothesis is said to be demonstrated when the facts are shown to be in entire accordance with it. If that is not scientific proof, there are no merely inductive conclusions which can be said to be proved. And the doctrine of evolution at the present time rests upon exactly as secure a foundation as the Copernican theory of the motions of the heavenly bodies did at the time of its promulgation. Its logical basis is precisely of the same character—the coincidence of the observed facts with theoretical requirements.

The only way of escape, if it be a way of escape, from the conclusions which I have just indicated, is the supposition that all these different equine forms have been created separately at separate epochs of time; and, I repeat, that of such an hypothesis as this there neither is, nor can be, any scientific evidence; and, assuredly so far as I know, there is none which is supported, or pretends to be supported, by evidence or authority of any other kind. I can but think that the time will come when such suggestions as these, such obvious attempts to escape the force of demonstration, will be put upon the same footing as the supposition made by some writers, who are, I believe, not completely extinct at present, that fossils are mere simulacra, are no indications of the former existence of the animals to which they seem to belong; but that they are either sports of Nature, or special creations, intended—as I heard suggested the other day—to test our faith.

In fact, the whole evidence is in favour of evolution, and there is none against it. And I say this, although perfectly well aware of the seeming difficulties which have been built up upon what appears to the uninformed to be a solid foundation. I meet constantly with the argument that the doctrine of evolution cannot be well founded, because it requires the lapse of a very vast period of time; while the duration of life upon the earth thus implied is inconsistent with the conclusions arrived at by the astronomer and the physicist. I may venture to say that I am familiar with those conclusions, inasmuch as, some years ago, when President of the Geological Society of London, I took the liberty of criticising them, and of showing in what respects, as it appeared to me, they lacked complete and thorough demonstration. But, putting that point aside, suppose that, as the astronomers, or some of them, and some physical philosophers, tell us, it is impossible that life could have endured upon the earth for as long a period as is required by the doctrine of evolution— supposing that to be proved—I desire to be informed what is the foundation for the statement that evolution does require so great a time? The biologist knows nothing whatever of the amount of time which may be required for the process of evolution. It is a matter of fact that the equine forms which I have described to you occur, in the order stated, in the Tertiary formations. But I have not the slightest means of guessing whether it took a million of years, or ten millions, or a hundred millions, or a thousand millions of years, to give rise to that series of changes. A biologist has no means of arriving at any conclusion as to the amount of time which may be needed for a certain quantity of organic change. He takes his time from the geologist. The geologist, considering the rate at which deposits are formed and the rate at which denudation goes on upon the surface of the earth, arrives at more or less justifiable conclusions as to the time which is required for the deposit of a certain thickness of rocks; and if he tells me that the Tertiary formations required 500,000,000 years for their deposit, I suppose he has good ground for what he says, and I take that as a measure of the duration of the evolution of the horse from the *Orohippus* up to its present condition. And, if he is right, undoubtedly evolution is a very slow process and requires a great deal of time. But suppose, now, that an astronomer or a physicist—for instance, my friend Sir William Thomson—tells me that my geological authority is quite wrong, and that he has weighty evidence to show that life could not possibly have existed upon the surface of the earth 500,000,000 years ago, because the earth would have then been too hot to allow of life, my reply is : " That is not my affair; settle that with the geologist, and when you have come to an agreement among yourselves I will adopt your conclusion." We take our time from the geologists and physicists; and it is monstrous that, having taken our time from the physical philosopher's clock, the physical philosopher should turn round upon us and say we are too fast or too slow. What we desire to know is, is it a fact that evolution took place? As to the amount of time which evolution may have occupied, we are in the hands of the physicist and the astronomer, whose business it is to deal with those questions.

I have now, ladies and gentlemen, arrived at the conclusion of the task which I set before myself when I undertook to deliver these lectures. My purpose has been, not to enable those among you who have paid no attention to these subjects before to leave this room in a condition to decide upon the validity or the invalidity of the hypothesis of evolution; but I have desired to put before you the principles upon which all hypotheses respecting the history of Nature must be judged; and, furthermore, to make apparent the nature of the evidence and the amount of cogency which is to be expected and may be obtained from it. To this end, I have not hesitated to regard you as genuine students and persons desirous of knowing the truth. I have not shrunk from taking you through long discussions, that I fear may have sometimes tried your patience; and I have inflicted upon you details which were indispensable, but which may well have been wearisome. But I shall rejoice—I shall consider that I have done you the greatest service which it was in my power to do —if I have thus convinced you that the great question which we have been discussing is not one to be dealt with by rhetorical flourishes, or by loose and superficial talk; but that it requires the keen attention of the trained intellect and the patience of the accurate observer.

ON THE PHYSICAL BASIS OF LIFE

[1868]

IN order to make the title of this discourse generally intelligible, I have translated the term " Protoplasm," which is the scientific name of the substance
of which I am about to speak, by the words " the
physical basis of life." I suppose that to many the
idea that there is such a thing as a physical basis, or
matter, of life may be novel—so widely spread is
the conception of life as a something which works
through matter, but is independent of it; and even
those who are aware that matter and life are insepar-
ably connected, may not be prepared for the conclusion plainly suggested by the phrase, " *the* physical
basis or matter of life," that there is some one kind
of matter which is common to all living beings, and
that their endless diversities are bound together by
a physical, as well as an ideal, unity. In fact, when
first apprehended, such a doctrine as this appears
almost shocking to common sense.

What, truly, can seem to be more obviously
different from one another, in faculty, in form, and
in substance, than the various kinds of living beings?
What community of faculty can there be between
the brightly-coloured lichen, which so nearly resembles a mere mineral incrustation of the bare rock
on which it grows, and the painter, to whom it is
instinct with beauty, or the botanist, whom it feeds
with knowledge?

Again, think of the microscopic fungus—a mere
infinitesimal ovoid particle, which finds space and
duration enough to multiply into countless millions
in the body of a living fly; and then of the wealth of
foliage, the luxuriance of flower and fruit, which lies
between this bald sketch of a plant and the giant
pine of California, towering to the dimensions of a

cathedral spire, or the Indian fig, which covers acres with its profound shadow, and endures while nations and empires come and go around its vast circumference.   Or, turning to the other half of the world of life, picture to yourselves the great Finner whale, hugest of beasts that live, or have lived, disporting his eighty or ninety feet of bone, muscle, and blubber, with easy roll, among waves in which the stoutest ship that ever left dockyard would flounder hopelessly; and contrast him with the invisible animalcules—mere gelatinous specks, multitudes of which could, in fact, dance upon the point of a needle with the same ease as the angels of the Schoolmen could, in imagination. With these images before your minds, you may well ask, what community of form, or structure, is there between the animalcule and the whale; or between the fungus and the fig-tree? And, *a fortiori*, between all four?

Finally, if we regard substance, or material composition, what hidden bond can connect the flower which a girl wears in her hair and the blood which courses through her youthful veins; or, what is there in common between the dense and resisting mass of the oak, or the strong fabric of the tortoise, and those broad disks of glassy jelly which may be seen pulsating through the waters of a calm sea, but which drain away to mere films in the hand which raises them out of their element?

Such objections as these must, I think, arise in the mind of every one who ponders, for the first time, upon the conception of a single physical basis of life underlying all the diversities of vital existence; but I propose to demonstrate to you that, notwithstanding these apparent difficulties, a threefold unity—namely, a unity of power or faculty, a unity of form, and a unity of substantial composition —does pervade the whole living world.

No very abstruse argumentation is needed, in the first place, to prove that the powers, or faculties, of all kinds of living matter, diverse as they may be in degree, are substantially similar in kind.

Goethe has condensed a survey of all powers of mankind into the well-known epigram :—

> " Warum treibt sich das Volk so und schreit ? Es will sich ernähren
> Kinder zeugen, und die nähren so gut es vermag.
>   *   *   *   *   *   *
> Weiter bringt es kein Mensch, stell' er sich wie er auch will."

In physiological language this means that all the multifarious and complicated activities of man are comprehensible under three categories. Either they are immediately directed towards the maintenance and development of the body, or they effect transitory changes in the relative positions of parts of the body, or they tend towards the continuance of the species. Even those manifestations of intellect, of feeling, and of will which we rightly name the higher faculties are not excluded from this classification, inasmuch as to every one but the subject of them they are known only as transitory changes in the relative positions of parts of the body. Speech, gesture, and every other form of human action are, in the long run, resolvable into muscular contraction, and muscular contraction is but a transitory change in the relative positions of the parts of a muscle. But the scheme which is large enough to embrace the activities of the highest form of life covers all those of the lower creatures. The lowest plant, or animalcule, feeds, grows, and reproduces its kind. In addition, all animals manifest those transitory changes of form which we class under irritability and contractility; and it is more than probable that, when the vegetable world is thoroughly explored, we shall find all plants in possession of the same powers, at one time or other of their existence.

I am not now alluding to such phenomena, at once rare and conspicuous, as those exhibited by the leaflets of the sensitive plants, or the stamens of the barberry, but to much more widely spread, and at the same time more subtle and hidden, manifestations of vegetable contractility. You are doubtless aware that the common nettle owes its stinging property to the innumerable stiff and needle-like, though exquisitely delicate, hairs which cover its surface. Each stinging-needle tapers from a broad base to a slender summit, which, though rounded at the end, is of such microscopic fineness that it readily penetrates, and breaks off in, the skin. The whole hair consists of a very delicate outer case of wood, closely applied to the inner surface of which is a layer of semi-fluid matter, full of innumerable granules of extreme minuteness. This semi-fluid lining is protoplasm, which thus constitutes a kind of bag, full of a limpid liquid, and roughly corresponding in form with the interior of the hair which it fills. When viewed with a sufficiently high magnifying power, the protoplasmic layer of the nettle hair is seen to be in a condition of unceasing activity. Local contractions of the whole thickness of its substance pass slowly and gradually from point to point, and give rise to the appearance of progressive waves, just as the bending of successive stalks of corn by a breeze produces the apparent billows of a cornfield.

But, in addition to these movements, and independently of them, the granules are driven, in relatively rapid streams, through channels in the protoplasm which seem to have a considerable amount of persistence. Most commonly, the currents in adjacent parts of the protoplasm take similar directions; and thus there is a general stream up one side of the hair and down the other: But this does not prevent the existence of partial currents which take different routes; and sometimes trains of granules may be seen coursing swiftly in opposite directions within a twenty-thousandth of an inch of one another; while occasionally opposite streams come into direct collision, and after a longer or shorter struggle one predominates. The cause of these currents seems to lie in contractions of the protoplasm which bounds the channels in which they flow, but which are so minute that the best microscopes show only their effects, and not themselves.

The spectacle afforded by the wonderful energies prisoned within the compass of the microscopic hair of a plant, which we commonly regard as a merely passive organism, is not easily forgotten by one who has watched its display, continued hour after hour, without pause or sign of weakening. The possible complexity of many other organic forms, seemingly as simple as the protoplasm of the nettle, dawns upon one; and the comparison of such a protoplasm to a body with an internal circulation, which has been put forward by an eminent physiologist, loses much of its startling character. Currents similar to those of the hairs of the nettle have been observed in a great multitude of very different plants, and weighty authorities have suggested that they probably occur, in more or less perfection, in all young vegetable cells. If such be the case, the wonderful noonday silence of a tropical forest is, after all, due only to the dulness of our hearing; and could our ears catch the murmur of these tiny Maelstroms, as they whirl in the innumerable myriads of living cells which constitute each tree, we should be stunned, as with the roar of a great city.

Among the lower plants, it is the rule rather than the exception that contractility should be still more openly manifested at some periods of their existence. The protoplasm of *Algæ* and *Fungi* becomes, under many circumstances, partially, or completely, freed from its woody case, and exhibits movements of its whole mass, or is propelled by the contractility of one or more hair-like prolongations of its body, which are called vibratile cilia. And, so far as the conditions of the manifestation of the phenomena of contractility have yet been studied, they are the same for the plant as for the animal. Heat and electric shocks influence both, and in the same way, though it may be in different degrees. It is by no means my intention to suggest that there is no difference in faculty between the lowest plant and the highest, or between plants and animals. But the difference between the powers of the lowest plant, or animal, and those of the highest, is one of degree, not of kind, and depends, as Milne-Edwards long ago so well pointed out, upon the extent to which the principle of the division of labour is carried out in the living economy. In the lowest organism all parts are competent to perform all functions, and one and the same portion of protoplasm may successfully take on the function of feeding, moving, or reproducing apparatus. In the highest, on the contrary, a great number of parts combine to perform each function, each part doing its allotted share of the work with great accuracy and efficiency, but being useless for any other purpose.

On the other hand, notwithstanding all the fundamental resemblances which exist between the powers of the protoplasm in plants and in animals, they present a striking difference (to which I shall advert more at length presently), in the fact that plants can manufacture fresh protoplasm out of mineral compounds, whereas animals are obliged to procure it ready made, and hence, in the long run, depend upon plants. Upon what condition this difference in the powers of the two great divisions of the world of life depends, nothing is at present known.

With such qualification as arises out of the last-mentioned fact, it may be truly said that the acts of all living things are fundamentally one. Is any such unity predicable of their forms? Let us seek in easily verified facts for a reply to this question. If a drop of blood be drawn by pricking one's finger, and viewed with proper precautions, and under a sufficiently high microscopic power, there will be seen, among the innumerable multitude of little, circular, discoidal bodies, or corpuscles, which float in it and give it its colour, a comparatively small number of colourless corpuscles, of somewhat larger size and very irregular shape. If the drop of blood be kept at the temperature of the body, these colourless corpuscles will be seen to exhibit a marvellous activity, changing their forms with great rapidity, drawing in and thrusting out prolongations of their substance, and creeping about as if they were independent organisms.

The substance which is thus active is a mass of protoplasm, and its activity differs in detail, rather than in principle, from that of the protoplasm of the nettle. Under sundry circumstances the corpuscle dies and becomes distended into a round mass, in the midst of which is seen a smaller spherical body, which existed, but was more or less hidden, in the living corpuscle, and is called its *nucleus*. Corpuscles of essentially similar structure are to be found in the skin, in the lining of the mouth, and scattered through the whole framework of the body. Nay, more; in the earliest condition of the human organism, in that state in which it has but just become distinguishable from the egg in which it arises, it is nothing but an aggregation of such corpuscles, and every organ of the body was once no more than such an aggregation.

Thus a nucleated mass of protoplasm turns out to be what may be termed the structural unit of the human body. As a matter of fact, the body, in its earliest state, is a mere multiple of such units; and in its perfect condition it is a multiple of such units, variously modified.

But does the formula which expresses the essential structural character of the highest animal cover all the rest, as the statement of its powers and faculties covered that of all others? Very nearly. Beast and fowl, reptile and fish, mollusk, worm, and polype, are all composed of structural units of the same character—namely, masses of protoplasm with a nucleus. There are sundry very low animals, each of which, structurally, is a mere colourless blood-corpuscle, leading an independent life. But at the very bottom of the animal scale even this simplicity becomes simplified, and all the phenomena of life are manifested by a particle of protoplasm without a nucleus. Nor are such organisms insignificant by reason of their want of complexity. It is a fair question whether the protoplasm of those simplest forms of life which people an immense extent of the bottom of the sea would not outweigh that of all the higher living beings which inhabit the land put together. And in ancient times, no less than at the present day, such living beings as these have been the greatest of rock-builders.

What has been said of the animal world is no less true of plants. Embedded in the protoplasm at the broad, or attached, end of the nettle hair there lies a spheroidal nucleus. Careful examination further proves that the whole substance of the nettle is made up of a repetition of such masses of nucleated proto-plasm, each contained in a wooden case, which is modified in form, sometimes into a woody fibre, sometimes into a duct or spiral vessel, sometimes into a pollen grain, or an ovule. Traced back to its earliest state, the nettle arises as the man does, in a particle of nucleated protoplasm. And in the lowest plants, as in the lowest animals, a single mass of such protoplasm may constitute the whole plant, or the protoplasm may exist without a nucleus.

Under these circumstances it may well be asked, how is one mass of non-nucleated protoplasm to be distinguished from another? why call one " plant " and the other " animal "?

The only reply is that, so far as form is concerned, plants and animals are not separable, and that in many cases it is a mere matter of convention whether we call a given organism an animal or a plant. There is a living body called *Æthalium septicum*, which appears upon decaying vegetable substances, and in one of its forms is common upon the surfaces of tan-

pits. In this condition it is, to all intents and purposes, a fungus, and formerly was always regarded
as such; but the remarkable investigations of De
Bary have shown that in another condition the
Æthalium is an actively locomotive creature, and
takes in solid matters, upon which, apparently, it
feeds, thus exhibiting the most characteristic feature
of animality. Is this a plant; or is it an animal?
Is it both; or is it neither? Some decide in favour
of the last supposition, and establish an intermediate
kingdom, a sort of biological No Man's Land for all
these questionable forms. But, as it is admittedly
impossible to draw any distinct boundary line between
this No Man's Land and the vegetable world, on the
one hand, or the animal, on the other, it appears to
me that this proceeding merely doubles the difficulty
which, before, was single.

Protoplasm, simple or nucleated, is the formal
basis of all life. It is the clay of the potter : which,
bake it and paint it as he will, remains clay, separated by artifice, and not by nature, from the commonest brick or sun-dried clod.

Thus it becomes clear that all living powers are
cognate, and that all living forms are fundamentally
of one character. The researches of the chemist
have revealed a no less striking uniformity of material
composition in living matter.

In perfect strictness, it is true that chemical investigation can tell us little or nothing, directly, of the
composition of living matter, inasmuch as such matter
must needs die in the act of analysis—and upon this
very obvious ground, objections, which I confess
seem to me to be somewhat frivolous, have been
raised to the drawing of any conclusions whatever
respecting the composition of actually living matter,
from that of the dead matter of life, which alone is
accessible to us. But objectors of this class do not
seem to reflect that it is also, in strictness, true that
we know nothing about the composition of any body
whatever, as it is. The statement that a crystal of

calc-spar consists of carbonate of lime is quite true, if we only mean that, by appropriate processes, it may be resolved into carbonic acid and quicklime. If you pass the same carbonic acid over the very quicklime thus obtained, you will obtain carbonate of lime again; but it will not be calc-spar, nor anything like it. Can it, therefore, be said that chemical analysis teaches nothing about the chemical composition of calc-spar? Such a statement would be absurd; but it is hardly more so than the talk one occasionally hears about the uselessness of applying the results of chemical analysis to the living bodies which have yielded them.

One fact, at any rate, is out of reach of such refinements, and this is, that all the forms of protoplasm which have yet been examined contain the four elements, carbon, hydrogen, oxygen, and nitrogen, in very complex union, and that they behave similarly towards several reagents. To this complex combination, the nature of which has never been determined with exactness, the name of Protein has been applied. And if we use this term with such caution as may properly arise out of our comparative ignorance of the things for which it stands, it may be truly said that all protoplasm is proteinaceous, or, as the white, or albumen, of an egg is one of the commonest examples of a nearly pure proteine matter, we may say that all living matter is more or less albuminoid.

Perhaps it would not yet be safe to say that all forms of protoplasm are affected by the direct action of electric shocks; and yet the number of cases in which the contraction of protoplasm is shown to be affected by this agency increases every day.

Nor can it be affirmed with perfect confidence that all forms of protoplasm are liable to undergo that peculiar coagulation at a temperature of 40–50° centigrade, which has been called " heat-stiffening," though Kühne's beautiful researches have proved this occurrence to take place in so many and such diverse living beings, that it is hardly rash to expect that the law holds good for all.

Enough has perhaps been said to prove the existence of a general uniformity in the character of the protoplasm, or physical basis of life, in whatever group of living beings it may be studied. But it will be understood that this general uniformity by no means excludes any amount of special modifications of the fundamental substance. The mineral, carbonate of lime, assumes an immense diversity of characters, though no one doubts that, under all these Protean changes, it is one and the same thing.

And now, what is the ultimate fate, and what the origin, of the matter of life?

Is it, as some of the older naturalists supposed, diffused throughout the universe in molecules, which are indestructible and unchangeable in themselves; but, in endless transmigration, unite in innumerable permutations, into the diversified forms of life we know? Or, is the matter of life composed of ordinary matter, differing from it only in the manner in which its atoms are aggregated? Is it built up of ordinary matter, and again resolved into ordinary matter when its work is done?

Modern science does not hesitate a moment between these alternatives. Physiology writes over the portals of life—

" Debemur morti nos nostraque,"

with a profounder meaning than the Roman poet attached to that melancholy line. Under whatever disguise it takes refuge, whether fungus or oak, worm or man, the living protoplasm not only ultimately dies and is resolved into its mineral and lifeless constituents, but is always dying, and, strange as the paradox may sound, could not live unless it died.

In the wonderful story of the " Peau de Chagrin," the hero becomes possessed of a magical wild ass' skin, which yields him the means of gratifying all his wishes. But its surface represents the duration of the proprietor's life; and for every satisfied desire the skin shrinks in proportion to the intensity of fruition, until at length life and the last hand-breadth of the *peau de chagrin* disappear with the gratification of a last wish.

Balzac's studies had led him over a wide range of thought and speculation, and his shadowing forth of physiological truth in this strange story may have been intentional. At any rate, the matter of life is a veritable *peau de chagrin*, and for every vital act it is somewhat the smaller. All work implies waste, and the work of life results, directly or indirectly, in the waste of protoplasm.

Every word uttered by a speaker costs him some physical loss; and, in the strictest sense, he burns that others may have light—so much eloquence, so much of his body resolved into carbonic acid, water, and urea. It is clear that this process of expenditure cannot go on for ever. But, happily, the protoplasmic *peau de chagrin* differs from Balzac's in its capacity of being repaired, and brought back to its full size, after every exertion.

For example, this present lecture, whatever its intellectual worth to you, has a certain physical value to me, which is, conceivably, expressible by the number of grains of protoplasm and other bodily substance wasted in maintaining my vital processes during its delivery. My *peau de chagrin* will be distinctly smaller at the end of the discourse than it was at the beginning. By and by I shall probably have recourse to the substance commonly called mutton, for the purpose of stretching it back to its original size. Now this mutton was once the living protoplasm, more or less modified, of another animal —a sheep. As I shall eat it, it is the same matter altered, not only by death, but by exposure to sundry artificial operations in the process of cooking.

But these changes, whatever be their extent, have

not rendered it incompetent to resume its old functions as matter of life. A singular inward laboratory, which I possess, will dissolve a certain portion of the modified protoplasm; the solution so formed will pass into my veins; and the subtle influences to which it will then be subjected will convert the dead protoplasm into living protoplasm, and transubstantiate sheep into man.

Nor is this all. If digestion were a thing to be trifled with, I might sup upon lobster, and the matter of life of the crustacean would undergo the same wonderful metamorphosis into humanity. And were I to return to my own place by sea, and undergo shipwreck, the crustacean might, and probably would, return the compliment, and demonstrate our common nature by turning my protoplasm into living lobster. Or, if nothing better were to be had, I might supply my wants with mere bread, and I should find the protoplasm of the wheat-plant to be convertible into man, with no more trouble than that of the sheep, and with far less, I fancy, than that of the lobster.

Hence it appears to be a matter of no great moment what animal, or what plant, I lay under contribution for protoplasm, and the fact speaks volumes for the general identity of that substance in all living beings. I share this catholicity of assimilation with other animals, all of which, so far as we know, could thrive equally well on the protoplasm of any of their fellows, or of any plant; but here the assimilative powers of the animal world cease. A solution of smelling-salts in water, with an infinitesimal proportion of some other saline matters, contains all the elementary bodies which enter into the composition of protoplasm; but, as I need hardly say, a hogshead of that fluid would not keep a hungry man from starving, nor would it save any animal whatever from a like fate. An animal cannot make protoplasm, but must take it ready-made from some other animal, or some plant—the animal's highest feat of constructive chemistry being to convert dead protoplasm into that living matter of life which is appropriate to itself.

Therefore, in seeking for the origin of protoplasm, we must eventually turn to the vegetable world. A fluid containing carbonic acid, water, and nitrogenous salts, which offers such a Barmecide feast to the animal, is a table richly spread to multitudes of plants; and with a due supply of only such materials many a plant will not only maintain itself in vigour, but grow and multiply until it has increased a million-fold, or a million million-fold, the quantity of protoplasm which it originally possessed; in this way building up the matter of life, to an indefinite extent, from the common matter of the universe.

Thus, the animal can only raise the complex substance of dead protoplasm to the higher power, as one may say, of living protoplasm; while the plant can raise the less complex substances—carbonic acid, water, and nitrogenous salts—to the same stage of living protoplasm, if not to the same level. But the plant also has its limitations. Some of the fungi, for example, appear to need higher compounds to start with; and no known plant can live upon the uncompounded elements of protoplasm. A plant supplied with pure carbon, hydrogen, oxygen, and nitrogen, phosphorus, sulphur, and the like, would as infallibly die as the animal in his bath of smelling-salts, though it would be surrounded by all the constituents of protoplasm. Nor, indeed, need the process of simplification of vegetable food be carried so far as this in order to arrive at the limit of the plant's thaumaturgy. Let water, carbonic acid, and all the other needful constituents be supplied except nitrogenous salts, and an ordinary plant will still be unable to manufacture protoplasm.

Thus the matter of life, so far as we know it (and we have no right to speculate on any other), breaks up, in consequence of that continual death which is the condition of its manifesting vitality, into carbonic acid, water, and nitrogenous compounds, which certainly possess no properties but those of ordinary matter. And out of these same forms of ordinary matter, and from none which are simpler, the vegetable world builds up all the protoplasm which keeps the animal world a-going. Plants are the accumulators of the power which animals distribute and disperse.

But it will be observed that the existence of the matter of life depends on the pre-existence of certain compounds; namely, carbonic acid, water, and certain nitrogenous bodies. Withdraw any one of these three from the world, and all vital phenomena come to an end. They are as necessary to the protoplasm of the plant as the protoplasm of the plant is to that of the animal. Carbon, hydrogen, oxygen, and nitrogen are all lifeless bodies. Of these, carbon and oxygen unite, in certain proportions and under certain conditions, to give rise to carbonic acid; hydrogen and oxygen produce water; nitrogen and other elements give rise to nitrogenous salts. These new compounds, like the elementary bodies of which they are composed, are lifeless. But when they are brought together, under certain conditions, they give rise to the still more complex body, protoplasm, and this protoplasm exhibits the phenomena of life.

I see no break in this series of steps in molecular complication, and I am unable to understand why the language which is applicable to any one term of the series may not be used of any of the others. We think fit to call different kinds of matter carbon, oxygen, hydrogen, and nitrogen, and to speak of the various powers and activities of these substances as the properties of the matter of which they are composed.

When hydrogen and oxygen are mixed in a certain proportion, and an electric spark is passed through them, they disappear, and a quantity of water, equal in weight to the sum of their weights, appears in their place. There is not the slightest parity between the passive and active powers of the water and those of the oxygen and hydrogen which have given rise to it. At 32° Fahrenheit, and far below that temperature, oxygen and hydrogen are elastic gaseous bodies, whose particles tend to rush away from one another with great force. Water at the same temperature is a strong though brittle solid, whose particles tend to cohere into definite geometrical shapes, and sometimes build up frosty imitations of the most complex forms of vegetable foliage.

Nevertheless we call these, and many other strange phenomena, the properties of the water, and we do not hesitate to believe that, in some way or another, they result from the properties of the component elements of the water. We do not assume that a something called " aquosity " entered into and took possession of the oxidated hydrogen as soon as it was formed, and then guided the aqueous particles to their places in the facets of the crystal, or amongst the leaflets of the hoar frost. On the contrary, we live in the hope and in the faith that, by the advance of molecular physics, we shall by and by be able to see our way as clearly from the constituents of water to the properties of water, as we are now able to deduce the operations of a watch from the form of its parts and the manner in which they are put together.

Is the case in any way changed when carbonic acid, water, and nitrogenous salts disappear, and in their place, under the influence of pre-existing living protoplasm, an equivalent weight of the matter of life makes its appearance?

It is true that there is no sort of parity between the properties of the components and the properties of the resultant, but neither was there in the case of the water. It is also true that what I have spoken of as the influence of pre-existing living matter is something quite unintelligible; but does anybody quite comprehend the *modus operandi* of an electric spark, which traverses a mixture of oxygen and hydrogen?

What justification is there, then, for the assumption of the existence in the living matter of a some-thing which has no representative, or correlative, in the not living matter which gave rise to it? What better philosophical status has "vitality" than "aquosity"? And why should "vitality" hope for a better fate than the other "itys" which have disappeared since Martinus Scriblerus accounted for the operation of the meat-jack by its inherent "meat-roasting quality," and scorned the "materialism" of those who explained the turning of the spit by a certain mechanism worked by the draught of the chimney?

If scientific language is to possess a definite and constant signification whenever it is employed, it seems to me that we are logically bound to apply to the protoplasm, or physical basis of life, the same conceptions as those which are held to be legitimate elsewhere. If the phenomena exhibited by water are its properties, so are those presented by proto-plasm, living or dead, its properties.

If the properties of water may be properly said to result from the nature and disposition of its com-ponent molecules, I can find no intelligible ground for refusing to say that the properties of protoplasm result from the nature and disposition of its molecules.

But I bid you beware that, in accepting these con-clusions, you are placing your feet on the first rung of a ladder which, in most people's estimation, is the reverse of Jacob's, and leads to the antipodes of heaven. It may seem a small thing to admit that the dull vital actions of a fungus, or a foraminifer, are the properties of their protoplasm, and are the direct results of the nature of the matter of which they are composed. But if, as I have endeavoured to prove to you, their protoplasm is essentially identical with, and most readily converted into, that of any animal, I can discover no logical halting-place between the admission that such is the case, and the further concession that all vital action may, with equal propriety, be said to be the result of the molecular forces of the protoplasm which displays it. And if so, it must be true, in the same sense and to the same extent, that the thoughts to which I am now giving utterance, and your thoughts regarding them, are the expression of molecular changes in that matter of life which is the source of our other vital phenomena.

Past experience leads me to be tolerably certain that, when the propositions I have just placed before you are accessible to public comment and criticism, they will be condemned by many zealous persons, and perhaps by some few of the wise and thoughtful. I should not wonder if " gross and brutal materialism " were the mildest phrase applied to them in certain quarters. And, most undoubtedly, the terms of the propositions are distinctly materialistic. Nevertheless, two things are certain : the one, that I hold the statements to be substantially true; the other, that I, individually, am no materialist, but, on the contrary, believe materialism to involve grave philosophical error.

This union of materialistic terminology with the repudiation of materialistic philosophy I share with some of the most thoughtful men with whom I am acquainted. And when I first undertook to deliver the present discourse, it appeared to me to be a fitting opportunity to explain how such a union is not only consistent with, but necessitated by, sound logic. I purposed to lead you through the territory of vital phenomena to the materialistic slough in which you find yourselves now plunged, and then to point out to you the sole path by which, in my judgment, extrication is possible.

An occurrence of which I was unaware until my arrival here last night renders this line of argument singularly opportune. I found in your papers the eloquent address " On the Limits of Philosophical Inquiry," which a distinguished prelate of the English Church delivered before the members of the Philosophical Institution on the previous day. My argument also turns upon this very point of the limits of philosophical inquiry; and I cannot bring out my own views better than by contrasting them with those so plainly and, in the main, fairly stated by the Archbishop of York.

But I may be permitted to make a preliminary comment upon an occurrence that greatly astonished me. Applying the name of the " New Philosophy " to that estimate of the limits of philosophical inquiry which I, in common with many other men of science, hold to be just, the Archbishop opens his address by identifying this " New Philosophy " with the Positive Philosophy of M. Comte (of whom he speaks as its " founder "); and then proceeds to attack that philosopher and his doctrines vigorously.

Now, so far as I am concerned, the most reverend prelate might dialectically hew M. Comte in pieces, as a modern Agag, and I should not attempt to stay his hand. In so far as my study of what specially characterises the Positive Philosophy has led me, I find therein little or nothing of any scientific value, and a great deal which is as thoroughly antagonistic to the very essence of science as anything in ultramontane Catholicism. In fact, M. Comte's philosophy, in practice, might be compendiously described as Catholicism *minus* Christianity.

But what has Comtism to do with the " New Philosophy," as the Archbishop defines it in the following passage?

" Let me briefly remind you of the leading principles of this new philosophy.

" All knowledge is experience of facts acquired by the senses. The traditions of older philosophies have obscured our experience by mixing with it much that the senses cannot observe, and until these additions are discarded, our knowledge is impure. Thus metaphysics tell us that one fact which we observe is a cause, and another is the effect of that cause; but, upon a rigid analysis, we find that our senses observe nothing of cause or effect: they observe, first, that one fact succeeds another, and, after some opportunity, that this fact has never failed to follow—that for cause and effect we should substitute invariable succession. An older philosophy teaches us to define an object by distinguishing its essential from its accidental qualities; but experience knows nothing of essential and accidental; she sees only that certain marks attach to an object, and, after many observations, that some of them attach invariably, whilst others may at times be absent. . . . As all knowledge is relative, the notion of anything being necessary must be banished with other traditions." [1]

There is much here that expresses the spirit of the "New Philosophy," if by that term be meant the spirit of modern science; but I cannot but marvel that the assembled wisdom and learning of Edinburgh should have uttered no sign of dissent when Comte was declared to be the founder of these doctrines. No one will accuse Scotchmen of habitually forgetting their great countrymen; but it was enough to make David Hume turn in his grave, that here, almost within earshot of his house, an instructed audience should have listened without a murmur while his most characteristic doctrines were attributed to a French writer of fifty years later date, in whose dreary and verbose pages we miss alike the vigour of thought and the exquisite clearness of style of the man whom I make bold to term the most acute thinker of the eighteenth century—even though that century produced Kant.

But I did not come to Scotland to vindicate the honour of one of the greatest men she has ever produced. My business is to point out to you that the only way of escape out of the "crass materialism" in which we just now landed, is the adoption and strict working out of the very principles which the Archbishop holds up to reprobation.

Let us suppose that knowledge is absolute, and not relative, and therefore that our conception of matter represents that which it really is. Let us suppose, further, that we do know more of cause and effect than a certain definite order of succession among facts, and that we have a knowledge of the

---

[1] *The Limits of Philosophical Inquiry*, pp. 4 and 5.

necessity of that succession—and hence, of necessary laws—and I, for my part, do not see what escape there is from utter materialism and necessarianism. For it is obvious that our knowledge of what we call the material world is, to begin with, at least as certain and definite as that of the spiritual world, and that our acquaintance with law is of as old a date as our knowledge of spontaneity. Further, I take it to be demonstrable that it is utterly impossible to prove that anything whatever may not be the effect of a material and necessary cause, and that human logic is equally incompetent to prove that any act is really spontaneous. A really spontaneous act is one which, by the assumption, has no cause; and the attempt to prove such a negative as this is, on the face of the matter, absurd. And while it is thus a philosophical impossibility to demonstrate that any given phenomenon is not the effect of a material cause, any one who is acquainted with the history of science will admit that its progress has, in all ages, meant, and now more than ever means, the extension of the province of what we call matter and causation, and the concomitant gradual banishment from all regions of human thought of what we call spirit and spontaneity.

I have endeavoured, in the first part of this discourse, to give you a conception of the direction towards which modern physiology is tending; and I ask you, what is the difference between the conception of life as the product of a certain disposition of material molecules, and the old notion of an Archæus governing and directing blind matter within each living body, except this—that here, as elsewhere, matter and law have devoured spirit and spontaneity? And as surely as every future grows out of past and present, so will the physiology of the future gradually extend the realm of matter and law until it is co-extensive with knowledge, with feeling, and with action.

The consciousness of this great truth weighs like

a nightmare, I believe, upon many of the best minds of these days. They watch what they conceive to be the progress of materialism, in such fear and powerless anger as a savage feels when, during an eclipse, the great shadow creeps over the face of the sun. The advancing tide of matter threatens to drown their souls; the tightening grasp of law impedes their freedom; they are alarmed lest man's moral nature be debased by the increase of his wisdom.

If the " New Philosophy " be worthy of the reprobation with which it is visited, I confess their fears seem to me to be well founded. While, on the contrary, could David Hume be consulted, I think he would smile at their perplexities, and chide them for doing even as the heathen, and falling down in terror before the hideous idols their own hands have raised.

For, after all, what do we know of this terrible " matter," except as a name for the unknown and hypothetical cause of states of our own consciousness? And what do we know of that " spirit " over whose threatened extinction by matter a great lamentation is arising, like that which was heard at the death of Pan, except that it is also a name for an unknown and hypothetical cause, or condition, of states of consciousness? In other words, matter and spirit are but names for the imaginary substrata of groups of natural phenomena.

And what is the dire necessity and " iron " law under which men groan? Truly, most gratuitously invented bugbears. I suppose if there be an " iron " law, it is that of gravitation; and if there be a physical necessity, it is that a stone, unsupported, must fall to the ground. But what is all we really know, and can know, about the latter phenomena? Simply that in all human experience stones have fallen to the ground under these conditions; that we have not the smallest reason for believing that any stone so circumstanced will not fall to the ground; and that we have, on the contrary, every reason to believe that it will so fall. It is very convenient to indicate that all the conditions of belief have been fulfilled in this case, by calling the statement that unsupported stones will fall to the ground, " a law of Nature." But when, as commonly happens, we change *will* into *must*, we introduce an idea of necessity which most assuredly does not lie in the observed facts, and has no warranty that I can discover elsewhere. For my part, I utterly repudiate and anathematise the intruder. Fact I know; and Law I know; but what is this Necessity, save an empty shadow of my own mind's throwing?

But, if it is certain that we can have no knowledge of the nature of either matter or spirit, and that the notion of necessity is something illegitimately thrust into the perfectly legitimate conception of law, the materialistic position that there is nothing in the world but matter, force, and necessity is as utterly devoid of justification as the most baseless of theological dogmas. The fundamental doctrines of materialism, like those of spiritualism, and most other " isms," lie outside " the limits of philosophical inquiry," and David Hume's great service to humanity is his irrefragable demonstration of what these limits are. Hume called himself a sceptic, and therefore others cannot be blamed if they apply the same title to him; but that does not alter the fact that the name, with its existing implications, does him gross injustice.

If a man asks me what the politics of the inhabitants of the moon are, and I reply that I do not know; that neither I, nor any one else, has any means of knowing; and that, under these circumstances, I decline to trouble myself about the subject at all, I do not think he has any right to call me a sceptic. On the contrary, in replying thus, I conceive that I am simply honest and truthful, and show a proper regard for the economy of time. So Hume's strong and subtle intellect takes up a great many problems about which we are naturally curious, and shows us that they are essentially questions of lunar politics, in their essence incapable of being answered, and therefore not worth the attention of men who have work to do in the world. And he thus ends one of his essays :—

" If we take in hand any volume of Divinity, or school metaphysics, for instance, let us ask, *Does it contain any abstract reasoning concerning quantity or number?* No. *Does it contain any experimental reasoning concerning matter of fact and existence?* No. Commit it then to the flames; for it can contain nothing but sophistry and illusion." [1]

Permit me to enforce this most wise advice. Why trouble ourselves about matters of which, however important they may be, we do know nothing, and can know nothing? We live in a world which is full of misery and ignorance, and the plain duty of each and all of us is to try to make the little corner he can influence somewhat less miserable and somewhat less ignorant than it was before he entered it. To do this effectually it is necessary to be fully possessed of only two beliefs : the first, that the order of Nature is ascertainable by our faculties to an extent which is practically unlimited; the second, that our volition [2] counts for something as a condition of the course of events.

Each of these beliefs can be verified experimentally, as often as we like to try. Each, therefore, stands upon the strongest foundation upon which any belief can rest, and forms one of our highest truths. If we find that the ascertainment of the order of nature is facilitated by using one terminology, or one set of symbols, rather than another, it is our clear duty to use the former; and no harm can accrue, so long as we bear in mind that we are dealing merely with terms and symbols.

[1] Hume's Essay, " Of the Academical or Sceptical Philosophy," in the *Inquiry concerning the Human Understanding.* [Many critics of this passage seem to forget that the subject-matter of Ethics and Æsthetics consists of matters of fact and existence.—1892.]

[2] Or, to speak more accurately, the physical state of which volition is the expression.—[1892.]

In itself it is of little moment whether we express the phenomena of matter in terms of spirit, or the phenomena of spirit in terms of matter : matter may be regarded as a form of thought, thought may be regarded as a property of matter—each statement has a certain relative truth. But with a view to the progress of science, the materialistic terminology is in every way to be preferred. For it connects thought with the other phenomena of the universe, and suggests inquiry into the nature of those physical conditions, or concomitants of thought, which are more or less accessible to us, and a knowledge of which may, in future, help us to exercise the same kind of control over the world of thought as we already possess in respect of the material world; whereas the alternative, or spiritualistic, terminology is utterly barren, and leads to nothing but obscurity and confusion of ideas.

Thus there can be little doubt that the further science advances, the more extensively and consistently will all the phenomena of Nature be represented by materialistic formulæ and symbols.

But the man of science, who, forgetting the limits of philosophical inquiry, slides from these formulæ and symbols into what is commonly understood by materialism, seems to me to place himself on a level with the mathematician, who should mistake the x's and y's with which he works his problems for real entities—and with this further disadvantage, as compared with the mathematician, that the blunders of the latter are of no practical consequence, while the errors of systematic materialism may paralyse the energies and destroy the beauty of a life.

NATURALISM
AND SUPERNATURALISM

[FROM PROLOGUE TO CONTROVERTED
QUESTIONS, 1892.]

THERE is a single problem with different aspects of which thinking men have been occupied ever since they began seriously to consider the wonderful frame of things in which their lives are set, and to seek for trustworthy guidance among its intricacies.

Experience speedily taught them that the shifting scenes of the world's stage have a permanent background; that there is order amidst the seeming confusion, and that many events take place according to unchanging rules. To this region of familiar steadiness and customary regularity they gave the name of Nature. But, at the same time, their infantile and untutored reason, little more, as yet, than the playfellow of the imagination, led them to believe that this tangible, commonplace, orderly world of Nature was surrounded and interpenetrated by another intangible and mysterious world, no more bound by fixed rules than, as they fancied, were the thoughts and passions which coursed through their minds and seemed to exercise an intermittent and capricious rule over their bodies. They attributed to the entities with which they peopled this dim and dreadful region an unlimited amount of that power of modifying the course of events of which they themselves possessed a small share, and thus came to regard them as not merely beyond, but above, Nature.

Hence arose the conception of a " Supernature " antithetic to " Nature "—the primitive dualism of a natural world " fixed in fate " and a supernatural, left to the free play of volition—which has pervaded all later speculation, and for thousands of years has exercised a profound influence on practice. For it is obvious that, on this theory of the Universe, the successful conduct of life must demand careful attention to both worlds; and, if either is to be neglected, it may be safer that it should be Nature. In any given contingency, it must doubtless be desirable to know what may be expected to happen in the ordinary course of things; but it must be quite as necessary to have some inkling of the line likely to be taken by supernatural agencies able, and possibly willing, to suspend or reverse that course. Indeed, logically developed, the dualistic theory must needs end in almost exclusive attention to Supernature, and in trust that its over-ruling strength will be exerted in favour of those who stand well with its denizens. On the other hand, the lessons of the great schoolmaster, experience, have hardly seemed to accord with this conclusion. They have taught, with considerable emphasis, that it does not answer to neglect Nature; and that, on the whole, the more attention paid to her dictates the better men fare.

Thus the theoretical antithesis brought about a practical antagonism. From the earliest times of which we have any knowledge, Naturalism and Supernaturalism have, consciously or unconsciously, competed and struggled with one another; and the varying fortunes of the contest are written in the records of the course of civilisation, from those of Egypt and Babylonia, six thousand years ago, down to those of our own time and people.

These records inform us that, so far as men have paid attention to Nature, they have been rewarded for their pains. They have developed the Arts which have furnished the conditions of civilised existence; and the Sciences, which have been a progressive revelation of reality, and have afforded the best discipline of the mind in the methods of discovering truth. They have accumulated a vast body of universally accepted knowlege; and the conceptions of man and of society, of morals and of law, based upon that knowledge, are every day more and more, either openly or tacitly, acknowledged to be the foundations of right action.

History also tells us that the field of the supernatural has rewarded its cultivators with a harvest, perhaps not less luxuriant, but of a different character. It has produced an almost infinite diversity of Religions. These, if we set aside the ethical concomitants upon which natural knowledge also has a claim, are composed of information about Supernature; they tell us of the attributes of supernatural beings, of their relations with Nature, and of the operations by which their interference with the ordinary course of events can be secured or averted. It does not appear, however, that supernaturalists have attained to any agreement about these matters or that history indicates a widening of the influence of supernaturalism on practice, with the onward flow of time. On the contrary, the various religions are, to a great extent, mutually exclusive; and their adherents delight in charging each other, not merely with error, but with criminality, deserving and ensuing punishment of infinite severity. In singular contrast with natural knowledge, again, the acquaintance of mankind with the supernatural appears the more extensive and the more exact, and the influence of supernatural doctrines upon conduct the greater, the further back we go in time and the lower the stage of civilisation submitted to investigation. Historically, indeed, there would seem to be an inverse relation between supernatural and natural knowledge. As the latter has widened, gained in precision and in trustworthiness, so has the former shrunk, grown vague and questionable; as the one has more and more filled the sphere of action, so has the other retreated into the region of meditation, or vanished behind the screen of mere verbal recognition.

Whether this difference of the fortunes of Naturalism and of Supernaturalism is an indication of the progress, or of the regress, of humanity; of a fall from, or an advance towards, the higher life; is a matter of opinion. The point to which I wish to direct attention is that the difference exists, and is making itself felt. Men are growing to be seriously alive to the fact that the historical evolution of humanity which is generally, and I venture to think not unreasonably, regarded as progress, has been, and is being, accompanied by a co-ordinate elimination of the supernatural from its originally large occupation of men's thoughts. The question—How far is this process to go?—is, in my apprehension, the Controverted Question of our time.

Controversy on this matter—prolonged, bitter, and fought out with the weapons of the flesh, as well as with those of the spirit—is no new thing to Englishmen. We have been more or less occupied with it these five hundred years. And during that time we have made attempts to establish a *modus vivendi* between the antagonists, some of which have had a worldwide influence; though, unfortunately, none have proved universally and permanently satisfactory.

In the fourteenth century, the controverted question among us was, whether certain portions of the Supernaturalism of mediæval Christianity were wellfounded. John Wicliff proposed a solution of the problem which, in the course of the following two hundred years, acquired wide popularity and vast historical importance : Lollards, Hussites, Lutherans, Calvinists, Zwinglians, Socinians, and Anabaptists, whatever their disagreements, concurred in the proposal to reduce the Supernaturalism of Christianity within the limits sanctioned by the Scriptures. None of the chiefs of Protestantism called in question either the supernatural origin and infallible authority of the Bible, or the exactitude of the account of the supernatural world given in its pages. In fact, they could not afford to entertain any doubt about these points, since the infallible Bible was the fulcrum of the lever with which they were endeavouring to upset the

Chair of St. Peter. The "freedom of private judgment" which they proclaimed meant no more, in
practice, than permission to themselves to make free
with the public judgment of the Roman Church, in
respect of the canon and of the meaning to be attached
to the words of canonical books. Private judgment—
that is to say, reason—was (theoretically, at any rate)
at liberty to decide what books were and what were
not to take the rank of " Scripture "; and to determine the sense of any passage in such books. But
this sense, once ascertained to the mind of the sectary,
was to be taken for pure truth—for the very word of
God. The controversial efficiency of the principle of
biblical infallibility lay in the fact that the conservative adversaries of the Reformers were not in a
position to contravene it without entangling themselves in serious difficulties; while, since both Papists
and Protestants agreed in taking efficient measures
to stop the mouths of any more radical critics, these
did not count.

The impotence of their adversaries, however, did
not remove the inherent weakness of the position of
the Protestants. The dogma of the infallibility of the
Bible is no more self-evident than is that of the
infallibility of the Pope. If the former is held by
" faith," then the latter may be. If the latter is to
be accepted, or rejected, by private judgment, why
not the former? Even if the Bible could be proved
anywhere to assert its own infallibility, the value of
that self-assertion to those who dispute the point is
not obvious. On the other hand, if the infallibility
of the Bible was rested on that of a " primitive
Church," the admission that the " Church " was
formerly infallible was awkward in the extreme for
those who denied its present infallibility. Moreover,
no sooner was the Protestant principle applied to
practice than it became evident that even an infallible
text, when manipulated by private judgment, will
impartially countenance contradictory deductions;
and furnish forth creeds and confessions as diverse

as the quality and the information of the intellects which exercise, and the prejudices and passions which sway, such judgments. Every sect, confident in the derivative infallibility of its wire-drawing of infallible materials, was ready to supply its contingent of martyrs; and to enable history once more to illustrate the truth that steadfastness under persecution says much for the sincerity, and still more for the tenacity, of the believer, but very little for the objective truth of that which he believes. No martyrs have sealed their faith with their blood more steadfastly than the Anabaptists.

Last, but not least, the Protestant principle contained within itself the germs of the destruction of the finality which the Lutheran, Calvinistic, and other Protestant Churches fondly imagined they had reached. Since their creeds were professedly based on the canonical Scriptures, it followed that, in the long run, whoso settled the canon defined the creed. If the private judgment of Luther might legitimately conclude that the Epistle of James was contemptible, while the Epistles of Paul contained the very essence of Christianity, it must be permissible for some other private judgment, on as good or as bad grounds, to reverse these conclusions; the critical process which excluded the Apocrypha could not be barred, at any rate by people who rejected the authority of the Church, from extending its operations to Daniel, the Canticles, and Ecclesiastes; nor, having got so far, was it easy to allege any good ground for staying the further progress of criticism. In fact, the logical development of Protestantism could not fail to lay the authority of the Scriptures at the feet of Reason; and in the hands of latitudinarian and rationalistic theologians, the despotism of the Bible was rapidly converted into an extremely limited monarchy. Treated with as much respect as ever, the sphere of its practical authority was minimised; and its decrees were valid only so far as they were countersigned by common sense, the responsible minister.

The champions of Protestantism are much given to glorify the Reformation of the sixteenth century as the emancipation of Reason; but it may be doubted if their contention has any solid ground; while there is a good deal of evidence to show that aspirations after intellectual freedom had nothing whatever to do with the movement. Dante, who struck the Papacy as hard blows as Wicliff; Wicliff himself and Luther himself, when they began their work; were far enough from any intention of meddling with even the most irrational of the dogmas of mediæval Supernaturalism. From Wicliff to Socinus, or even to Münzer, Rothmann, and John of Leyden, I fail to find a trace of any desire to set Reason free. The most that can be discovered is a proposal to change masters. From being the slave of the Papacy, the intellect was to become the serf of the Bible; or, to speak more accurately, of somebody's interpretation of the Bible, which, rapidly shifting its attitude from the humility of a private judgment to the arrogant Cæsaro-papistry of a state-enforced creed, had no more hesitation about forcibly extinguishing opponent private judgments and judges than had the old-fashioned Pontiff-papistry.

It was the iniquities, and not the irrationalities, of the Papal system that lay at the bottom of the revolt of the laity; which was, essentially, an attempt to shake off the intolerable burden of certain practical deductions from a Supernaturalism in which everybody, in principle, acquiesced. What was the gain to intellectual freedom of abolishing transubstantiation, image-worship, indulgences, ecclesiastical infallibility; if consubstantiation, real-unreal presence mystifications, the bibliolatry, the " inner-light " pretensions, and the demonology, which are fruits of the same supernaturalistic tree, remained in enjoyment of the spiritual and temporal support of a new infallibility? One does not free a prisoner by merely scraping away the rust from his shackles.

It will be asked, perhaps, was not the Reformation

one of the products of that great outbreak of many-sided free mental activity included under the general head of the Renascence? Melanchthon, Ulrich von Hutten, Beza, were they not all humanists? Was not the arch-humanist, Erasmus, fautor-in-chief of the Reformation, until he got frightened and basely deserted it?

From the language of Protestant historians, it would seem that they often forget that Reformation and Protestantism are by no means convertible terms. There were plenty of sincere and indeed zealous reformers, before, during, and after the birth and growth of Protestantism, who would have nothing to do with it. Assuredly, the rejuvenescence of science and of art; the widening of the field of Nature by geographical and astronomical discovery; the revelation of the noble ideals of antique literature by the revival of classical learning; the stir of thought, throughout all classes of society, by the printers' work, loosened traditional bonds and weakened the hold of mediæval Supernaturalism. In the interests of liberal culture and of national welfare, the humanists were eager to lend a hand to anything which tended to the discomfiture of their sworn enemies, the monks, and they willingly supported every movement in the direction of weakening ecclesiastical interference with civil life. But the bond of a common enemy was the only real tie between the humanist and the protestant; their alliance was bound to be of short duration, and, sooner or later, to be replaced by internecine warfare. The goal of the humanists, whether they were aware of it or not, was the attainment of the complete intellectual freedom of the antique philosopher, than which nothing could be more abhorrent to a Luther, a Calvin, a Beza, or a Zwingli.

The key to the comprehension of the conduct of Erasmus seems to me to lie in the clear apprehension of this fact. That he was a man of many weaknesses may be true; in fact, he was quite aware of them, and professed himself no hero. But he never deserted that reformatory movement which he originally contemplated; and it was impossible he should have deserted the specifically Protestant reformation in which he never took part. He was essentially a theological whig, to whom radicalism was as hateful as it is to all whigs; or, to borrow a still more appropriate comparison from modern times, a broad churchman who refused to enlist with either the High Church or the Low Church zealots, and paid the penalty of being called coward, time-server, and traitor, by both. Yet really there is a good deal in his pathetic remonstrance that he does not see why he is bound to become a martyr for that in which he does not believe; and a fair consideration of the circumstances and the consequences of the Protestant Reformation seems to me to go a long way towards justifying the course he adopted.

Few men had better means of being acquainted with the condition of Europe; none could be more competent to gauge the intellectual shallowness and self-contradiction of the Protestant criticism of Catholic doctrine; and to estimate at its proper value the fond imagination that the waters let out by the Renascence would come to rest amidst the blind alleys of the new ecclesiasticism. The bastard, whilom poor student and monk, become the familiar of bishops and princes, at home in all grades of society, could not fail to be aware of the gravity of the social position, of the dangers imminent from the profligacy and indifference of the ruling classes, no less than from the anarchical tendencies of the people who groaned under their oppression. The wanderer who had lived in Germany, in France, in England, in Italy, and who counted many of the best and most influential men in each country among his friends, was not likely to estimate wrongly the enormous forces which were still at the command of the Papacy. Bad as the churchmen might be, the statesmen were worse; and a person of far more sanguine temperament than

Erasmus might have seen no hope for the future, except in gradually freeing the ubiquitous organisation of the Church from the corruptions which alone, as he imagined, prevented it from being as beneficent as it was powerful. The broad tolerance of the scholar and man of the world might well be revolted by the ruffianism, however genial, of one great light of Protestantism, and the narrow fanaticism, however learned and logical, of others, and to a cautious thinker, by whom, whatever his shortcomings, the ethical ideal of the Christian evangel was sincerely prized, it really was a fair question whether it was worth while to bring about a political and social deluge, the end of which no mortal could foresee, for the purpose of setting up Lutheran, Zwinglian, and other Peterkins in the place of the actual claimant to the reversion of the spiritual wealth of the Galilean fisherman.

Let us suppose that, at the beginning of the Lutheran and Zwinglian movement, a vision of its immediate consequences had been granted to Erasmus; imagine that to the spectre of the fierce outbreak of Anabaptist communism which opened the apocalypse had succeeded, in shadowy procession, the reign of terror and of spoliation in England, with the judicial murders of his friends, More and Fisher; the bitter tyranny of evangelistic clericalism in Geneva and in Scotland; the long agony of religious wars, persecutions, and massacres, which devastated France and reduced Germany almost to savagery; finishing with the spectacle of Lutheranism in its native country sunk into mere dead Erastian formalism, before it was a century old; while Jesuitry triumphed over Protestantism in three-fourths of Europe, bringing in its train a recrudescence of all the corruptions Erasmus and his friends sought to abolish; might not he have quite honestly thought this a somewhat too heavy price to pay for Protestantism; more especially since no one was in a better position than himself to know how little the dogmatic foundation of the new

confessions was able to bear the light which the
inevitable progress of humanistic criticism would
throw upon them? As the wiser of his contemporaries
saw, Erasmus was, at heart, neither Protestant nor
Papist, but an " Independent Christian "; and, as
the wiser of his modern biographers have discerned,
he was the precursor, not of sixteenth-century reform,
but of eighteenth-century " enlightenment "; a sort
of broad-church Voltaire, who held by his " Independent Christianity " as stoutly as Voltaire by his Deism.

In fact, the stream of the Renascence, which bore
Erasmus along, left Protestantism stranded amidst
the mudbanks of its articles and creeds; while its true
course became visible to all men two centuries later.
By this time, those in whom the movement of the
Renascence was incarnate became aware what spirit
they were of; and they attacked Supernaturalism in
its Biblical stronghold, defended by Protestants and
Romanists with equal zeal. In the eyes of the
" Patriarch," Ultramontanism, Jansenism, and Calvin-
ism were merely three persons of the one " Infâme "
which it was the object of his life to crush. If he
hated one more than another, it was probably the
last; while D'Holbach and the extreme left of the
free-thinking host were disposed to show no more
mercy to Deism and Pantheism.

The sceptical insurrection of the eighteenth century
made a terrific noise, and frightened not a few worthy
people out of their wits; but cool judges might have
foreseen, at the outset, that the efforts of the later
rebels were no more likely than those of the earlier to
furnish permanent resting-places for the spirit of
scientific inquiry. However worthy of admiration
may be the acuteness, the common sense, the wit, the
broad humanity, which abound in the writings of
the best of the free-thinkers; there is rarely much to
be said for their work as an example of the adequate
treatment of a grave and difficult investigation. I do
not think any impartial judge will assert that, from
this point of view, they are much better than their

adversaries. It must be admitted that they share to the full the fatal weakness of *a priori* philosophising, no less than the moral frivolity common to their age; while a singular want of appreciation of history, as the record of the moral and social evolution of the human race, permitted them to resort to preposterous theories of imposture, in order to account for the religious phenomena which are natural products of that evolution.

For the most part, the Romanist and Protestant adversaries of the free-thinkers met them with arguments no better than their own; and with vituperation so far inferior that it lacked the wit. But one great Christian Apologist fairly captured the guns of the free-thinking array, and turned their batteries upon themselves. Speculative " infidelity " of the eighteenth-century type was mortally wounded by the *Analogy ;* while the progress of the historical and psychological sciences brought to light the important part played by the mythopœic faculty; and, by demonstrating the extreme readiness of men to impose upon themselves, rendered the calling in of sacerdotal co-operation, in most cases, a superfluity.

Again, as in the fourteenth and the sixteenth centuries, social and political influences came into play. The free-thinking *philosophes*, who objected to Rousseau's sentimental religiosity almost as much as they did to *L'Infâme*, were credited with the responsibility for all the evil deeds of Rousseau's Jacobin disciples, with about as much justification as Wicliff was held responsible for the Peasants' revolt, or Luther for the *Bauern-krieg*. In England, though our *ancien régime* was not altogether lovely, the social edifice was never in such a bad way as in France; it was still capable of being repaired; and our forefathers, very wisely, preferred to wait until that operation could be safely performed, rather than pull it all down about their ears in order to build a philosophically planned house on brand-new speculative foundations. Under these circumstances, it is not wonderful that, in this country, practical men preferred the Gospel of Wesley and Whitfield to that of Jean Jacques; while enough of the old leaven of Puritanism remained to ensure the favour and support of a large number of religious men to a revival of evangelical supernaturalism. Thus, by degrees, the free-thinking, or the indifference, prevalent among us in the first half of the eighteenth century was replaced by a strong supernaturalistic reaction, which submerged the work of the free-thinkers; and even seemed, for a time, to have arrested the naturalistic movement of which that work was an imperfect indication. Yet, like Lollardry four centuries earlier, free-thought merely took to running underground, safe, sooner or later, to return to the surface.

My memory, unfortunately, carries me back to the fourth decade of the nineteenth century, when the evangelical flood had a little abated and the tops of certain mountains were soon to appear, chiefly in the neighbourhood of Oxford; but when, nevertheless, bibliolatry was rampant; when church and chapel alike proclaimed as the oracles of God the crude assumptions of the worst informed and, in natural sequence, the most presumptuously bigoted of all theological schools.

In accordance with promises made on my behalf, but certainly without my authorisation, I was very early taken to hear " sermons in the vulgar tongue." And vulgar enough often was the tongue in which some preacher, ignorant alike of literature, of history, of science, and even of theology, outside that patronised by his own narrow school, poured forth, from the safe entrenchment of the pulpit, invectives against those who deviated from his notion of orthodoxy. From dark allusions to " sceptics " and " infidels," I became aware of the existence of people who trusted in carnal reason; who audaciously doubted that the world was made in six natural days, or that the deluge was universal; perhaps even went so far as to question the literal accuracy of the story of Eve's temptation, or of Balaam's ass; and from the horror of the tones in which they were mentioned, I should have been justified in drawing the conclusion that these rash men belonged to the criminal classes. At the same time, those who were more directly responsible for providing me with the knowledge essential to the right guidance of life (and who sincerely desired to do so), imagined they were discharging that most sacred duty by impressing upon my childish mind the necessity, on pain of reprobation in this world and damnation in the next, of accepting, in the strict and literal sense, every statement contained in the Protestant Bible. I was told to believe, and I did believe, that doubt about any of them was a sin, not less reprehensible than a moral delict. I suppose that, out of a thousand of my contemporaries, nine hundred at least had their minds systematically warped and poisoned, in the name of the God of truth, by like discipline. I am sure that, even a score of years later, those who ventured to question the exact historical accuracy of any part of the Old Testament and *a fortiori* of the Gospels had to expect a pitiless shower of verbal missiles, to say nothing of the other disagreeable consequences which visit those who in any way run counter to that chaos of prejudices called public opinion.

My recollections of this time have recently been revived by the perusal of a remarkable document,[1] signed by as many as thirty-eight out of the twenty odd thousand clergymen of the Established Church. It does not appear that the signatories are officially accredited spokesmen of the ecclesiastical corporation to which they belong; but I feel bound to take their word for it that they are " stewards of the Lord, who have received the Holy Ghost," and, therefore, to accept this memorial as evidence that, though the Evangelicism of my early days may be deposed from

[1] *Declaration on the Truth of Holy Scripture. The Times,* 18th December, 1891.

its place of power, though so many of the colleagues
of the thirty-eight even repudiate the title of Protestants, yet the green bay tree of bibliolatry flourishes
as it did sixty years ago.   And, as in those good old
times, whoso refuses to offer incense to the idol is
held to be guilty of " a dishonour to God," imperilling
his salvation.

It is to the credit of the perspicacity of the
memorialists that they discern the real nature of the
Controverted Question of the age.   They are awake
to the unquestionable fact that, if Scripture has been
discovered " not to be worthy of unquestioning
belief," faith " in the supernatural itself " is, so far,
undermined.   And I may congratulate myself upon
such weighty confirmation of an opinion in which I
have had the fortune to anticipate them.   But
whether it is more to the credit of the courage, than
to the intelligence, of the thirty-eight that they
should go on to proclaim that the canonical scriptures
of the Old and New Testaments " declare incontrovertibly the actual historical truth in all records, both
of past events and of the delivery of predictions to
be thereafter fulfilled," must be left to the coming
generation to decide.

The interest which attaches to this singular document will, I think, be based by most thinking men,
not upon what it is, but upon that of which it is a
sign.   It is an open secret that the memorial is put
forth as a counterblast to a manifestation of opinion
of a contrary character on the part of certain members
of the same ecclesiastical body, who therefore have,
as I suppose, an equal right to declare themselves
" stewards of the Lord and recipients of the Holy
Ghost."   In fact, the stream of tendency towards
Naturalism, the course of which I have briefly traced,
has of late years flowed so strongly that even the
Churches have begun, I dare not say to drift, but at
any rate to swing at their moorings.   Within the pale
of the Anglican establishment, I venture to doubt
whether, at this moment, there are as many thorough-

going defenders of " plenary inspiration " as there were timid questioners of that doctrine half a century ago. Commentaries, sanctioned by the highest authority, give up the " actual historical truth " of the cosmogonical and diluvial narratives. University professors of deservedly high repute accept the critical decision that the Hexateuch is a compilation, in which the share of Moses, either as author or as editor, is not quite so clearly demonstrable as it might be; highly placed Divines tell us that the pre-Abrahamic Scripture narratives may be ignored; that the Book of Daniel may be regarded as a patriotic romance of the second century B.C.; that the words of the writer of the fourth Gospel are not always to be distinguished from those which he puts into the mouth of Jesus. Conservative, but conscientious, revisers decide that whole passages, some of dogmatic and some of ethical importance, are interpolations. An uneasy sense of the weakness of the dogma of Biblical infallibility seems to be at the bottom of a prevailing tendency once more to substitute the authority of the " Church " for that of the Bible. In my old age, it has happened to me to be taken to task for regarding Christianity as a " religion of a book " as gravely as, in my youth, I should have been reprehended for doubting that proposition. It is a no less interesting symptom that the State Church seems more and more anxious to repudiate all complicity with the principles of the Protestant Reformation and to call itself " Anglo-Catholic." Inspiration, deprived of its old intelligible sense, is watered down into a mystification. The Scriptures are, indeed, inspired; but they contain a wholly undefined and indefinable " human element "; and this unfortunate intruder is converted into a sort of biblical whipping-boy. Whatsoever scientific investigation, historical or physical, proves to be erroneous, the " human element " bears the blame; while the divine inspiration of such statements as by their nature are out of reach of proof or disproof is still asserted with all the vigour inspired by conscious.

safety from attack. Though the proposal to treat the Bible " like any other book," which caused so much scandal forty years ago, may not yet be generally accepted, and though Bishop Colenso's criticisms may still lie, formally, under ecclesiastical ban, yet the Church has not wholly turned a deaf ear to the voice of the scientific tempter; and many a coy divine, while crying " I will ne'er consent," has consented to the proposals of that scientific criticism which the memorialists renounce and denounce.

A humble layman, to whom it would seem the height of presumption to assume even the unconsidered dignity of a " steward of science," may well find this conflict of apparently equal ecclesiastical authorities perplexing—suggestive, indeed, of the wisdom of postponing attention to either, until the question of precedence between them is settled. And this course will probably appear the more advisable, the more closely the fundamental position of the memorialists is examined.

" No opinion of the fact or form of Divine Revelation, founded on literary criticism [and I suppose I may add historical, or physical, criticism] of the Scriptures themselves, can be admitted to interfere with the traditionary testimony of the Church, when that has been once ascertained and verified by appeal to antiquity." [1]

Grant that it is " the traditionary testimony of the Church " which guarantees the canonicity of each and all of the books of the Old and New Testaments. Grant also that canonicity means infallibility; yet, according to the thirty-eight, this " traditionary testimony " has to be " ascertained and verified by appeal to antiquity." But " ascertainment and verification " are purely intellectual processes, which must be conducted according to the strict rules of scientific investigation, or be self-convicted of worthlessness. Moreover, before we can set about the appeal to " antiquity," the exact sense of that usefully

[1] *Declaration*, Article 10.

vague term must be defined by similar means.
" Antiquity " may include any number of centuries,
great or small; and whether " antiquity " is to com-
prise the Council of Trent, or to stop a little beyond
that of Nicæa, or to come to an end in the time of
Irenæus, or in that of Justin Martyr, are knotty
questions which can be decided, if at all, only by those
critical methods which the signatories treat so
cavalierly. And yet the decision of these questions
is fundamental, for as the limits of the canonical
scriptures vary, so may the dogmas deduced from
them require modification. Christianity is one thing,
if the fourth Gospel, the Epistle to the Hebrews, the
pastoral Epistles, and the Apocalypse are canonical
and (by the hypothesis) infallibly true; and another
thing if they are not. As I have already said, whoso
defines the canon defines the creed.

Now it is quite certain with respect to some of these
books, such as the Apocalypse and the Epistle to the
Hebrews, that the Eastern and the Western Church
differed in opinion for centuries; and yet neither the
one branch nor the other can have considered its judgment infallible, since they eventually agreed to a
transaction by which each gave up its objection to
the book patronised by the other. Moreover, the
" fathers " argue (in a more or less rational manner)
about the canonicity of this or that book, and are by
no means above producing evidence, internal and
external, in favour of the opinions they advocate.
In fact, imperfect as their conceptions of scientific
method may be, they not unfrequently used it to the
best of their ability. Thus it would appear that
though science, like Nature, may be driven out with
a fork, ecclesiastical or other, yet she surely comes
back again. The appeal to " antiquity " is, in fact,
an appeal to science, first to define what antiquity
is; secondly, to determine what " antiquity," so
defined, says about canonicity; thirdly, to prove that
canonicity means infallibility. And when science,
largely in the shape of the abhorred " criticism," has

answered this appeal, and has shown that " antiquity " used her own methods, however clumsily and imperfectly, she naturally turns round upon the appellants, and demands that they should show cause why, in these days, science should not resume the work the ancients did so imperfectly, and carry it out efficiently.

But no such cause can be shown. If " antiquity " permitted Eusebius, Origen, Tertullian, Irenæus, to argue for the reception of this book into the canon and the rejection of that, upon rational grounds, " antiquity " admitted the whole principle of modern criticism. If Irenæus produces ridiculous reasons for limiting the Gospels to four, it was open to any one else to produce good reasons (if he had them) for cutting them down to three, or increasing them to five. If the Eastern branch of the Church had a right to reject the Apocalypse and accept the Epistle to the Hebrews, and the Western an equal right to accept the Apocalypse and reject the Epistle, down to the fourth century, any other branch would have an equal right, on cause shown, to reject both or, as the Catholic Church afterwards actually did, to accept both.

Thus I cannot but think that the thirty-eight are hoist with their own petard. Their "appeal to antiquity " turns out to be nothing but a roundabout way of appealing to the tribunal the jurisdiction of which they affect to deny. Having rested the world of Christian supernaturalism on the elephant of biblical infallibility, and furnished the elephant with standing ground on the tortoise of " antiquity," they, like their famous Hindoo analogue, have been content to look no further; and have thereby been spared the horror of discovering that the tortoise rests on a grievously fragile construction, to a great extent the work of that very intellectual operation which they anathematise and repudiate.

Moreover, there is another point to be considered. It is of course true that a Christian Church (whether the Christian Church, or not, depends on the connotation of the definite article) existed before the

Christian scriptures; and that the infallibility of
these depends upon the infallibility of the judgment
of the persons who selected the books of which they
are composed, out of the mass of literature current
among the early Christians. The logical acumen of
Augustine showed him that the authority of the
Gospel he preached must rest on that of the Church
to which he belonged.[1] But it is no less true that the
Hebrew and the Septuagint versions of most, if not
all, of the Old Testament books existed before the
birth of Jesus of Nazareth; and that their divine
authority is presupposed by, and therefore can hardly
depend upon, the religious body constituted by his
disciples. As everybody knows, the very conception
of a " Christ " is purely Jewish. The validity of the
argument from the Messianic prophecies vanishes
unless their infallible authority is granted; and, as a
matter of fact, whether we turn to the Gospels, the
Epistles, or the writings of the early Apologists, the
Jewish scriptures are recognised as the highest court
of appeal of the Christian.

The proposal to cite Christian " antiquity " as a
witness to the infallibility of the Old Testament, when
its own claims to authority vanish if certain propositions contained in the Old Testament are erroneous,
hardly satisfies the requirements of lay logic. It is
as if a claimant to be sole legatee, under another
kind of testament, should offer his assertion as sufficient evidence of the validity of the will. And, even
were not such a circular, or rather rotatory, argument,
that the infallibility of the Bible is testified by the
infallible Church, whose infallibility is testified by the
infallible Bible, too absurd for serious consideration,
it remains permissible to ask, Where and when the
Church, during the period of its infallibility, as limited
by Anglican dogmatic necessities, has officially decreed
the " actual historical truth of all records " in the

---

[1] Ego vero evangelio non crederem, nisi ecclesiæ Catholicæ
me commoveret auctoritas.—*Contra Epistolam Manichæi*,
cap. v.

Old Testament? Was Augustine heretical when he denied the actual historical truth of the record of the Creation? Father Suarez, standing on later Roman tradition, may have a right to declare that he was; but it does not lie in the mouth of those who limit their appeal to that early " antiquity," in which Augustine played so great a part, to say so.

Among the watchers of the course of the world of thought, some view with delight, and some with horror, the recrudescence of Supernaturalism which manifests itself among us, in shapes ranged along the whole flight of steps, which, in this case, separates the sublime from the ridiculous—from Neo-Catholicism and Inner-light mysticism, at the top, to unclean things, not worthy of mention in the same breath, at the bottom. In my poor opinion, the importance of these manifestations is often greatly over-estimated. The extant forms of Supernaturalism have deep roots in human nature, and will undoubtedly die hard; but in these latter days they have to cope with an enemy whose full strength is only just beginning to be put out, and whose forces, gathering strength year by year, are hemming them round on every side. This enemy is Science, in the acceptation of systematised natural knowledge, which during the last two centuries has extended those methods of investigation, the worth of which is confirmed by daily appeal to Nature, to every region in which the Supernatural has hitherto been recognised.

When scientific historical criticism reduced the annals of heroic Greece and of regal Rome to the level of fables; when the unity of authorship of the *Iliad* was successfully assailed by scientific literary criticism; when scientific physical criticism, after exploding the geocentric theory of the universe and reducing the solar system itself to one of millions of groups of like cosmic specks, circling at unimaginable distances from one another through infinite space, showed the supernaturalistic theories of the duration of the earth and of life upon it to be as inadequate as those of its relative dimensions and importance had been; it needed no prophetic gift to see that sooner or later the Jewish and the early Christian records would be treated in the same manner; that the authorship of the Hexateuch and of the Gospels would be as severely tested; and that the evidence in favour of the veracity of many of the statements found in the Scriptures would have to be strong indeed if they were to be opposed to the conclusions of physical science. In point of fact, so far as I can discover, no one competent to judge of the evidential strength of these conclusions ventures now to say that the biblical accounts of the Creation and of the Deluge are true in the natural sense of the words of the narratives. The most modern Reconcilers venture upon is to affirm that some quite different sense may be put upon the words; and that this non-natural sense may, with a little trouble, be manipulated into some sort of non-contradiction of scientific truth.

My purpose, in an essay [1] which treats of the narrative of the Deluge, was to prove, by physical criticism, that no such event as that described ever took place; to exhibit the untrustworthy character of the narrative demonstrated by literary criticism; and, finally, to account for its origin by producing a form of those ancient legends of pagan Chaldæa, from which the biblical compilation is manifestly derived. I have yet to learn that the main propositions of this essay can be seriously challenged.

In two essays [2] on the narrative of the Creation, I have endeavoured to controvert the assertion that modern science supports, either the interpretation put upon it by Mr. Gladstone, or any interpretation which is compatible with the general sense of the narrative, quite apart from particular details. The

[1] *Hasisadra's Adventure.*
[2] *The Interpreters of Genesis and the Interpreters of Nature* and *Mr. Gladstone and Genesis.*

first chapter of Genesis teaches the supernatural creation of the present forms of life; modern science teaches that they have come about by evolution. The first chapter of Genesis teaches the successive origin—firstly, of all the plants; secondly, of all the aquatic and aerial animals; thirdly, of all the terrestrial animals, which now exist—during distinct intervals of time; modern science teaches that, throughout all the duration of an immensely long past, so far as we have any adequate knowledge of it (that is as far back as the Silurian epoch), plants, aquatic, aerial, and terrestrial animals have co-existed; that the earliest known are unlike those which at present exist; and that the modern species have come into existence as the last terms of a series, the members of which have appeared one after another. Thus, far from confirming the account in Genesis, the results of modern science, so far as they go, are in principle, as in detail, hopelessly discordant with it.

Yet, if the pretensions to infallibility set up, not by the ancient Hebrew writings themselves, but by the ecclesiastical champions and friends from whom they may well pray to be delivered, thus shatter themselves against the rock of natural knowledge, in respect of the two most important of all events, the origin of things and the palingenesis of terrestrial life, what historical credit dare any serious thinker attach to the narratives of the fabrication of Eve, of the Fall, of the commerce between the *Bene Elohim* and the daughters of men, which lie between the creational and the diluvial legends? And, if these are to lose all historical worth, what becomes of the infallibility of those who, according to the later scriptures, have accepted them, argued from them, and staked far-reaching dogmatic conclusions upon their historical accuracy?

It is the merest ostrich policy for contemporary ecclesiasticism to try to hide its Hexateuchal head—in the hope that the inseparable connection of its body with pre-Abrahamic legends may be overlooked. The question will still be asked, If the first nine chapters of the Pentateuch are unhistorical, how is the historical accuracy of the remainder to be guaranteed? What more intrinsic claim has the story of the Exodus than that of the Deluge to belief? If God did not walk in the Garden of Eden, how can we be assured that he spoke from Sinai?

In other essays [1] I have endeavoured to show that sober and well-founded physical and literary criticism plays no less havoc with the doctrine that the canonical scriptures of the New Testament " declare incontrovertibly the actual historical truth in all records." We are told that the Gospels contain a true revelation of the spiritual world—a proposition which, in one sense of the word " spiritual," I should not think it necessary to dispute. But, when it is taken to signify that everything we are told about the world of spirits in these books is infallibly true; that we are bound to accept the demonology which constitutes an inseparable part of their teaching; and to profess belief in a Supernaturalism as gross as that of any primitive people—it is at any rate permissible to ask why? Science may be unable to define the limits of possibility, but it cannot escape from the moral obligation to weigh the evidence in favour of any alleged wonderful occurrence; and I have endeavoured to show that the evidence for the Gadarene miracle is altogether worthless. We have simply three, partially discrepant, versions of a story, about the primitive form, the origin, and the authority for which we know absolutely nothing. But the evidence in favour of the Gadarene miracle is as good as that for any other.

Elsewhere I have pointed out that it is utterly beside the mark to declaim against these conclusions on the ground of their asserted tendency to deprive

---

[1] *Agnosticism; The Value of Witness to the Miraculous; Agnosticism: a Rejoinder; Agnosticism and Christianity; The Keepers of the Herd of Swine;* and *Illustrations of Mr. Gladstone's Controversial Methods.*

mankind of the consolations of the Christian faith, and to destroy the foundations of morality : still less to brand them with the question-begging vituperative appellation of " infidelity." The point is not whether they are wicked; but whether, from the point of view of scientific method, they are irrefragably true. If they are, they will be accepted in time, whether they are wicked or not wicked. Nature, so far as we have been able to attain to any insight into her ways, recks little about consolation, and makes for righteousness by very round-about paths. And, at any rate, whatever may be possible for other people, it is becoming less and less possible for the man who puts his faith in scientific methods of ascertaining truth, and is accustomed to have that faith justified by daily experience, to be consciously false to his principle in any matter. But the number of such men, driven into the use of scientific methods of inquiry and taught to trust them, by their education, their daily professional and business needs, is increasing and will continually increase. The phraseology of Supernaturalism may remain on men's lips, but in practice they are Naturalists. The magistrate who listens with devout attention to the precept " Thou shalt not suffer a witch to live " on Sunday, on Monday dismisses, as intrinsically absurd, a charge of bewitching a cow brought against some old woman; the superintendent of a lunatic asylum who substituted exorcism for rational modes of treatment would have but a short tenure of office; even parish clerks doubt the utility of prayers for rain, so long as the wind is in the east; and an outbreak of pestilence sends men, not to the churches, but to the drains. In spite of prayers for the success of our arms and *Te Deums* for victory, our real faith is in big battalions and keeping our powder dry; in knowledge of the science of warfare; in energy, courage, and discipline. In these, as in all other practical affairs, we act on the aphorism " *Laborare est orare* " ; we admit that intelligent work is the only acceptable worship; and that, whether there be a Supernature or not, our business is with Nature.

It is important to note that the principle of the scientific Naturalism of the latter half of the nineteenth century, in which the intellectual movement of the Renascence has culminated, and which was first clearly formulated by Descartes, leads not to the denial of the existence of any Supernature; [1] but simply to the denial of the validity of the evidence adduced in favour of this, or of that, extant form of Supernaturalism.

Looking at the matter from the most rigidly scientific point of view, the assumption that, amidst the myriads of worlds scattered through endless space, there can be no intelligence as much greater than man's as his is greater than a blackbeetle's; no being endowed with powers of influencing the course of Nature as much greater than his as his is greater than a snail's, seems to me not merely baseless, but impertinent. Without stepping beyond the analogy of that which is known, it is easy to people the cosmos with entities, in ascending scale, until we reach something practically indistinguishable from omnipotence, omnipresence, and omniscience. If our intelligence can, in some matters, surely reproduce the past of thousands of years ago and anticipate the future thousands of years hence, it is clearly within the limits of possibility that some greater intellect, even of the same order, may be able to mirror the whole past and the whole future; if the universe is penetrated by a medium of such a nature that a magnetic needle on the earth answers to a commotion in the

---

[1] I employ the words "Supernature" and "Supernatural" in their popular senses. For myself, I am bound to say that the term "Nature" covers the totality of that which is. The world of psychical phenomena appears to me to be as much part of "Nature" as the world of physical phenomena; and I am unable to perceive any justification for cutting the Universe into two halves, one natural and one supernatural.

sun, an omnipresent agent is also conceivable; if our insignificant knowledge gives us some influence over events, practical omniscience may confer indefinably greater power. Finally, if evidence that a thing may be were equivalent to proof that it is, analogy might justify the construction of a naturalistic theology and demonology not less wonderful than the current supernatural; just as it might justify the peopling of Mars, or of Jupiter, with living forms to which terrestrial biology offers no parallel. Until human life is longer and the duties of the present press less heavily, I do not think that wise men will occupy themselves with Jovian, or Martian, natural history; and they will probably agree to a verdict of " not proven " in respect of naturalistic theology, taking refuge in that Agnostic confession, which appears to me to be the only position for people who object to say that they know what they are quite aware they do not know. As to the interests of morality, I am disposed to think that if mankind could be got to act up to this last principle in every relation of life, a reformation would be effected such as the world has not yet seen; an approximation to the millennium such as no supernaturalistic religion has ever yet succeeded, or seems likely ever to succeed, in effecting.

THE VALUE OF WITNESS TO THE MIRACULOUS

[1889]

CHARLES, or, more properly, Karl, King of the Franks, consecrated Roman Emperor in St. Peter's on Christmas Day, A.D. 800, and known to posterity as the Great (chiefly by his agglutinative Gallicised denomination of Charlemagne), was a man great in all ways, physically and mentally. Within a couple of centuries after his death Charlemagne became the centre of innumerable legends; and the myth-making process does not seem to have been sensibly interfered with by the existence of sober and truthful histories of the Emperor and of the times which immediately preceded and followed his reign, by a contemporary writer who occupied a high and confidential position in his court, and in that of his successor. This was one Eginhard, or Einhard, who appears to have been born about A.D. 770, and spent his youth at the court, being educated along with Charles's sons. There is excellent contemporary testimony not only to Eginhard's existence, but to his abilities, and to the place which he occupied in the circle of the intimate friends of the great ruler whose life he subsequently wrote. In fact, there is as good evidence of Eginhard's existence, of his official position, and of his being the author of the chief works attributed to him, as can reasonably be expected in the case of a man who lived more than a thousand years ago, and was neither a great king nor a great warrior. The works are—1. " The Life of the Emperor Karl." 2. " The Annals of the Franks." 3. " Letters." 4. " The History of the Translation of the Blessed Martyrs of Christ, SS. Marcellinus and Petrus."

It is to the last, as one of the most singular and

interesting records of the period during which the
Roman world passed into that of the Middle Ages,
that I wish to direct attention.[1] It was written in
the ninth century, somewhere, apparently, about the
year 830, when Eginhard, ailing in health and weary
of political life, had withdrawn to the monastery of
Seligenstadt, of which he was the founder.   A manu-
script copy of the work, made in the tenth century, and
once the property of the monastery of St. Bavon on
the Scheldt, of which Eginhard was abbot, is still
extant, and there is no reason to believe that in this
copy the original has been in any way interpolated or
otherwise tampered with.   The main features of the
strange story contained in the *Historia Translationis*
are set forth in the following pages, in which, in regard
to all matters of importance, I shall adhere as closely
as possible to Eginhard's own words.

While I was still at Court, busied with secular affairs, I
often thought of the leisure which I hoped one day to enjoy in
a solitary place, far away from the crowd, with which the
liberality of Prince Louis, whom I then served, had provided
me.   This place is situated in that part of Germany which
lies between the Neckar and the Maine,[2] and is nowadays
called the Odenwald by those who live in and about it.   And
here having built, according to my capacity and resources,
not only houses and permanent dwellings, but also a basilica
fitted for the performance of divine service and of no mean
style of construction, I began to think to what saint or
martyr I could best dedicate it.   A good deal of time had
passed while my thoughts fluctuated about this matter,
when it happened that a certain deacon of the Roman Church,
named Deusdona, arrived at the Court for the purpose of
seeking the favour of the King in some affairs in which he
was interested.   He remained some time; and then, having
transacted his business, he was about to return to Rome,
when one day, moved by courtesy to a stranger, we invited
him to a modest refection; and while talking of many things
at table, mention was made of the translation of the body of

---

[1] My citations are made from Teulet's *Einhardi omnia
quæ extant opera*, Paris, 1840–1843, which contains a biography
of the author, a history of the text, with translations into
French, and many valuable annotations.

[2] At present included in the Duchies of Hesse-Darmstadt
and Baden.

the blessed Sebastian,[1] and of the neglected tombs of the martyrs, of which there is such a prodigious number at Rome; and the conversation having turned towards the dedication of our new basilica, I began to inquire how it might be possible for me to obtain some of the true relics of the saints which rest at Rome. He at first hesitated, and declared that he did not know how that could be done. But observing that I was both anxious and curious about the subject, he promised to give me an answer some other day.

When I returned to the question some time afterwards, he immediately drew from his bosom a paper, which he begged me to read when I was alone, and to tell him what I was disposed to think of that which was therein stated. I took the paper and, as he desired, read it alone and in secret. (Cap. 1, 2, 3.)

I shall have occasion to return to Deacon Deusdona's conditions, and to what happened after Eginhard's acceptance of them. Suffice it, for the present, to say that Eginhard's notary, Ratleicus (Ratleig), was despatched to Rome, and succeeded in securing two bodies, supposed to be those of the holy martyrs Marcellinus and Petrus; and when he had got as far on his homeward journey as the Burgundian town of Solothurn, or Soleure,[2] notary Ratleig despatched to his master, at St. Bavon, a letter announcing the success of his mission.

As soon as by reading it I was assured of the arrival of the saints, I despatched a confidential messenger to Maestricht to gather together priests, other clerics, and also laymen, to go out to meet the coming saints as speedily as possible. And he and his companions, having lost no time, after a few days met those who had charge of the saints at Solothurn. Joined with them, and with a vast crowd of people who gathered from all parts, singing hymns, and amidst great and universal rejoicings, they travelled quickly to the city of Argentoratum, which is now called Strasburg. Thence embarking on the Rhine, they came to the place called Portus,[3] and landing on the east bank of the river, at the fifth station thence they

---

[1] This took place in the year 826 A.D. The relics were brought from Rome and deposited in the Church of St. Medardus at Soissons.

[2] Now included in Western Switzerland.

[3] Probably, according to Teulet, the present Sandhofer-fahrt, a little below the embouchure of the Neckar.

arrived at Michilinstadt,[1] accompanied by an immense multitude, praising God. This place is in that forest of Germany which in modern times is called the Odenwald, and about six leagues from the Maine. And here, having found a basilica recently built by me, but not yet consecrated, they carried the sacred remains into it and deposited them therein, as if it were to be their final resting-place. As soon as all this was reported to me I travelled thither as quickly as I could. (Cap. ii. 14.)

Three days after Eginhard's arrival began the series of wonderful events which he narrates, and for which we have his personal guarantee. The first thing that he notices is the dream of a servant of Ratleig, the notary, who, being set to watch the holy relics in the church after vespers, went to sleep and, during his slumbers, had a vision of two pigeons, one white and one grey and white, which came and sat upon the bier over the relics; while, at the same time, a voice ordered the man to tell his master that the holy martyrs had chosen another resting-place and desired to be transported thither without delay.

Unfortunately, the saints seem to have forgotten to mention where they wished to go; and, with the most anxious desire to gratify their smallest wishes, Eginhard was naturally greatly perplexed what to do. While in this state of mind, he was one day contemplating his "great and wonderful treasure, more precious than all the gold in the world," when it struck him that the chest in which the relics were contained was quite unworthy of its contents; and, after vespers, he gave orders to one of the sacristans to take the measure of the chest in order that a more fitting shrine might be constructed. The man, having lighted a wax candle and raised the pall which covered the relics, in order to carry out his master's orders, was astonished and terrified to observe that the chest was covered with a blood-like exudation (*loculum mirum in modum humore sanguineo undique distillantem*), and at once sent a message to Eginhard.

---

[1] The present Michilstadt, thirty miles N.E. of Heidelberg.

Then I and those priests who accompanied me beheld this stupendous miracle, worthy of all admiration. For just as when it is going to rain, pillars and slabs and marble images exude moisture, and, as it were, sweat, so the chest which contained the most sacred relics was found moist with the blood exuding on all sides. (Cap. ii. 16.)

Three days' fast was ordained in order that the meaning of the portent might be ascertained. All that happened, however, was that at the end of that time the " blood," which had been exuding in drops all the while, dried up. Eginhard is careful to say that the liquid " had a saline taste, something like that of tears, and was thin as water, though of the colour of true blood," and he clearly thinks this satisfactory evidence that it was blood.

The same night, another servant had a vision, in which still more imperative orders for the removal of the relics were given; and from that time forth " not a single night passed without one, two, or even three of our companions receiving revelations in dreams that the bodies of the saints were to be transferred from that place to another." At last a priest, Hildfrid saw in a dream a venerable white-haired man in a priest's vestments, who bitterly reproached Eginhard for not obeying the repeated orders of the saints; and, upon this, the journey was commenced. Why Eginhard delayed obedience to these repeated visions so long does not appear. He does not say so, in so many words, but the general tenor of the narrative leads one to suppose that Mulinheim (afterwards Seligenstadt) is the " solitary place " in which he had built the church which awaited dedication. In that case, all the people about him would know that he desired that the saints should go there. If a glimmering of secular sense led him to be a little suspicious about the real cause of the unanimity of the visionary beings who manifested themselves to his *entourage* in favour of moving on, he does not say so.

At the end of the first day's journey the precious relics were deposited in the church of St. Martin, in the village of Ostheim. Hither, a paralytic nun

(*sanctimonialis quædam paralytica*) of the name of
Ruodlang was brought, in a car, by her friends and
relatives from a monastery a league off. She spent
the night watching and praying by the bier of the
saints; " and health returning to all her members, on
the morrow she went back to her place whence she
came, on her feet, nobody supporting her, or in any
way giving her assistance."   (Cap. ii. 19.)

On the second day the relics were carried to Upper
Mulinheim; and finally, in accordance with the orders
of the martyrs, deposited in the church of that place,
which was therefore renamed Seligenstadt. Here,
Daniel, a beggar boy of fifteen, and so bent that " he
could not look at the sky without lying on his back,"
collapsed and fell down during the celebration of the
Mass.   " Thus he lay a long time, as if asleep, and all
his limbs straightening and his flesh strengthening
(*recepta firmitate nervorum*), he arose before our eyes,
quite well."   (Cap. ii. 20.)

Some time afterwards an old man entered the
church on his hands and knees, being unable to use
his limbs properly :—

He, in presence of all of us, by the power of God and the
merits of the blessed martyrs, in the same hour in which he
entered was so perfectly cured that he walked without so
much as a stick.   And he said that, though he had been deaf
for five years, his deafness had ceased along with the palsy.
(Cap. iii. 33.)

Eginhard was now obliged to return to the Court at
Aix-la-Chapelle, where his duties kept him through
the winter; and he is careful to point out that the
later miracles which he proceeds to speak of are known
to him only at second hand. But, as he naturally
observes, having seen such wonderful events with his
own eyes, why should he doubt similar narrations
when they are received from trustworthy sources?

Wonderful stories these are indeed, but as they are,
for the most part, of the same general character as
those already recounted, they may be passed over.
There is, however, an account of a possessed maiden

which is worth attention. This is set forth in a
memoir, the principal contents of which are the
speeches of a demon who declared himself to possess
the singular appellation of " Wiggo," and revealed
himself in the presence of many witnesses, before the
altar, close to the relics of the blessed martyrs. It is
noteworthy that the revelations appear to have been
made in the shape of replies to the questions of the
exorcising priest; and there is no means of judging
how far the answers are, really, only the questions to
which the patient replied yes or no.

The possessed girl, about sixteen years of age, was
brought by her parents to the basilica of the martyrs.

When she approached the tomb containing the sacred
bodies, the priest, according to custom, read the formula of
exorcism over her head. When he began to ask how and
when the demon had entered her, she answered not in the
tongue of the barbarians, which alone the girl knew, but in
the Roman tongue. And when the priest was astonished
and asked how she came to know Latin, when her parents,
who stood by, were wholly ignorant of it, " Thou hast never
seen my parents," was the reply. To this the priest,
" Whence art thou, then, if these are not thy parents? "
And the demon, by the mouth of the girl, " I am a follower
and disciple of Satan, and for a long time I was gate-keeper
(janitor) in hell; but, for some years, along with eleven
companions, I have ravaged the kingdom of the Franks."
(Cap. v. 49.)

He then goes on to tell how they blasted the crops and
scattered pestilence among beasts and men, because
of the prevalent wickedness of the people.[1]

The enumeration of all these iniquities in oratorical
style takes up a whole octavo page; and at the end
it is stated, " All these things the demon spoke in
Latin by the mouth of the girl."

And when the priest imperatively ordered him to come
out, " I shall go," said he, " not in obedience to you, but on
account of the power of the saints, who do not allow me to
remain any longer." And, having said this, he threw the
girl down on the floor and there compelled her to lie prostrate

---

[1] In the Middle Ages one of the most favourite accusations
against witches was that they committed just these enormities.

for a time, as though she slumbered.   After a little while, however, he going away, the girl, by the power of Christ and the merits of the blessed martyrs, as it were awaking from sleep, rose up quite well, to the astonishment of all present; nor after the demon had gone out was she able to speak Latin : so that it was plain enough that it was not she who had spoken in that tongue, but the demon by her mouth. (Cap. v. 51.)

If the *Historia Translationis* contained nothing more than has been laid before the reader up to this time, disbelief in the miracles of which it gives so precise and full a record might well be regarded as hyper-scepticism.   It might fairly be said, Here you have a man whose high character, acute intelligence, and large instruction are certified by eminent contemporaries; a man who stood high in the confidence of one of the greatest rulers of any age, and whose other works prove him to be an accurate and judicious narrator of ordinary events.   This man tells you, in language which bears the stamp of sincerity, of things which happened within his own knowledge, or within that of persons in whose veracity he has entire confidence, while he appeals to his sovereign and the court as witnesses of others; what possible ground can there be for disbelieving him?

Well, it is hard upon Eginhard to say so, but it is exactly the honesty and sincerity of the man which are his undoing as a witness to the miraculous.   He himself makes it quite obvious that when his profound piety comes on the stage, his good sense, and even his perception of right and wrong, make their exit.   Let us go back to the point at which we left him, secretly perusing the letter of Deacon Deusdona.   As he tells us, its contents were

that he [the deacon] had many relics of saints at home, and that he would give them to me if I would furnish him with the means of returning to Rome; he had observed that I had two mules, and if I would let him have one of them and would despatch with him a confidential servant to take charge of the relics, he would at once send them to me.   This plausibly expressed proposition pleased me, and I made up my mind to test the value of the somewhat ambiguous promise at once; [1] so giving him the mule and money for his journey I ordered my notary Ratleig (who already desired to go to Rome to offer his devotions there) to go with him. Therefore, having left Aix-la-Chapelle (where the Emperor and his Court resided at the time) they came to Soissons. Here they spoke with Hildoin, abbot of the monastery of St. Medardus, because the said deacon had assured him that he had the means of placing in his possession the body of the blessed Tiburtius the Martyr. Attracted by which promises he (Hildoin) sent with them a certain priest, Hunus by name, a sharp man (*hominem callidum*), whom he ordered to receive and bring back the body of the martyr in question. And so, resuming their journey, they proceeded to Rome as fast as they could. (Cap. i. 3.)

Unfortunately, a servant of the notary, one Reginbald, fell ill of a tertian fever, and impeded the progress of the party. However, this piece of adversity had its sweet uses; for three days before they reached Rome, Reginbald had a vision. Somebody habited as a deacon appeared to him and asked why his master was in such a hurry to get to Rome; and when Reginbald explained their business, this visionary deacon, who seems to have taken the measure of his brother in the flesh with some accuracy, told him not by any means to expect that Deusdona would fulfil his promises. Moreover, taking the servant by the hand, he led him to the top of a high mountain and, showing him Rome (where the man had never been), pointed out a church, adding, " Tell Ratleig the thing he wants is hidden there; let him get it as quickly as he can and go back to his master." By way of a sign that the order was authoritative, the servant was promised that from that time forth his fever should disappear. And as the fever did vanish to return no more, the faith of Eginhard's people in Deacon Deusdona naturally vanished with it (*et fidem diaconi promissis non haberent*). Nevertheless, they put up at the deacon's house near St. Peter ad Vincula. But

---

[1] It is pretty clear that Eginhard had his doubts about the deacon, whose pledges he qualifies as *sponsiones incertæ*. But, to be sure, he wrote after events which fully justified scepticism.

time went on and no relics made their appearance, while the notary and the priest were put off with all sorts of excuses—the brother to whom the relics had been confided was gone to Beneventum and not expected back for some time, and so on—until Ratleig and Hunus began to despair, and were minded to return, *infecto negotio*.

But my notary calling to mind his servant's dream proposed to his companion that they should go to the cemetery which their host had talked about without him. So, having found and hired a guide, they went in the first place to the basilica of the blessed Tiburtius in the Via Labicana, about three thousand paces from the town, and cautiously and carefully inspected the tomb of that martyr, in order to discover whether it could be opened without any one being the wiser. Then they descended into the adjoining crypt, in which the bodies of the blessed martyrs of Christ, Marcellinus and Petrus, were buried; and, having made out the nature of their tomb, they went away thinking their host would not know what they had been about. But things fell out differently from what they had imagined. (Cap. i. 7.)

In fact, Deacon Deusdona, who doubtless kept an eye on his guests, knew all about their manœuvres and made haste to offer his services, in order that, " with the help of God " (*si Deus votis eorum favere dignaretur*), they should all work together. The deacon was evidently alarmed lest they should succeed without *his* help.

So, by way of preparation for the contemplated *vol avec affraction*, they fasted three days; and then, at night, without being seen, they betook themselves to the basilica of St. Tiburtius, and tried to break open the altar erected over his remains. But the marble proving too solid, they descended to the crypt, and, " having evoked our Lord Jesus Christ and adored the holy martyrs," they proceeded to prise off the stone which covered the tomb, and thereby exposed the body of the most sacred martyr, Marcellinus, " whose head rested on a marble tablet on which his name was inscribed." The body was taken up with the greatest veneration, wrapped in a rich covering, and given over to the keeping of the deacon and his brother, Lunison, while the stone was replaced with such care that no sign of the theft remained.

As sacrilegious proceedings of this kind were punishable with death by the Roman law, it seems not unnatural that Deacon Deusdona should have become uneasy, and have urged Ratleig to be satisfied with what he had got and be off with his spoils. But the notary having thus cleverly captured the blessed Marcellinus, thought it a pity he should be parted from the blessed Petrus, side by side with whom he had rested, for five hundred years and more, in the same sepulchre (as Eginhard pathetically observes); and the pious man could neither eat, drink, nor sleep, until he had compassed his desire to reunite the saintly colleagues. This time, apparently in consequence of Deusdona's opposition to any further resurrectionist doings, he took counsel with a Greek monk, one Basil, and accompanied by Hunus, but saying nothing to Deusdona, they committed another sacrilegious burglary, securing this time, not only the body of the blessed Petrus, but a quantity of dust, which they agreed the priest should take, and tell his employer that it was the remains of the blessed Tiburtius. How Deusdona was " squared," and what he got for his not very valuable complicity in these transactions, does not appear. But at last the relics were sent off in charge of Lunison, the brother of Deusdona, and the priest Hunus, as far as Pavia, while Ratleig stopped behind for a week to see if the robbery was discovered, and, presumably, to act as a blind if any hue and cry was raised. But, as everything remained quiet, the notary betook himself to Pavia, where he found Lunison and Hunus awaiting his arrival. The notary's opinion of the character of his worthy colleagues, however, may be gathered from the fact that, having persuaded them to set out in advance along a road which he told them he was about to take, he immediately adopted another route, and, travelling by way of St. Maurice and the Lake of Geneva, eventually reached Soleure.

Eginhard tells all this story with the most naïve air of unconsciousness that there is anything remarkable about an abbot, and a high officer of state to boot, being an accessory, both before and after the fact, to a most gross and scandalous act of sacrilegious and burglarious robbery. And an amusing sequel to the story proves that where relics were concerned, his friend Hildoin, another high ecclesiastical dignitary, was even less scrupulous than himself.

On going to the palace early one morning, after the saints were safely bestowed at Seligenstadt, he found Hildoin waiting for an audience in the Emperor's antechamber, and began to talk to him about the miracle of the bloody exudation. In the course of conversation, Eginhard happened to allude to the remarkable fineness of the garment of the blessed Marcellinus. Whereupon Abbot Hildoin observed (to Eginhard's stupefaction) that his observation was quite correct. Much astonished at this remark from a person who was supposed not to have seen the relics, Eginhard asked him how he knew that? Upon this, Hildoin saw that he had better make a clean breast of it, and he told the following story, which he had received from his priestly agent, Hunus. While Hunus and Lunison were at Pavia, waiting for Eginhard's notary, Hunus (according to his own account) had robbed the robbers. The relics were placed in a church; and a number of laymen and clerics, of whom Hunus was one, undertook to keep watch over them. One night, however, all the watchers, save the wide-awake Hunus, went to sleep; and then, according to the story which this " sharp " ecclesiastic foisted upon his patron,

it was borne in upon his mind that there must be some great reason why all the people, except himself, had suddenly become somnolent; and, determining to avail himself of the opportunity thus offered (*oblata occasione utendum*), he rose and, having lighted a candle, silently approached the chests. Then, having burnt through the threads of the seals with the flame of the candle, he quickly opened the chests, which had no locks; [1] and, taking out portions of each of the bodies which were thus exposed, he closed the chests and connected the burnt ends of the threads with the seals again, so that they appeared not to have been touched; and, no one having seen him, he returned to his place. (Cap. iii. 23.)

Hildoin went on to tell Eginhard that Hunus at first declared to him that these purloined relics belonged to St. Tiburtius; but afterwards confessed, as a great secret, how he had come by them, and he wound up his discourse thus:

They have a place of honour beside St. Medardus, where they are worshipped with great veneration by all the people; but whether we may keep them or not is for your judgment. (Cap. iii. 23.)

Poor Eginhard was thrown into a state of great perturbation of mind by this revelation. An acquaintance of his had recently told him of a rumour that was spread about that Hunus had contrived to abstract *all* the remains of SS. Marcellinus and Petrus while Eginhard's agents were in a drunken sleep; and that, while the real relics were in Abbot Hildoin's hands at St. Medardus, the Shrine at Seligenstadt contained nothing but a little dust. Though greatly annoyed by this " execrable rumour, spread everywhere by the subtlety of the devil," Eginhard had doubtless comforted himself by his supposed knowledge of its falsity, and he only now discovered how considerable a foundation there was for the scandal. There was nothing for it but to insist upon the return of the stolen treasures. One would have thought that the holy man, who had admitted himself to be knowingly a receiver of stolen goods, would have made instant restitution and begged only for absolution. But Eginhard intimates that he had very great difficulty in getting his brother abbot to see that even restitution was necessary.

Hildoin's proceedings were not of such a nature as

[1] The words are *scrinia sine clave*, which seems to mean " having no key." But the circumstances forbid the idea of breaking open.

to lead any one to place implicit confidence in anything he might say; still less had his agent, priest Hunus, established much claim to confidence; and it is not surprising that Eginhard should have lost no time in summoning his notary and Lunison to his presence, in order that he might hear what they had to say about the business. They, however, at once protested that priest Hunus's story was a parcel of lies, and that after the relics left Rome no one had any opportunity of meddling with them. Moreover, Lunison, throwing himself at Eginhard's feet, confessed with many tears what actually took place. It will be remembered that after the body of St. Marcellinus was abstracted from its tomb, Ratleig deposited it in the house of Deusdona, in charge of the latter's brother, Lunison. But Hunus, being very much disappointed that he could not get hold of the body of St. Tiburtius, and afraid to go back to his abbot empty-handed, bribed Lunison with four pieces of gold and five of silver to give him access to the chest. This Lunison did, and Hunus helped himself to as much as would fill a gallon-measure (*vas sextarii mensuram*) of the sacred remains. Eginhard's indignation at the "rapine" of this "*nequissimus nebulo*" is exquisitely droll. It would appear that the adage about the receiver being as bad as the thief was not current in the ninth century.

Let us now briefly sum up the history of the acquisition of the relics. Eginhard makes a contract with Deusdona for the delivery of certain relics which the latter says he possesses. Eginhard makes no inquiry how he came by them; otherwise, the transaction is innocent enough.

Deusdona turns out to be a swindler, and has no relics. Thereupon Eginhard's agent, after due fasting and prayer, breaks open the tombs and helps himself.

Eginhard discovers by the self-betrayal of his brother abbot, Hildoin, that portions of his relics have been stolen and conveyed to the latter. With much ado he succeeds in getting them back.

Hildoin's agent, Hunus, in delivering these stolen goods to him, at first declared they were the relics of St. Tiburtius, which Hildoin desired him to obtain; but afterwards invented a story of their being the product of a theft, which the providential drowsiness of his companions enabled him to perpetrate, from the relics which Hildoin well knew were the property of his friend.

Lunison, on the contrary, swears that all this story is false, and that he himself was bribed by Hunus to allow him to steal what he pleased from the property confided to his own and his brother's care by their guest Ratleig. And the honest notary himself seems to have no hesitation about lying and stealing to any extent, where the acquisition of relics is the object in view.

For a parallel to these transactions one must read a police report of the doings of a " long firm " or of a set of horse-coupers; yet Eginhard seems to be aware of nothing, but that he has been rather badly used by his friend Hildoin, and the " *nequissimus nebulo* " Hunus.

It is not easy for a modern Protestant, still less for any one who has the least tincture of scientific culture, whether physical or historical, to picture to himself the state of mind of a man of the ninth century, however cultivated, enlightened, and sincere he may have been. His deepest convictions, his most cherished hopes, were bound up with the belief in the miraculous. Life was a constant battle between saints and demons for the possession of the souls of men. The most superstitious among our modern countrymen turn to supernatural agencies only when natural causes seem insufficient; to Eginhard and his friends the supernatural was the rule; and the sufficiency of natural causes was allowed only when there was nothing to suggest others.

Moreover, it must be recollected that the possession of miracle-working relics was greatly coveted, not only on high, but on very low, grounds. To a man like Eginhard, the mere satisfaction of the religious sentiment was obviously a powerful attraction. But, more than this, the possession of such a treasure was an immense practical advantage. If the saints were duly flattered and worshipped, there was no telling what benefits might result from their interposition on your behalf. For physical evils, access to the shrine was like the grant of the use of a universal pill and ointment manufactory; and pilgrimages thereto might suffice to cleanse the performers from any amount of sin. A letter to Lupus, subsequently Abbot of Ferrara, written while Eginhard was smarting under the grief caused by the loss of his much-loved wife Imma, affords a striking insight into the current view of the relation between the glorified saints and their worshippers. The writer shows that he is anything but satisfied with the way in which he has been treated by the blessed martyrs whose remains he has taken such pains to " convey " to Seligenstadt, and to honour there as they would never have been honoured in their Roman obscurity.

It is an aggravation of my grief and a reopening of my wound, that our vows have been of no avail, and that the faith which we placed in the merits and intervention of the martyrs has been utterly disappointed.

We may admit, then, without impeachment of Eginhard's sincerity, or of his honour under all ordinary circumstances, that when piety, self-interest, the glory of the Church in general, and that of the church at Seligenstadt in particular, all pulled one way, even the workaday principles of morality were disregarded; and, *a fortiori*, anything like proper investigation of the reality of alleged miracles was thrown to the winds.

And if this was the condition of mind of such a man as Eginhard, what is it not legitimate to suppose may have been that of Deacon Deusdona, Lunison, Hunus, and company, thieves and cheats by their own confession, or of the probably hysterical nun, or of the professional beggars, for whose in-

capacity to walk and straighten themselves there is
no guarantee but their own? Who is to make sure
that the exorcist of the demon Wiggo was not just
such another priest as Hunus; and is it not at least
possible, when Eginhard's servants dreamed, night
after night, in such a curiously coincident fashion,
that a careful inquirer might have found they were
very anxious to please their master?

Quite apart from deliberate and conscious fraud
(which is a rarer thing than is often supposed),
people whose mythopœic faculty is once stirred are
capable of saying the thing that is not, and of acting
as they should not, to an extent which is hardly
imaginable by persons who are not so easily affected
by the contagion of blind faith. There is no falsity
so gross that honest men and, still more, virtuous
women, anxious to promote a good cause, will not
lend themselves to it without any clear consciousness
of the moral bearings of what they are doing. The
cases of miraculously-effected cures of which Eginhard is ocular witness appear to belong to classes of
disease in which malingering is possible or hysteria
presumable. Without modern means of diagnosis,
the names given to them are quite worthless. One
" miracle," however, in which the patient, a woman,
was cured by the mere sight of the church in which
the relics of the blessed martyrs lay, is an unmistakable case of dislocation of the lower jaw; and it is
obvious that, as not unfrequently happens in such
accidents in weakly subjects, the jaw slipped suddenly
back into place, perhaps in consequence of a jolt,
as the woman rode towards the church. (Cap. v.
53.) [1]

There is also a good deal said about a very questionable blind man—one Albricus (Alberich?)—who,

---

[1] Eginhard speaks with lofty contempt of the *vana ac
superstitiosa præsumptio* of the poor woman's companions
in trying to alleviate her sufferings with " herbs and frivolous
incantations." Vain enough, no doubt, but the *mulier-
culæ* might have returned the epithet " superstitious " with
interest.

having been cured, not of his blindness, but of another disease under which he laboured, took up his quarters at Seligenstadt, and came out as a prophet, inspired by the Archangel Gabriel. Eginhard intimates that his prophecies were fulfilled; but as he does not state exactly what they were, or how they were accomplished, the statement must be accepted with much caution. It is obvious that he was not the man to hesitate to " ease " a prophecy until it fitted, if the credit of the shrine of his favourite saints could be increased by such a procedure. There is no impeachment of his honour in the supposition. The logic of the matter is quite simple, if somewhat sophistical. The holiness of the Church of the martyrs guarantees the reality of the appearance of the Archangel Gabriel there; and what the archangel says must be true. Therefore if anything seem to be wrong, that must be the mistake of the transmitter; and, in justice to the archangel, it must be suppressed or set right. This sort of " reconciliation " is not unknown in quite modern times, and among people who would be very much shocked to be compared with a " benighted papist " of the ninth century.

The readers of this essay are, I imagine, very largely composed of people who would be shocked to be regarded as anything but enlightened Protestants. It is not unlikely that those of them who have accompanied me thus far may be disposed to say, " Well, this is all very amusing as a story, but what is the practical interest of it? We are not likely to believe in the miracles worked by the spolia of SS. Marcellinus and Petrus, or by those of any other saints in the Roman Calendar."

The practical interest is this : if you do not believe in these miracles recounted by a witness whose character and competency are firmly established, whose sincerity cannot be doubted, and who appeals to his sovereign and other contemporaries as witnesses of the truth of what he says in a document of which a MS. copy exists, probably dating within a century of the author's death, why do you profess to believe in stories of a like character, which are found in documents of the dates and of the authorship of which nothing is certainly determined, and no known copies of which come within two or three centuries of the events they record? If it be true that the four Gospels and the Acts were written by Matthew, Mark, Luke, and John, all that we know of these persons comes to nothing in comparison with our knowledge of Eginhard; and not only is there no proof that the traditional authors of these works wrote them, but very strong reasons to the contrary may be alleged. If, therefore, you refuse to believe that "Wiggo" was cast out of the possessed girl on Eginhard's authority, with what justice can you profess to believe that the legion of devils were cast out of the man among the tombs of the Gadarenes? And if, on the other hand, you accept Eginhard's evidence, why do you laugh at the supposed efficacy of relics and the saint-worship of the modern Romanists? It cannot be pretended, in the face of all evidence, that the Jews of the year 30 A.D. or thereabouts were less imbued with the belief in the supernatural than were the Franks of the year 800 A.D. The same influences were at work in each case, and it is only reasonable to suppose that the results were the same. If the evidence of Eginhard is insufficient to lead reasonable men to believe in the miracles he relates, *a fortiori* the evidence afforded by the Gospels and the Acts must be so.[1]

But it may be said that no serious critic denies the genuineness of the four great Pauline Epistles— Galatians, First and Second Corinthians, and Romans —and that in three out of these four Paul lays claim

---

[1] Of course there is nothing new in this argument; but it does not grow weaker by age. And the case of Eginhard is far more instructive than that of Augustine, because the former has so very frankly, though incidentally, revealed to us not only his own mental and moral habits, but those of the people about him.

to the power of working miracles.[1] Must we suppose, therefore, that the Apostle to the Gentiles has stated that which is false? But to how much does this so-called claim amount? It may mean much or little. Paul nowhere tells us what he did in this direction; and in his sore need to justify his assumption of apostleship against the sneers of his enemies, it is hardly likely that, if he had any very striking cases to bring forward, he would have neglected evidence so well calculated to put them to shame. And, without the slightest impeachment of Paul's veracity, we must further remember that his strongly-marked mental characteristics, displayed in unmistakable fashion in these Epistles, are anything but those which would justify us in regarding him as a critical witness respecting matters of fact, or as a trustworthy interpreter of their significance. When a man testifies to a miracle, he not only states a fact, but he adds an interpretation of the fact. We may admit his evidence as to the former, and yet think his opinion as to the latter worthless. If Eginhard's calm and objective narrative of the historical events of his time is no guarantee for the soundness of his judgment where the supernatural is concerned, the heated rhetoric of the Apostle of the Gentiles, his absolute confidence in the " inner light," and the extraordinary conceptions of the nature and requirements of logical proof which he betrays, in page after page of his Epistles, afford still less security.

There is a comparatively modern man who shared to the full Paul's trust in the " inner light," and who, though widely different from the fiery evangelist of Tarsus in various obvious particulars, yet, if I am not mistaken, shares his deepest characteristics. I speak of George Fox, who separated himself from the current Protestantism of England in the seventeenth century, as Paul separated himself from the Judaism of the first century, at the bidding of the " inner light "; who went through persecutions as

[1] See 1 Cor. xii. 10–28; 2 Cor. vi. 12; Rom. xv. 19.

serious as those which Paul enumerates; who was beaten, stoned, cast out for dead, imprisoned nine times, sometimes for long periods, who was in perils on land and perils at sea. George Fox was an even more widely-travelled missionary; while his success in founding congregations, and his energy in visiting them, not merely in Great Britain and Ireland and the West India Islands, but on the continent of Europe and that of North America, were no less remarkable. A few years after Fox began to preach, there were reckoned to be a thousand Friends in prison in the various gaols of England; at his death, less than fifty years after the foundation of the sect, there were seventy thousand Quakers in the United Kingdom. The cheerfulness with which these people —women as well as men—underwent martyrdom in this country and in the New England States is one of the most remarkable facts in the history of religion.

No one who reads the voluminous autobiography of " Honest George " can doubt the man's utter truthfulness; and though in his multitudinous letters he but rarely rises far above the incoherent commonplaces of a street preacher, there can be no question of his power as a speaker, nor any doubt as to the dignity and attractiveness of his personality, or of his possession of a large amount of practical good sense and governing faculty.

But that George Fox had full faith in his own powers as a miracle-worker, the following passage of his autobiography (to which others might be added) demonstrates :—

Now after I was set at liberty from Nottingham gaol (where I had been kept a prisoner a pretty long time) I travelled as before, in the work of the Lord. And coming to Mansfield Woodhouse, there was a distracted woman, under a doctor's hand, with her hair let loose all about her ears; and he was about to let her blood, she being first bound, and many people being about her, holding her by violence; but he could get no blood from her. And I desired them to unbind her and let her alone; for they could not touch the spirit in her by which she was tormented. So they did unbind her, and I was moved to speak to her, and in the name of the Lord to bid her be quiet and still. And she was so. And the Lord's power settled her mind and she mended; and afterwards received the truth and continued in it to her death. And the Lord's name was honoured; to whom the glory of all His works belongs. Many great and wonderful things were wrought by the heavenly power in those days. For the Lord made bare His omnipotent arm and manifested His power to the astonishment of many; by the healing virtue whereof many have been delivered from great infirmities, and the devils were made subject through His name: of which particular instances might be given beyond what this unbelieving age is able to receive or bear.[1]

It needs no long study of Fox's writings, however, to arrive at the conviction that the distinction between subjective and objective verities had not the same place in his mind as it has in that of an ordinary mortal. When an ordinary person would say, " I thought so and so," or " I made up my mind to do so and so," George Fox says, " It was opened to me," or " At the command of God I did so and so." " Then at the command of God on the ninth day of the seventh month 1643 (Fox being just nineteen), I left my relations and brake off all familiarity or friendship with young or old." " About the beginning of the year 1647 I was moved of the Lord to go into Darbyshire." Fox hears voices and he sees visions, some of which he brings before the reader with apocalyptic power in the simple and strong English, alike untutored and undefiled, of which, like John Bunyan, his contemporary, he was a master.

" And one morning, as I was sitting by the fire, a great cloud came over me and a temptation beset me; and I sate still. And it was said, *All things come by Nature*. And the elements and stars came over me; so that I was in a manner quite clouded with it. . . . And as I sate still under it, and let it alone, a living hope arose in me and a true voice arose in me which said, *There is a living God who made all things.*

---

[1] *A Journal or Historical Account of the Life, Travels, Sufferings, and Christian Experiences, &c., of George Fox.* Ed. 1694, pp. 27, 28.

And immediately the cloud and the temptation vanished away, and life rose over it all, and my heart was glad and I praised the living God " (p. 13).

If George Fox could speak, as he proves in this and some other passages he could write, his astounding influence on the contemporaries of Milton and of Cromwell is no mystery. But this modern reproduction of the ancient prophet, with his " Thus saith the Lord," " This is the work of the Lord," steeped in supernaturalism and glorying in blind faith, is the mental antipodes of the philosopher, founded in naturalism and a fanatic for evidence, to whom these affirmations inevitably suggest the previous question : How do you know that the Lord saith it ? How do you know that the Lord doeth it ? and who is compelled to demand that rational ground for belief, without which, to the man of science, assent is merely an immoral pretence.

And it is this rational ground of belief which the writers of the Gospels, no less than Paul, and Eginhard, and Fox, so little dream of offering that they would regard the demand for it as a kind of blasphemy.

AGNOSTICISM

[1889]

WITHIN the last few months [1889] the public has received much and varied information on the subject of Agnostics, their tenets, and even their future. Agnosticism exercised the orators of the Church Congress at Manchester.[1] It has been furnished with a set of " articles," fewer, but not less rigid, and certainly not less consistent than the Thirty-Nine; its nature has been analysed, and its future severely predicted by the most eloquent of that prophetical school whose Samuel is Auguste Comte. It may still be a question, however, whether the public is as much the wiser as might be expected, considering all the trouble that has been taken to enlighten it. Not only are the three accounts of the Agnostic position sadly out of harmony with one another, but I propose to show cause for my belief that all three must be seriously questioned by any one who employs the term " Agnostic " in the sense in which it was originally used. The learned Principal of King's College, who brought the topic of Agnosticism before the Church Congress, took a short and easy way of settling the business :—

But if this be so, for a man to urge, as an escape from this article of belief, that he has no means of a scientific knowledge of the unseen world, or of the future, is irrelevant. His difference from Christians lies not in the fact that he has no knowledge of these things, but that he does not believe the authority on which they are stated. He may prefer to call himself an agnostic; but his real name is an older one—he is an infidel; that is to say, an unbeliever. The word infidel, perhaps, carries an unpleasant significance. Perhaps it is right that it should. It is, and it ought to be, an unpleasant

---

[1] See the *Official Report of the Church Congress held at Manchester*, October 1888, pp. 253, 254.

thing for a man to have to say plainly that he does not believe in Jesus Christ.[1]

So much of Dr. Wace's address either explicitly or implicitly concerns me, that I take upon myself to deal with it; but, in doing so, it must be understood that I speak for myself alone. I am not aware that there is any sect of Agnostics; and if there be, I am not its acknowledged prophet or pope. I desire to leave to the Comtists the entire monopoly of the manufacture of imitation ecclesiasticism.

Let us calmly and dispassionately consider Dr. Wace's appreciation of Agnosticism. The Agnostic, according to his view, is a person who says he has no means of attaining a scientific knowledge of the unseen world or of the future; by which somewhat loose phraseology Dr. Wace presumably means the theological unseen world and future. I cannot think this description happy, either in form or substance; but for the present it may pass. Dr. Wace continues that is not " his difference from Christians." Are there then any Christians who say that they know nothing about the unseen world and the future? I was ignorant of the fact, but I am ready to accept it on the authority of a professional theologian, and I proceed to Dr. Wace's next proposition.

The real state of the case, then, is that the Agnostic " does not believe the authority " on which " these things " are stated, which authority is Jesus Christ. He is simply an old-fashioned " infidel " who is afraid

---

[1] [In this place and in *Illustrations of Mr. Gladstone's Controversial Methods*, there are references to the late Archbishop of York which are of no importance to my main argument, and which I have expunged because I desire to obliterate the traces of a temporary misunderstanding with a man of rare ability, candour, and wit, for whom I entertained a great liking and no less respect. I rejoice to think now of the (then) Bishop's cordial hail the first time we met after our little skirmish, " Well, is it to be peace or war? " I replied, " A little of both." But there was only peace when we parted, and ever after.]

to own to his right name. As "presbyter is priest writ large," so is "Agnostic" the mere Greek equivalent for the Latin "infidel." There is an attractive simplicity about this solution of the problem; and it has that advantage of being somewhat offensive to the persons attacked, which is so dear to the less refined sort of controversialist. The Agnostic says, "I cannot find good evidence that so and so is true." "Ah," says his adversary, seizing his opportunity, "then you declare that Jesus Christ was untruthful, for he said so and so;" a very telling method of rousing prejudice. But suppose that the value of the evidence as to what Jesus may have said and done, and as to the exact nature and scope of his authority, is just that which the Agnostic finds it most difficult to determine. If I venture to doubt that the Duke of Wellington gave the command "Up, Guards, and at 'em!" at Waterloo, I do not think that even Dr. Wace would accuse me of disbelieving the Duke. Yet it would be just as reasonable to do this as to accuse any one of denying what Jesus said, before the preliminary question as to what he did say is settled.

Now, the question as to what Jesus really said and did is strictly a scientific problem, which is capable of solution by no other methods than those practised by the historian and the literary critic. It is a problem of immense difficulty, which has occupied some of the best heads in Europe for the last century; and it is only of late years that their investigations have begun to converge towards one conclusion.[1]

---

[1] Dr. Wace tells us, " It may be asked how far we can rely on the accounts we possess of our Lord's teaching on these subjects." And he seems to think the question appropriately answered by the assertion that it " ought to be regarded as settled by M. Renan's practical surrender of the adverse case." I thought I knew M. Renan's works pretty well, but I have contrived to miss this " practical " (I wish Dr. Wace had defined the scope of that useful adjective) surrender. However, as Dr. Wace can find no difficulty in pointing out

That kind of faith which Dr. Wace describes and lauds is of no use here. Indeed, he himself takes pains to destroy its evidential value.

" What made the Mahommedan world? Trust and faith in the declarations and assurances of Mahommed. And what made the Christian world? Trust and faith in the declarations and assurances of Jesus Christ and His Apostles " (*l.c.* p. 253). The triumphant tone of this imaginary catechism leads me to suspect that its author has hardly appreciated its full import. Presumably, Dr. Wace regards Mahommed as an unbeliever, or, to use the term which he prefers, infidel; and considers that his assurances have given rise to a vast delusion which has led, and is leading, millions of men straight to everlasting punishment. And this being so, the " trust and faith " which have " made the Mahommedan world," in just the same sense as they have " made the Christian world," must be trust and faith in falsehood. No man who has studied history, or even attended to the occurrences of everyday life, can doubt the enormous practical value of trust and faith; but as little will he be inclined to deny that this practical value has not the least relation to the reality of the objects of that trust and faith. In examples of patient constancy of faith and of unswerving trust, the " *Acta Martyrum* " do not excel the annals of Babism.[1]

The discussion upon which we have now entered goes so thoroughly to the root of the whole matter;

the passage of M. Renan's writings, by which he feels justified in making his statement, I shall wait for further enlightenment, contenting myself, for the present, with remarking that if M. Renan were to retract and do penance in Notre Dame tomorrow for any contributions to Biblical criticism that may be specially his property, the main results of that criticism, as they are set forth in the works of Strauss, Baur, Reuss, and Volkmar, for example, could not be sensibly affected.

[1] [See De Gobineau, *Les Religions et les Philosophies dans l'Asie Centrale;* and the recently published work of Mr. E. G. Browne, *The Episode of the Bab.*]

the question of the day is so completely, as the author of *Robert Elsmere* says, the value of testimony, that I shall offer no apology for following it out somewhat in detail; and, by way of giving substance to the argument, I shall base what I have to say upon a case, the consideration of which lies strictly within the province of natural science, and of that particular part of it known as the physiology and pathology of the nervous system.

I find, in the second Gospel (chap. v.), a statement, to all appearance intended to have the same evidential value as any other contained in that history. It is the well-known story of the devils who were cast out of a man, and ordered, or permitted, to enter into a herd of swine, to the great loss and damage of the innocent Gerasene, or Gadarene, pig-owners. There can be no doubt that the narrator intends to convey to his readers his own conviction that this casting out and entering in were effected by the agency of Jesus of Nazareth; that, by speech and action, Jesus enforced this conviction; nor does any inkling of the legal and moral difficulties of the case manifest itself.

On the other hand, everything that I know of physiological and pathological science leads me to entertain a very strong conviction that the phenomena ascribed to possession are as purely natural as those which constitute small-pox; everything that I know of anthropology leads me to think that the belief in demons and demoniacal possession is a mere survival of a once-universal superstition, and that its persistence at the present time is pretty much in the inverse ratio of the general instruction, intelligence, and sound judgment of the population among whom it prevails. Everything that I know of law and justice convinces me that the wanton destruction of other people's property is a misdemeanour of evil example. Again, the study of history, and especially of that of the fifteenth, sixteenth, and seventeenth centuries, leaves no shadow of doubt on my mind that the belief in the reality of possession and of witchcraft, justly based, alike by Catholics and Protestants, upon this and innumerable other passages in both the Old and New Testaments, gave rise, through the special influence of Christian ecclesiastics, to the most horrible persecutions and judicial murders of thousands upon thousands of innocent men, women, and children. And when I reflect that the record of a plain and simple declaration upon such an occasion as this, that the belief in witchcraft and possession is wicked nonsense, would have rendered the long agony of mediæval humanity impossible, I am prompted to reject, as dishonouring, the supposition that such declaration was withheld out of condescension to popular error.

"Come forth, thou unclean spirit, out of the man" (Mark v. 8) [1] are the words attributed to Jesus. If I declare, as I have no hesitation in doing, that I utterly disbelieve in the existence of "unclean spirits," and, consequently, in the possibility of their "coming forth" out of a man, I suppose that Dr. Wace will tell me I am disregarding the testimony "of our Lord." For, if these words were really used, the most resourceful of reconcilers can hardly venture to affirm that they are compatible with a disbelief "in these things." As the learned and fair-minded, as well as orthodox, Dr. Alexander remarks, in an editorial note to the article "Demoniacs," in the *Biblical Cyclopædia* (Vol. I. p. 664, note) :—

. . . On the lowest grounds on which our Lord and His Apostles can be placed they must, at least, be regarded as *honest* men. Now, though honest speech does not require that words should be used always and only in their etymological sense, it does require that they should not be used so as to affirm what the speaker knows to be false. Whilst, therefore, our Lord and His Apostles might use the word δαιμονίζεσθαι, or the phrase, δαιμόνιον ἔχειν, as a popular description of certain diseases, without giving in to the

---

[1] Here, as always, the Revised Version is cited.

belief which lay at the source of such a mode of expression, they could not speak of demons entering into a man, or being cast out of him, without pledging themselves to the belief of an actual possession of the man by the demons. (Campbell, *Prel. Diss*. vi. 1, 10.) If, consequently, they did not hold this belief, they spoke not as honest men.

The story which we are considering does not rest on the authority of the second Gospel alone. The third confirms the second, especially in the matter of commanding the unclean spirit to come out of the man (Luke viii. 29); and, although the first Gospel either gives a different version of the same story, or tells another of like kind, the essential point remains : " If thou cast us out, send us away into the herd of swine. And He said unto them : Go ! " (Matt. viii. 31, 32).

If the concurrent testimony of the three synoptics, then, is really sufficient to do away with all rational doubt as to the matter of fact of the utmost practical and speculative importance—belief or disbelief in which may affect, and has affected, men's lives and their conduct towards other men, in the most serious way—then I am bound to believe that Jesus implicitly affirmed himself to possess a " knowledge of the unseen world," which afforded full confirmation of the belief in demons and possession current among his contemporaries. If the story is true, the mediæval theory of the invisible world may be, and probably is, quite correct; and the witch-finders, from Sprenger to Hopkins and Mather, are much-maligned men.

On the other hand, humanity, noting the frightful consequences of this belief; common sense, observing the futility of the evidence on which it is based, in all cases that have been properly investigated; science, more and more seeing its way to inclose all the phenomena of so-called " possession " within the domain of pathology, so far as they are not to be relegated to that of the police—all these powerful influences concur in warning us, at our peril, against accepting the belief without the most careful scrutiny of the authority on which it rests.

I can discern no escape from this dilemma : either Jesus said what he is reported to have said, or he did not. In the former case, it is inevitable that his authority on matters connected with the " unseen world " should be roughly shaken; in the latter, the blow falls upon the authority of the Synoptic Gospels. If their report on a matter of such stupendous and far-reaching practical import as this is untrustworthy, how can we be sure of its trustworthiness in other cases? The favourite " earth " in which the hard-pressed reconciler takes refuge, that the Bible does not profess to teach science,[1] is stopped in this instance. For the question of the existence of demons and of possession by them, though it lies strictly within the province of science, is also of the deepest moral and religious significance. If physical and mental disorders are caused by demons, Gregory of Tours and his contemporaries rightly considered that relics and exorcists were more useful than doctors; the gravest questions arise as to the legal and moral responsibilities of persons inspired by demoniacal impulses; and our whole conception of the universe and of our relations to it becomes totally different from what it would be on the contrary hypothesis.

The theory of life of an average mediæval Christian was as different from that of an average nineteenth-

---

[1] Does any one really mean to say that there is any internal or external criterion by which the reader of a biblical statement, in which scientific matter is contained, is enabled to judge whether it is to be taken *au sérieux* or not? Is the account of the Deluge, accepted as true in the New Testament, less precise and specific than that of the call of Abraham, also accepted as true therein ? By what mark does the story of the feeding with manna in the wilderness, which involves some very curious scientific problems, show that it is meant merely for edification, while the story of the inscription of the Law on stone by the hand of Jahveh is literally true? If the story of the Fall is not the true record of an historical occurrence, what becomes of Pauline theology. Yet the story of the Fall as directly conflicts with probability, and is as devoid of trustworthy evidence, as that of the Creation or that of the Deluge, with which it forms an harmoniously legendary series.

century Englishman as that of a West African negro is now, in these respects. The modern world is slowly, but surely, shaking off these and other monstrous survivals of savage delusions; and, whatever happens, it will not return to that wallowing in the mire. Until the contrary is proved, I venture to doubt whether, at this present moment, any Protestant theologian who has a reputation to lose will say that he believes the Gadarene story.

The choice then lies between discrediting those who compiled the Gospel biographies and disbelieving the Master, whom they, simple souls, thought to honour by preserving such traditions of the exercise of his authority over Satan's invisible world. This is the dilemma. No deep scholarship, nothing but a knowledge of the Revised Version (on which it is to be supposed all that mere scholarship can do has been done), with the application thereto of the commonest canons of common sense, is needful to enable us to make a choice between its alternatives. It is hardly doubtful that the story, as told in the first Gospel, is merely a version of that told in the second and third. Nevertheless, the discrepancies are serious and irreconcilable; and, on this ground alone, a suspension of judgment, at the least, is called for. But there is a great deal more to be said. From the dawn of scientific biblical criticism until the present day, the evidence against the long-cherished notion that the three Synoptic Gospels are the works of three independent authors, each prompted by divine inspiration, has steadily accumulated, until at the present time there is no visible escape from the conclusion that each of the three is a compilation consisting of a groundwork common to all three—the threefold tradition; and of a superstructure, consisting, firstly, of matter common to it with one of the others, and, secondly, of matter special to each. The use of the terms " groundwork " and " superstructure " by no means implies that the latter must be of later date than the former. On the contrary, some parts of it may be, and probably are, older than some parts of the groundwork.[1]

The story of the Gadarene swine belongs to the groundwork; at least, the essential part of it, in which the belief in demoniac possession is expressed, does; and therefore the compilers of the first, second, and third Gospels, whoever they were, certainly accepted that belief (which, indeed, was universal among both Jews and pagans at that time), and attributed it to Jesus.

What, then, do we know about the originator, or originators, of this groundwork—of that threefold tradition which all three witnesses (in Paley's phrase) agree upon—that we should allow their mere statements to outweigh the counter-arguments of humanity, of common sense, of exact science, and to imperil the respect which all would be glad to be able to render to their Master?

Absolutely nothing.[2] There is no proof, nothing more than a fair presumption, that any one of the Gospels existed, in the state in which we find it in the Authorised Version of the Bible, before the second century, or, in other words, sixty or seventy years after the events recorded. And between that time and the date of the oldest extant manuscripts of the Gospels, there is no telling what additions and alterations and interpolations may have been made. It may be said that this is all mere speculation, but it is a good deal more. As competent scholars and honest men, our revisers have felt compelled to point

[1] See, for an admirable discussion of the whole subject, Dr. Abbott's article on the Gospels in the *Encyclopædia Britannica;* and the remarkable monograph by Professor Volkmar, *Jesus Nazarenus und die erste christliche Zeit* (1882). Whether we agree with the conclusions of these writers or not, the method of critical investigation which they adopt is unimpeachable.

[2] Notwithstanding the hard words shot at me from behind the hedge of anonymity by a writer in a recent number of the *Quarterly Review,* I repeat, without the slightest fear of refutation, that the four Gospels, as they have come to us, are the work of unknown writers.

out that such things have happened even since the date of the oldest known manuscripts. The oldest two copies of the second Gospel end with the eighth verse of the sixteenth chapter; the remaining twelve verses are spurious, and it is noteworthy that the maker of the addition has not hesitated to introduce a speech in which Jesus promises his disciples that " in My name shall they cast out devils."

The other passage " rejected to the margin " is still more instructive. It is that touching apologue, with its profound ethical sense, of the woman taken in adultery—which, if internal evidence were an infallible guide, might well be affirmed to be a typical example of the teachings of Jesus. Yet, say the revisers, pitilessly, " Most of the ancient authorities omit John vii. 53–viii. 11." Now let any reasonable man ask himself this question: If, after an approximate settlement of the canon of the New Testament, and even later than the fourth and fifth centuries, literary fabricators had the skill and the audacity to make such additions and interpolations as these, what may they have done when no one had thought of a canon; when oral tradition, still unfixed, was regarded as more valuable than such written records as may have existed in the latter portion of the first century? Or, to take the other alternative, if those who gradually settled the canon did not know of the existence of the oldest codices which have come down to us; or if, knowing them, they rejected their authority, what is to be thought of their competency as critics of the text?

People who object to free criticism of the Christian scriptures forget that they are what they are in virtue of very free criticism; unless the advocates of inspiration are prepared to affirm that the majority of influential ecclesiastics during several centuries were safeguarded against error. For, even granting that some books of the period were inspired, they were certainly few amongst many, and those who selected the canonical books, unless they themselves were also inspired, must be regarded in the light of mere critics, and, from the evidence they have left of their intellectual habits, very uncritical critics. When one thinks that such delicate questions as those involved fell into the hands of men like Papias (who believed in the famous millenarian grape story); of Irenæus, with his " reasons " for the existence of only four Gospels; and of such calm and dispassionate judges as Tertullian, with his *Credo quia impossibile* : the marvel is that the selection which constitutes our New Testament is as free as it is from obviously objectionable matter. The apocryphal Gospels certainly deserve to be apocryphal; but one may suspect that a little more critical discrimination would have enlarged the Apocrypha not inconsiderably.

At this point a very obvious objection arises, and deserves full and candid consideration. It may be said that critical scepticism carried to the length suggested is historical pyrrhonism; that if we are altogether to discredit an ancient or a modern historian, because he has assumed fabulous matter to be true, it will be as well to give up paying any attention to history. It may be said, and with great justice, that Eginhard's *Life of Charlemagne* is none the less trustworthy because of the astounding revelation of credulity, of lack of judgment, and even of respect for the eighth commandment, which he has unconsciously made in the *History of the Translation of the Blessed Martyrs Marcellinus and Paul*. Or, to go no further back than the last number of the *Nineteenth Century*, surely that excellent lady, Miss Strickland, is not to be refused all credence because of the myth about the second James's remains, which she seems to have unconsciously invented.

Of course this is perfectly true. I am afraid there is no man alive whose witness could be accepted if the condition precedent were proof that he had never invented and promulgated a myth. In the minds of all of us there are little places here and there, like the indistinguishable spots on a rock which give

oothold to moss or stonecrop, on which, if the germ
of a myth fall, it is certain to grow, without in the
least degree affecting our accuracy or truthfulness
elsewhere. Sir Walter Scott knew that he could not
repeat a story without, as he said, " giving it a new
hat and stick." Most of us differ from Sir Walter
only in not knowing about this tendency of the
mythopœic faculty to break out unnoticed. But it
is also perfectly true that the mythopœic faculty is
not equally active in all minds, nor in all regions and
under all conditions of the same mind. David Hume
was certainly not so liable to temptation as the
Venerable Bede, or even as some recent historians
who could be mentioned; and the most imaginative
of debtors, if he owes five pounds, never makes an
obligation to pay a hundred out of it. The rule of
common sense is *prima facie* to trust a witness in all
matters, in which neither his self-interest, his passions, his prejudices, nor that love of the marvellous
which is inherent to a greater or less degree in all
mankind, are strongly concerned; and, when they
are involved, to require corroborative evidence in
exact proportion to the contravention of probability
by the thing testified.

Now, in the Gadarene affair, I do not think I am
unreasonably sceptical if I say that the existence of
demons who can be transferred from a man to a pig
does thus contravene probability. Let me be perfectly candid. I admit I have no *a priori* objection
to offer. There are physical things, such as *tæniæ*
and *trichinæ*, which can be transferred from men to
pigs, and *vice versa*, and which do undoubtedly produce most diabolical and deadly effects on both.
For anything I can absolutely prove to the contrary,
there may be spiritual things capable of the same
transmigration, with like effects. Moreover, I am
bound to add that perfectly truthful persons, for
whom I have the greatest respect, believe in stories
about spirits of the present day quite as improbable
as that we are considering.

So I declare, as plainly as I can, that I am unable to show cause why these transferable devils should not exist; nor can I deny that, not merely the whole Roman Church, but many Wacean "infidels" of no mean repute, do honestly and firmly believe that the activity of such-like demonic beings is in full swing in this year of grace 1889.

Nevertheless, as good Bishop Butler says, "probability is the guide of life"; and it seems to me that this is just one of the cases in which the canon of credibility and testimony, which I have ventured to lay down, has full force. So that, with the most entire respect for many (by no means for all) of our witnesses for the truth of demonology, ancient and modern, I conceive their evidence on this particular matter to be ridiculously insufficient to warrant their conclusion.[1]

After what has been said, I do not think that any sensible man, unless he happen to be angry, will accuse me of "contradicting the Lord and His Apostles" if I reiterate my total disbelief in the whole Gadarene story. But, if that story is discredited, all the other stories of demoniac possession fall under suspicion. And if the belief in demons and demoniac possession, which forms the sombre background of the whole picture of primitive Christi-

[1] Their arguments, in the long run, are always reducible to one form. Otherwise trustworthy witnesses affirm that such and such events took place. These events are inexplicable, except the agency of "spirits" is admitted. Therefore "spirits" were the cause of the phenomena.

And the heads of the reply are always the same. Remember Goethe's aphorism: *Alles factische ist schon Theorie.* Trustworthy witnesses are constantly deceived, or deceive themselves, in their interpretation of sensible phenomena. No one can prove that the sensible phenomena, in these cases, could be caused only by the agency of spirits: and there is abundant ground for believing that they may be produced in other ways. Therefore, the utmost that can be reasonably asked for, on the evidence as it stands, is suspension of judgment. And, on the necessity for even that suspension, reasonable men may differ, according to their views of probability.

anity, presented to us in the New Testament, is shaken. what is to be said, in any case, of the uncorroborated testimony of the Gospels with respect to " the unseen world " ?

I am not aware that I have been influenced by any more bias in regard to the Gadarene story than I have been in dealing with other cases of like kind the investigation of which has interested me. I was brought up in the strictest school of evangelical orthodoxy; and when I was old enough to think for myself I started upon my journey of inquiry with little doubt about the general truth of what I had been taught; and with that feeling of the unpleasantness of being called an " infidel " which, we are told, is so right and proper. Near my journey's end, I find myself in a condition of something more than mere doubt about these matters.

In the course of other inquiries, I have had to do with fossil remains which looked quite plain at a distance, and became more and more indistinct as I tried to define their outline by close inspection. There was something there—something which, if I could win assurance about it, might mark a new epoch in the history of the earth; but, study as long as I might, certainty eluded my grasp. So has it been with me in my efforts to define the grand figure of Jesus as it lies in the primary strata of Christian literature. Is he the kindly, peaceful Christ depicted in the Catacombs? Or is he the stern Judge who frowns above the altar of SS. Cosmas and Damianus? Or can he be rightly represented by the bleeding ascetic, broken down by physical pain, of too many mediæval pictures? Are we to accept the Jesus of the second, or the Jesus of the fourth Gospel, as the true Jesus? What did he really say and do; and how much that is attributed to him, in speech and action, is the embroidery of the various parties into which his followers tended to split themselves within twenty years of his death, when even the threefold tradition was only nascent?

If any one will answer these questions for me with something more to the point than feeble talk about the " cowardice of Agnosticism," I shall be deeply his debtor. Unless and until they are satisfactorily answered, I say of Agnosticism in this matter, " *J'y suis, et j'y reste.*"

But, as we have seen, it is asserted that I have no business to call myself an Agnostic; that, if I am not a Christian, I am an infidel; and that I ought to call myself by that name of " unpleasant significance." Well, I do not care much what I am called by other people, and if I had at my side all those who, since the Christian era, have been called infidels by other folks, I could not desire better company. If these are my ancestors, I prefer, with the old Frank, to be with them wherever they are. But there are several points in Dr. Wace's contention which must be elucidated before I can even think of undertaking to carry out his wishes. I must, for instance, know what a Christian is. Now what is a Christian? By whose authority is the signification of that term defined? Is there any doubt that the immediate followers of Jesus, the " sect of the Nazarenes," were strictly orthodox Jews differing from other Jews not more than the Sadducees, the Pharisees, and the Essenes differed from one another; in fact, only in the belief that the Messiah, for whom the rest of their nation waited, had come? Was not their chief, " James, the brother of the Lord," reverenced alike by Sadducee, Pharisee, and Nazarene? At the famous conference which, according to the Acts, took place at Jerusalem, does not James declare that " myriads " of Jews, who, by that time, had become Nazarenes, were " all zealous for the Law "? Was not the name of " Christian " first used to denote the converts to the doctrine promulgated by Paul and Barnabas at Antioch? Does the subsequent history of Christianity leave any doubt that, from this time forth, the " little rift within the lute " caused by the new teaching, developed, if not inaugurated, at

Antioch, grew wider and wider, until the two types of doctrine irreconcilably diverged? Did not the primitive Nazarenism, or Ebionism, develop into the Nazarenism, and Ebionism, and Elkasaitism of later ages, and finally die out in obscurity and condemnation, as damnable heresy; while the younger doctrine throve and pushed out its shoots into that endless variety of sects, of which the three strongest survivors are the Roman and Greek Churches and modern Protestantism?

Singular state of things! If I were to profess the doctrine which was held by " James, the brother of the Lord," and by every one of the " myriads " of his followers and co-religionists in Jerusalem up to twenty or thirty years after the Crucifixion (and one knows not how much later at Pella), I should be condemned with unanimity, as an ebionising heretic by the Roman, Greek, and Protestant Churches! And probably this hearty and unanimous condemnation of the creed, held by those who were in the closest personal relation with their Lord, is almost the only point upon which they would be cordially of one mind. On the other hand, though I hardly dare imagine such a thing, I very much fear that the " pillars " of the primitive Hierosolymitan Church would have considered Dr. Wace an infidel. No one can read the famous second chapter of Galatians and the Book of Revelation without seeing how narrow was even Paul's escape from a similar fate. And, if ecclesiastical history is to be trusted, the Thirty-Nine Articles, be they right or wrong, diverge from the primitive doctrine of the Nazarenes vastly more than even Pauline Christianity did.

But, further than this, I have great difficulty in assuring myself that even James, " the brother of the Lord," and his " myriads " of Nazarenes, properly represented the doctrines of their Master. For it is constantly asserted by our modern " pillars " that one of the chief features of the work of Jesus was the instauration of religion by the abolition of what our sticklers for articles and liturgies, with unconscious humour, call the narrow restrictions of the Law. Yet, if James knew this, how could the bitter controversy with Paul have arisen; and why did not one or the other side quote any of the various sayings of Jesus, recorded in the Gospels, which directly bear on the question—sometimes, apparently, in opposite directions?

So, if I am asked to call myself an "infidel," I reply : To what doctrine do you ask me to be faithful? Is it that contained in the Nicene and the Athanasian Creeds? My firm belief is that the Nazarenes, say of the year 40, headed by James, would have stopped their ears and thought worthy of stoning the audacious man who propounded it to them. Is it contained in the so-called Apostles' Creed ! I am pretty sure that even that would have created a recalcitrant commotion at Pella in the year 70, among the Nazarenes of Jerusalem, who had fled from the soldiers of Titus. And yet, if the unadulterated tradition of the teachings of "the Nazarene" were to be found anywhere, it surely should have been amidst those not very aged disciples who may have heard them as they were delivered.

Therefore, however sorry I may be to be unable to demonstrate that, if necessary, I should not be afraid to call myself an "infidel," I cannot do it. "Infidel" is a term of reproach, which Christians and Mahommedans, in their modesty, agree to apply to those who differ from them. If he had only thought of it, Dr. Wace might have used the term "miscreant," which, with the same etymological signification, has the advantage of being still more "unpleasant" to the persons to whom it is applied. But why should a man be expected to call himself a "miscreant" or an "infidel"? That St. Patrick "had two birthdays because he was a twin" is a reasonable and intelligible utterance beside that of the man who should declare himself to be an infidel on the ground of denying his own belief. It may be logically, if not ethically, defensible that a Christian should call a Mahommedan an infidel and *vice versa ;* but, on Dr. Wace's principles, both ought to call themselves infidels, because each applies the term to the other.

Now I am afraid that all the Mahommedan world would agree in reciprocating that appellation to Dr. Wace himself. I once visited the Hazar Mosque, the great University of Mahommedanism, in Cairo, in ignorance of the fact that I was unprovided with proper authority. A swarm of angry undergraduates, as I suppose I ought to call them, came buzzing about me and my guide; and if I had known Arabic, I suspect that " dog of an infidel " would have been by no means the most " unpleasant " of the epithets showered upon me, before I could explain and apologise for the mistake. If I had had the pleasure of Dr. Wace's company on that occasion, the undiscriminative followers of the Prophet would, I am afraid, have made no difference between us; not even if they had known that he was the head of an orthodox Christian seminary. And I have not the smallest doubt that even one of the learned mollahs, if his grave courtesy would have permitted him to say anything offensive to men of another mode of belief, would have told us that he wondered we did not find it " very unpleasant " to disbelieve in the Prophet of Islam.

From what precedes, I think it becomes sufficiently clear that Dr. Wace's account of the origin of the name of " Agnostic " is quite wrong. Indeed, I am bound to add that very slight effort to discover the truth would have convinced him that, as a matter of fact, the term arose otherwise. I am loath to go over an old story once more; but more than one object which I have in view will be served by telling it a little more fully than it has yet been told.

Looking back nearly fifty years, I see myself as a boy, whose education has been interrupted, and who intellectually was left, for some years, altogether to his own devices. At that time I was a voracious and omnivorous reader; a dreamer and speculator of the first water, well endowed with that splendid courage in attacking any and every subject which is the blessed compensation of youth and inexperience. Among the books and essays, on all sorts of topics from metaphysics to heraldry, which I read at this time, two left indelible impressions on my mind. One was Guizot's "History of Civilisation," the other was Sir William Hamilton's essay "On the Philosophy of the Unconditioned," which I came upon, by chance, in an odd volume of the *Edinburgh Review*. The latter was certainly strange reading for a boy, and I could not possibly have understood a great deal of it; [1] nevertheless I devoured it with avidity, and it stamped upon my mind the strong conviction that, on even the most solemn and important of questions, men are apt to take cunning phrases for answers; and that the limitation of our faculties, in a great number of cases, renders real answers to such questions, not merely actually impossible, but theoretically inconceivable.

Philosophy and history, having laid hold of me in this eccentric fashion, have never loosened their grip. I have no pretension to be an expert in either subject; but the turn for philosophical and historical reading, which rendered Hamilton and Guizot attractive to me, has not only filled many lawful leisure hours, and still more sleepless ones, with the repose of changed mental occupation, but has not unfrequently disputed my proper work-time with my liege lady, Natural Science. In this way I have found it possible to cover a good deal of ground in the territory of philosophy; and all the more easily that I have never cared much about A's or B's opinions, but have rather sought to know what answer he had to give to the questions I had to put to him—that of the

---

[1] Yet I must somehow have laid hold of the pith of the matter, for, many years afterwards, when Dean Mansel's Bampton Lectures were published, it seemed to me I already knew all that this eminently Agnostic thinker had to tell me.

limitation of possible knowledge being the chief. The ordinary examiner, with his " State the views of So-and-so," would have floored me at any time. If he had said, What do *you* think about any given problem? I might have got on fairly well.

The reader who has had the patience to follow the enforced, but unwilling, egotism of this veritable history (especially if his studies have led him in the same direction) will now see why my mind steadily gravitated towards the conclusions of Hume and Kant, so well stated by the latter in a sentence, which I have quoted elsewhere.

The greatest and perhaps the sole use of all philosophy of pure reason is, after all, merely negative, since it serves not as an organon for the enlargement [of knowledge], but as a discipline for its delimitation; and, instead of discovering truth, has only the modest merit of preventing error.[1]

When I reached intellectual maturity and began to ask myself whether I was an atheist, a theist, or a pantheist; a materialist or an idealist; a Christian or a freethinker; I found that the more I learned and reflected, the less ready was the answer; until, at last, I came to the conclusion that I had neither art nor part with any of these denominations, except the last. The one thing in which most of these good people were agreed was the one thing in which I differed from them. They were quite sure they had attained a certain " gnosis,"—had, more or less successfully, solved the problem of existence; while I was quite sure I had not, and had a pretty strong conviction that the problem was insoluble. And, with Hume and Kant on my side, I could not think myself presumptuous in holding fast by that opinion. Like Dante,

> Nel mezzo del cammin di nostra vita
> Mi ritrovai per una selva oscura,

but, unlike Dante, I cannot add,

> Che la diritta via era smarrita.

---

[1] *Kritik der reinen Vernunft.* Edit. Hartenstein, p. 256.

On the contrary, I had, and have, the firmest conviction that I never left the " *verace via* "—the straight road; and that this road led nowhere else but into the dark depths of a wild and tangled forest.   And though I have found leopards and lions in the path; though I have made abundant acquaintance with the hungry wolf, that " with privy paw devours apace and nothing said," as another great poet says of the ravening beast; and though no friendly spectre has even yet offered his guidance, I was, and am, minded to go straight on, until I either come out on the other side of the wood, or find there is no other side to it— at least, none attainable by me.

This was my situation when I had the good fortune to find a place among the members of that remarkable confraternity of antagonists, long since deceased, but of green and pious memory, the Metaphysical Society. Every variety of philosophical and theological opinion was represented there, and expressed itself with entire openness; most of my colleagues with -*ists* of one sort or another; and, however kind and friendly they might be, I, the man without a rag of a label to cover himself with, could not fail to have some of the uneasy feelings which must have beset the historical fox when, after leaving the trap in which his tail remained, he presented himself to his normally elongated companions. So I took thought, and invented what I conceived to be the appropriate title of " Agnostic."   It came into my head as suggestively antithetic to the " Gnostic " of Church history, who professed to know so much about the very things of which I was ignorant; and I took the earliest opportunity of parading it at our Society, to show that I, too, had a tail, like the other foxes.   To my great satisfaction, the term took; and when the *Spectator* had stood godfather to it, any suspicion in the minds of respectable people that a knowledge of its parentage might have awakened was, of course, completely lulled.

That is the history of the origin of the terms

"Agnostic" and "Agnosticism"; and it will be observed that it does not quite agree with the confident assertion of the reverend Principal of King's College, that "the adoption of the term Agnostic is only an attempt to shift the issue, and that it involves a mere evasion" in relation to the Church and Christianity.[1]

The last objection (I rejoice as much as my readers must do that it is the last) which I have to take to Dr. Wace's deliverance before the Church Congress arises, I am sorry to say, on a question of morality.

"It is, and it ought to be," authoritatively declares this official representative of Christian ethics, "an unpleasant thing for a man to have to say plainly that he does not believe in Jesus Christ" (*l.c.* p. 254).

Whether it is so depends, I imagine, a good deal on whether the man was brought up in a Christian household or not. I do not see why it should be "unpleasant" for a Mahommedan or Buddhist to say so. But that "it ought to be" unpleasant for any man to say anything which he sincerely, and after due deliberation, believes, is, to my mind, a proposition of the most profoundly immoral character. I verily believe that the great good which has been effected in the world by Christianity has been largely counteracted by the pestilent doctrine on which all the Churches have insisted, that honest disbelief in their more or less astonishing creeds is a moral offence, indeed a sin of the deepest dye, deserving and involving the same future retribution as murder and robbery. If we could only see, in one view, the torrents of hypocrisy and cruelty, the lies, the slaughter, the violations of every obligation of humanity, which have flowed from this source along the course of the history of Christian nations, our worst imaginations of Hell would pale beside the vision.

A thousand times, no! It ought *not* to be un-

---

[1] *Report of the Church Congress*, Manchester, 1888, p. 252.

pleasant to say that which one honestly believes or disbelieves. That it so constantly is painful to do so, is quite enough obstacle to the progress of mankind in that most valuable of all qualities, honesty of word or of deed, without erecting a sad concomitant of human weakness into something to be admired and cherished. The bravest of soldiers often, and very naturally, " feel it unpleasant " to go into action; but a court-martial which did its duty would make short work of the officer who promulgated the doctrine that his men *ought* to feel their duty unpleasant.

I am very well aware, as I suppose most thoughtful people are in these times, that the process of breaking away from old beliefs is extremely unpleasant; and I am much disposed to think that the encouragement, the consolation, and the peace afforded to earnest believers in even the worst forms of Christianity are of great practical advantage to them. What deductions must be made from this gain on the score of the harm done to the citizen by the ascetic other-worldliness of logical Christianity; to the ruler, by the hatred, malice, and all uncharitableness of sectarian bigotry; to the legislator, by the spirit of exclusiveness and domination of those that count themselves pillars of orthodoxy; to the philosopher by the restraints on the freedom of learning and teaching which every Church exercises, when it is strong enough; to the conscientious soul, by the introspective hunting after sins of the mint and cummin type, the fear of theological error, and the overpowering terror of possible damnation, which have accompanied the Churches like their shadow, I need not now consider; but they are assuredly not small. If Agnostics lose heavily on the one side, they gain a good deal on the other. People who talk about the comforts of belief appear to forget its discomforts; they ignore the fact that the Christianity of the Churches is something more than faith in the ideal personality of Jesus, which they create for themselves, *plus* so much as can be carried into practice, without disorganising civil society, of the maxims of the " Sermon on the Mount." Trip in morals or in doctrine (especially in doctrine), without due repentance or retractation, or fail to get properly baptized before you die, and a *plébiscite* of the Christians of Europe, if they were true to their creeds, would affirm your everlasting damnation by an immense majority.

Preachers, orthodox and heterodox, din into our ears that the world cannot get on without faith of some sort. There is a sense in which that is as eminently as obviously true; there is another in which, in my judgment, it is as eminently as obviously false, and it seems to me that the hortatory, or pulpit, mind is apt to oscillate between the false and the true meanings, without being aware of the fact.

It is quite true that the ground of every one of our actions, and the validity of all our reasonings, rest upon the great act of faith, which leads us to take the experience of the past as a safe guide in our dealings with the present and the future. From the nature of ratiocination, it is obvious, that the axioms on which it is based cannot be demonstrated by ratiocination. It is also a trite observation that in the business of life we constantly take the most serious action upon evidence of an utterly insufficient character. But it is surely plain that faith is not necessarily entitled to dispense with ratiocination because ratiocination cannot dispense with faith as a starting-point; and that because we are often obliged, by the pressure of events, to act on very bad evidence, it does not follow that it is proper to act on such evidence when the pressure is absent.

The writer of the Epistle to the Hebrews tells us that " faith is the assurance of things hoped for, the proving of things not seen." In the Authorised Version, " substance " stands for " assurance," and " evidence " for " proving." The question of the exact meaning of the two words, ὑπόστασις and ἔλεγχος, affords a fine field of discussion for the

scholar and the metaphysician. But I fancy we shall
be not far from the mark if we take the writer to
have had in his mind the profound psychological
truth, that men constantly feel certain about things
for which they strongly hope, but have no evidence,
in the legal or logical sense of the word; and he calls
this feeling " faith." I may have the most absolute
faith that a friend has not committed the crime of
which he is accused. In the early days of English
history, if my friend could have obtained a few more
compurgators of a like robust faith, he would have
been acquitted. At the present day, if I tendered
myself as a witness on that score, the judge would
tell me to stand down, and the youngest barrister
would smile at my simplicity. Miserable indeed is
the man who has not such faith in some of his fellow-
men—only less miserable than the man who allows
himself to forget that such faith is not, strictly speaking, evidence; and when his faith is disappointed, as
will happen now and again, turns Timon and blames
the universe for his own blunders. And so, if a man
can find a friend, the hypostasis of all his hopes, the
mirror of his ethical ideal, in the Jesus of any, or all,
of the Gospels, let him live by faith in that ideal.
Who shall or can forbid him? But let him not delude
himself with the notion that his faith is evidence of
the objective reality of that in which he trusts. Such
evidence is to be obtained only by the use of the
methods of science, as applied to history and to
literature, and it amounts at present to very little.

THE CHRISTIAN TRADITION IN RE-LATION TO JUDAIC CHRISTIANITY

[FROM " AGNOSTICISM : A REJOINDER," 1889]

THE most constant reproach which is launched against persons of my way of thinking is that it is all very well for us to talk about the deductions of scientific thought, but what are the poor and the uneducated to do? Has it ever occurred to those who talk in this fashion, that their creeds and the articles of their several confessions, their determination of the exact nature and extent of the teachings of Jesus, their expositions of the real meaning of that which is written in the Epistles (to leave aside all questions concerning the Old Testament), are nothing more than deductions which, at any rate, profess to be the result of strictly scientific thinking, and which are not worth attending to unless they really possess that character? If it is not historically true that such and such things happened in Palestine eighteen centuries ago, what becomes of Christianity? And what is historical truth but that of which the evidence bears strict scientific investigaton? I do not call to mind any problem of natural science which has come under my notice which is more difficult, or more curiously interesting as a mere problem, than that of the origin of the Synoptic Gospels and that of the historical value of the narratives which they contain. The Christianity of the Churches stands or falls by the results of the purely scientific investigation of these questions. They were first taken up, in a purely scientific spirit, about a century ago; they have been studied over and over again by men of vast knowledge and critical acumen; but he would be a rash man who should assert that any solution of these problems as yet formulated is exhaustive. The most that can be said is that certain prevalent solutions are certainly false, while others are more or less probably true.

If I am doing my best to rouse my countrymen out of their dogmatic slumbers, it is not that they may be amused by seeing who gets the best of it in a contest between a " scientist " and a theologian. The serious question is whether theological men of science or theological special pleaders are to have the confidence of the general public; it is the question whether a country in which it is possible for a body of excellent clerical and lay gentlemen to discuss, in public meeting assembled, how much it is desirable to let the congregations of the faithful know of the results of biblical criticism, is likely to wake up with anything short of the grasp of a rough lay hand upon its shoulder; it is the question whether the New Testament books, being, as I believe they were, written and compiled by people who, according to their lights, were perfectly sincere, will not, when properly studied as ordinary historical documents, afford us the means of self-criticism. And it must be remembered that the New Testament books are not responsible for the doctrine invented by the Churches that they are anything but ordinary historical documents. The author of the third Gospel tells us, as straightforwardly as a man can, that he has no claim to any other character than that of an ordinary compiler and editor, who had before him the works of many and variously qualified predecessors.

In my former papers, according to Dr. Wace, I have evaded giving an answer to his main proposition, which he states as follows—

Apart from all disputed points of criticism, no one practically doubts that our Lord lived, and that He died on the cross, in the most intense sense of filial relation to His Father in Heaven, and that He bore testimony to that Father's providence, love, and grace towards mankind. The Lord's Prayer affords a sufficient evidence on these points. If the Sermon on the Mount alone be added, the whole unseen world, of which the Agnostic refuses to know anything, stands unveiled before us. . . . If Jesus Christ preached that Sermon, made those promises, and taught that prayer, then any one who says that we know nothing of God, or of a future life, or of an unseen world, says that he does not believe Jesus Christ (pp. 354–355).

Again—

The main question at issue, in a word, is one which Professor Huxley has chosen to leave entirely on one side—whether, namely, allowing for the utmost uncertainty on other points of the criticism to which he appeals, there is any reasonable doubt that the Lord's Prayer and the Sermon on the Mount afford a true account of our Lord's essential belief and cardinal teaching (p. 355).

I certainly was not aware that I had evaded the questions here stated; indeed I should say that I have indicated my reply to them pretty clearly; but, as Dr. Wace wants a plainer answer, he shall certainly be gratified. If, as Dr. Wace declares it is, his " whole case is involved in " the argument as stated in the latter of these two extracts, so much the worse for his whole case. For I am of opinion that there is the gravest reason for doubting whether the " Sermon on the Mount " was ever preached, and whether the so-called " Lord's Prayer " was ever prayed, by Jesus of Nazareth. My reasons for this opinion are, among others, these : There is now no doubt that the three Synoptic Gospels, so far from being the work of three independent writers, are closely inter-dependent,[1] and that in one of two ways. Either all three contain, as their foundation, versions, to a large extent verbally identical, of one and the same tradition; or two of them are thus closely dependent on the third; and the opinion of the majority of the best critics has of late years more

[1] I suppose this is what Dr. Wace is thinking about when he says that I allege that there " is no visible escape " from the supposition of an *Ur-Marcus* (p. 367). That a " theologian of repute " should confound an indisputable fact with one of the modes of explaining that fact is not so singular as those who are unaccustomed to the ways of theologians might imagine.

and more converged towards the conviction that our
canonical second Gospel (the so-called " Mark's "
Gospel) is that which most closely represents the
primitive groundwork of the three.[1] That I take to
be one of the most valuable results of New Testament
criticism, of immeasurably greater importance than the
discussion about dates and authorship.

But if, as I believe to be the case, beyond any
rational doubt or dispute, the second Gospel is the
nearest extant representative of the oldest tradition,
whether written or oral, how comes it that it contains
neither the " Sermon on the Mount " nor the " Lord's
Prayer," those typical embodiments, according to
Dr. Wace, of the " essential belief and cardinal teaching " of Jesus ? Not only does " Mark's " Gospel
fail to contain the " Sermon on the Mount," or anything but a very few of the sayings contained in that
collection; but, at the point of the history of Jesus
where the " Sermon " occurs in " Matthew," there is
in " Mark " an apparently unbroken narrative from
the calling of James and John to the healing of
Simon's wife's mother. Thus the oldest tradition not
only ignores the " Sermon on the Mount," but, by
implication, raises a probability against its being
delivered when and where the later " Matthew "
inserts it in his compilation.

[1] Any examiner whose duty it has been to examine into a
case of " copying " will be particularly well prepared to
appreciate the force of the case stated in that most excellent
little book, *The Common Tradition of the Synoptic Gospels*,
by Dr. Abbott and Mr. Rushbrooke (Macmillan, 1884). To
those who have not passed through such painful experiences
I may recommend the brief discussion of the genuineness of
the " Casket Letters " in my friend Mr. Skelton's interesting
book, *Maitland of Lethington*. The second edition of Holtzmann's *Lehrbuch*, published in 1886, gives a remarkably fair
and full account of the present results of criticism. At
p. 366 he writes that the present burning question is whether
the " relatively primitive narrative and the root of the other
synoptic texts is contained in Matthew or in Mark. It is only
on this point that properly-informed (*sachkundige*) critics.
differ," and he decides in favour of Mark.

And still more weighty is the fact that the third Gospel, the author of which tells us that he wrote after " many " others had " taken in hand " the same enterprise; who should therefore have known the first Gospel (if it existed), and was bound to pay to it the deference due to the work of an apostolic eye-witness (if he had any reason for thinking it was so)— this writer, who exhibits far more literary competence than the other two, ignores any " Sermon on the Mount," such as that reported by " Matthew," just as much as the oldest authority does. Yet " Luke " has a great many passages identical, or parallel, with those in " Matthew's " " Sermon on the Mount," which are, for the most part, scattered about in a totally different connection.

Interposed, however, between the nomination of the Apostles and a visit to Capernaum; occupying, therefore, a place which answers to that of the " Sermon on the Mount," in the first Gospel, there is, in the third Gospel a discourse which is as closely similar to the " Sermon on the Mount " in some particulars as it is widely unlike it in others.

This discourse is said to have been delivered in a " plain " or " level place " (Luke vi. 17), and by way of distinction we may call it the " Sermon on the Plain."

I see no reason to doubt that the two Evangelists are dealing, to a considerable extent, with the same traditional material; and a comparison of the two " Sermons " suggests very strongly that " Luke's " version is the earlier. The correspondences between the two forbid the notion that they are independent. They both begin with a series of blessings, some of which are almost verbally identical. In the middle of each (Luke vi. 27–38, Matt. v. 43–48) there is a striking exposition of the ethical spirit of the command given in Leviticus xix. 18. And each ends with a passage containing the declaration that a tree is to be known by its fruit, and the parable of the house built on the sand. But while there are only

twenty-nine verses in the " Sermon on the Plain,"
there are one hundred and seven in the " Sermon on
the Mount "; the excess in length of the latter being
chiefly due to the long interpolations, one of thirty
verses before, and one of thirty-four verses after, the
middlemost parallelism with Luke. Under these circumstances it is quite impossible to admit that there
is more probability that " Matthew's " version of the
Sermon is historically accurate than there is that
" Luke's " version is so; and they cannot both be
accurate.

" Luke " either knew the collection of loosely-
connected and aphoristic utterances which appear
under the name of the " Sermon on the Mount " in
" Matthew "; or he did not. If he did not, he must
have been ignorant of the existence of such a document as our canonical " Matthew," a fact which does
not make for the genuineness, or the authority, of
that book. If he did, he has shown that he does not
care for its authority on a matter of fact of no small
importance; and that does not permit us to conceive
that he believed the first Gospel to be the work of an
authority to whom he ought to defer, let alone that
of an apostolic eye-witness.

The tradition of the Church about the second
Gospel, which I believe to be quite worthless, but
which is all the evidence there is for " Mark's "
authorship, would have us believe that " Mark " was
little more than the mouthpiece of the Apostle Peter.
Consequently, we are to suppose that Peter either did
not know, or did not care very much for, that
account of the " essential belief and cardinal teaching" of Jesus which is contained in the " Sermon
on the Mount "; and, certainly, he could not have
shared Dr. Wace's view of its importance.[1]

[1] Holtzmann (*Die synoptischen Evangelien*, 1863, p. 75),
following Ewald, argues that the " Source A " (= the threefold tradition, more or less) contained something that
answered to the " Sermon on the Plain " immediately after
the words of our present " Mark," " And he cometh into a
house " (iii. 19). But what conceivable motive could

I thought that all fairly attentive and intelligent students of the Gospels, to say nothing of theologians of reputation, knew these things. But how can any one who does know them have the conscience to ask whether there is " any reasonable doubt " that the " Sermon on the Mount " was preached by Jesus of Nazareth? If conjecture is permissible, where nothing else is possible, the most probable conjecture seems to be that " Matthew," having a *cento* of sayings attributed—rightly or wrongly it is impossible to say —to Jesus among his materials, thought they were, or might be, records of a continuous discourse, and put them in at the place he thought likeliest. Ancient historians of the highest character saw no harm in composing long speeches which never were spoken, and putting them into the mouths of statesmen and warriors; and I presume that whoever is represented by " Matthew " would have been grievously astonished to find that any one objected to his following the example of the best models accessible to him.

So with the " Lord's Prayer." Absent in our representative of the oldest tradition, it appears in both " Matthew " and " Luke." There is reason to believe that every pious Jew at the commencement of our era prayed three times a day, according to a formula which is embodied in the present " Schmone-Esre " [1] of the Jewish prayer-book. Jesus, who was assuredly, in all respects, a pious Jew, whatever else he may have been, doubtless did the same. Whether he modified the current formula, or whether the so-called " Lord's Prayer " is the prayer substituted for the " Schmone-Esre " in the congregations of the Gentiles, is a question which can hardly be answered.

In a subsequent passage of Dr. Wace's article

" Mark " have for omitting it? Holtzmann has no doubt, however, that the " Sermon on the Mount " is a compilation, or as he calls it in his recently-published *Lehrbuch* (p. 372), " an artificial mosaic work."

[1] See Schürer, *Geschichte des judischen Volkes*, Zweiter Theil, p. 384.

(p. 356) he adds to the list of the verities which he imagines to be unassailable, " The Story of the Passion." I am not quite sure what he means by this. I am not aware that any one (with the exception of certain ancient heretics) has propounded doubts as to the reality of the Crucifixion; and certainly I have no inclination to argue about the precise accuracy of every detail of that pathetic story of suffering and wrong. But if Dr. Wace means, as I suppose he does, that that which, according to the orthodox view, happened after the Crucifixion, and which is, in a dogmatic sense, the most important part of the story, is founded on solid historical proofs, I must beg leave to express a diametrically opposite conviction.

What do we find when the accounts of the events in question, contained in the three Synoptic Gospels, are compared together? In the oldest there is a simple, straightforward statement which, for anything that I have to urge to the contrary, may be exactly true. In the other two there is, round this possible and probable nucleus, a mass of accretions of the most questionable character.

The cruelty of death by crucifixion depended very much upon its lingering character. If there were a support for the weight of the body, as not unfrequently was the practice, the pain during the first hours of the infliction was not, necessarily, extreme; nor need any serious physical symptoms at once arise from the wounds made by the nails in the hands and feet, supposing they were nailed, which was not invariably the case. When exhaustion set in, and hunger, thirst, and nervous irritation had done their work, the agony of the sufferer must have been terrible; and the more terrible that, in the absence of any effectual disturbance of the machinery of physical life, it might be prolonged for many hours, or even days. Temperate, strong men, such as were the ordinary Galilean peasants, might live for several days on the cross. It is necessary to bear these facts in mind when we read the account contained in the fifteenth chapter of the second Gospel.

Jesus was crucified at the third hour (xv. 25), and the narrative seems to imply that he died immediately after the ninth hour (v. 34). In this case, he would have been crucified only six hours; and the time spent on the cross cannot have been much longer, because Joseph of Arimathæa must have gone to Pilate, made his preparations, and deposited the body in the rock-cut tomb before sunset, which, at that time of the year, was about the twelfth hour. That any one should die after only six hours' crucifixion could not have been at all in accordance with Pilate's large experience of the effects of that method of punishment. It, therefore, quite agrees with what might be expected, that Pilate " marvelled if he were already dead " and required to be satisfied on this point by the testimony of the Roman officer who was in command of the execution party. Those who have paid attention to the extraordinarily difficult question, What are the indisputable signs of death?—will be able to estimate the value of the opinion of a rough soldier on such a subject, even if his report to the Procurator were in no wise affected by the fact that the friend of Jesus, who anxiously awaited his answer, was a man of influence and of wealth.

The inanimate body, wrapped in linen, was deposited in a spacious,[1] cool rock chamber, the entrance of which was closed, not by a well-fitting door, but by a stone rolled against the opening, which would of course allow free passage of air. A little more than thirty-six hours afterwards (Friday, 6 P.M., to Sunday, 6 A.M., or a little after) three women visit the tomb and find it empty. And they are told by a young man " arrayed in a white robe " that Jesus is gone to his native country of Galilee, and that the disciples and Peter will find him there.

[1] Spacious, because a young man could sit in it " on the right side " (xv. 5), and therefore with plenty of room to spare.

Thus it stands, plainly recorded, in the oldest tradition that, for any evidence to the contrary, the sepulchre may have been emptied at any time during the Friday or Saturday nights. If it is said that no Jew would have violated the Sabbath by taking the former course, it is to be recollected that Joseph of Arimathæa might well be familiar with that wise and liberal interpretation of the fourth commandment, which permitted works of mercy to men—nay, even the drawing of an ox or an ass out of a pit—on the Sabbath. At any rate, the Saturday night was free to the most scrupulous of observers of the Law.

These are the facts of the case as stated by the oldest extant narrative of them. I do not see why any one should have a word to say against the inherent probability of that narrative; and, for my part, I am quite ready to accept it as an historical fact that so much and no more is positively known of the end of Jesus of Nazareth. On what grounds can a reasonable man be asked to believe any more? So far as the narrative in the first Gospel, on the one hand, and those in the third Gospel and the Acts, on the other, go beyond what is stated in the second Gospel, they are hopelessly discrepant with one another. And this is the more significant because the pregnant phrase " some doubted," in the first Gospel, is ignored in the third.

But it is said that we have the witness Paul speaking to us directly in the Epistles. There is little doubt that we have, and a very singular witness he is. According to his own showing, Paul, in the vigour of his manhood, with every means of becoming acquainted, at first hand, with the evidence of eye-witnesses, not merely refused to credit them, but " persecuted the Church of God and made havoc of it." The reasoning of Stephen fell dead upon the acute intellect of this zealot for the traditions of his fathers : his eyes were blind to the ecstatic illumination of the martyr's countenance " as it had been the face of an angel "; and when, at the words " Behold,

I see the heavens opened and the Son of Man standing on the right hand of God," the murderous mob rushed upon and stoned the rapt disciple of Jesus, Paul ostentatiously made himself their official accomplice.

Yet this strange man, because he has a vision one day, at once, and with equally headlong zeal, flies to the opposite pole of opinion. And he is most careful to tell us that he abstained from any re-examination of the facts.

> Immediately I conferred not with flesh and blood; neither went I up to Jerusalem to them which were Apostles before me; but I went away into Arabia. (Galatians i. 16, 17.)

I do not presume to quarrel with Paul's procedure. If it satisfied him, that was his affair; and if it satisfies any one else, I am not called upon to dispute the right of that person to be satisfied. But I certainly have the right to say that it would not satisfy me in like case; that I should be very much ashamed to pretend that it could, or ought to, satisfy me; and that I can entertain but a very low estimate of the value of the evidence of people who are to be satisfied in this fashion, when questions of objective fact, in which their faith is interested, are concerned. So that when I am called upon to believe a great deal more than the oldest Gospel tells me about the final events of the history of Jesus on the authority of Paul (1 Corinthians xv. 5–8), I must pause. Did he think it, at any subsequent time, worth while " to confer with flesh and blood," or, in modern phrase, to re-examine the facts for himself? or was he ready to accept anything that fitted in with his preconceived ideas? Does he mean, when he speaks of all the appearances of Jesus after the Crucifixion as if they were of the same kind, that they were all visions, like the manifestation to himself? And, finally, how is this account to be reconciled with those in the first and third Gospels—which, as we have seen, disagree with one another?

Until these questions are satisfactorily answered,

I am afraid that, so far as I am concerned, Paul's testimony cannot be seriously regarded, except as it may afford evidence of the state of traditional opinion at the time at which he wrote, say between 55 and 60 A.D.; that is, more than twenty years after the event; a period much more than sufficient for the development of any amount of mythology about matters of which nothing was really known. A few years later, among the contemporaries and neighbours of the Jews, and, if the most probable interpretation of the Apocalypse can be trusted, among the followers of Jesus also, it was fully believed, in spite of all the evidence to the contrary, that the Emperor Nero was not really dead, but that he was hidden away somewhere in the East, and would speedily come again at the head of a great army, to be revenged upon his enemies.[1]

Thus, I conceive that I have shown cause for the opinion that Dr. Wace's challenge touching the "Sermon on the Mount," the "Lord's Prayer," and the Passion was more valorous than discreet. After all this discussion, I am still at the Agnostic point. Tell me, first, what Jesus can be proved to have been, said, and done, and I will say whether I believe him, or in him,[2] or not. As Dr. Wace admits that I have dissipated his lingering shade of unbelief about the bedevilment of the Gadarene pigs, he might have done something to help mine. Instead of that, he manifests a total want of conception of the nature of the obstacles which impede the conversion of his "infidels."

---

[1] King Herod had not the least difficulty in supposing the resurrection of John the Baptist—" John, whom I beheaded, he is risen " (Mark vi. 16).

[2] I am very sorry for the interpolated " in," because citation ought to be accurate in small things as in great. But what difference it makes whether one " believes Jesus " or " believes in Jesus " much thought has not enabled me to discover. If you " believe him " you must believe him to be what he professed to be—that is, " believe in him; " and if you " believe in him " you must necessarily " believe him."

The truth I believe to be that the difficulties in the way of arriving at a sure conclusion as to these matters, from the "Sermon on the Mount," the "Lord's Prayer," or any other data offered by the Synoptic Gospels (and *a fortiori* from the fourth Gospel), are insuperable. Every one of these records is coloured by the prepossessions of those among whom the primitive traditions arose, and of those by whom they were collected and edited : and the difficulty of making allowance for these prepossessions is enhanced by our ignorance of the exact dates at which the documents were first put together; of the extent to which they have been subsequently worked over and interpolated; and of the historical sense, or want of sense, and the dogmatic tendencies of their compilers and editors. Let us see if there is any other road which will take us into something better than negation.

There is a widespread notion that the "primitive Church," while under the guidance of the Apostles and their immediate successors, was a sort of dogmatic dovecot, pervaded by the most loving unity and doctrinal harmony. Protestants, especially, are fond of attributing to themselves the merit of being nearer "the Church of the Apostles" than their neighbours; and they are the less to be excused for their strange delusion because they are great readers of the documents which prove the exact contrary. The fact is that, in the course of the first three centuries of its existence the Church rapidly underwent a process of evolution of the most remarkable character, the final stage of which is far more different from the first than Anglicanism is from Quakerism. The key to the comprehension of the problem of the origin of that which is now called "Christianity," and its relation to Jesus of Nazareth, lies here. Nor can we arrive at any sound conclusion as to what it is probable that Jesus actually said and did, without being clear on this head. By far the most important and subsequently influential steps in the evolution of Christianity took place in the course of the century, more or less, which followed upon the Crucifixion. It is almost the darkest period of Church history, but, most fortunately, the beginning and the end of the period are brightly illuminated by the contemporary evidence of two writers of whose historical existence there is no doubt,[1] and against the genuineness of whose most important works there is no widely-admitted objection. These are Justin, the philsopher and martyr, and Paul, the Apostle to the Gentiles. I shall call upon these witnesses only to testify to the condition of opinion among those who called themselves disciples of Jesus in their time.

Justin, in his Dialogue with Trypho the Jew, which was written somewhere about the middle of the second century, enumerates certain categories of persons who, in his opinion, will, or will not, be saved.[2] These are :—

1. Orthodox Jews who refuse to believe that Jesus is the Christ. *Not Saved.*

2. Jews who observe the Law; believe Jesus to be the Christ; but who insist on the observance of the Law by Gentile converts. *Not Saved.*

3. Jews who observe the Law; believe Jesus to be the Christ, and hold that Gentile converts need not observe the Law. *Saved* (in Justin's opinion; but some of his fellow-Christians think the contrary).

4. Gentile converts to the belief in Jesus as the Christ, who observe the Law. *Saved* (possibly).

5. Gentile believers in Jesus as the Christ, who do not observe the Law themselves (except so far as the refusal of idol sacrifices), but do not consider those who do observe it heretics. *Saved* (this is Justin's own view).

6. Gentile believers who do not observe the Law,

---

[1] True for Justin; but there is a school of theological critics who more or less question the historical reality of Paul and the genuineness of even the four cardinal epistles.

[2] See *Dial. cum Tryphone*, § 47 and § 35. It is to be understood that Justin does not arrange these categories in order, as I have done.

except in refusing idol sacrifices, and hold those who do observe it to be heretics. *Saved*.

7. Gentiles who believe Jesus to be the Christ and call themselves Christians, but who eat meats sacrificed to idols. *Not Saved*.

8. Gentiles who disbelieve in Jesus as the Christ. *Not Saved*.

Justin does not consider Christians who believe in the natural birth of Jesus, of whom he implies that there is a respectable minority, to be heretics, though he himself strongly holds the preternatural birth of Jesus and his pre-existence as the " Logos " or " Word." He conceives the Logos to be a second God, inferior to the first, unknowable God, with respect to whom Justin, like Philo, is a complete Agnostic. The Holy Spirit is not regarded by Justin as a separate personality, and is often mixed up with the " Logos." The doctrine of the natural immortality of the soul is, for Justin, a heresy; and he is as firm a believer in the resurrection of the body as in the speedy Second Coming and the establishment of the millennium.

This pillar of the Church in the middle of the second century—a much-travelled native of Samaria—was certainly well acquainted with Rome, probably with Alexandria; and it is likely that he knew the state of opinion throughout the length and breadth of the Christian world as well as any man of his time. If the various categories above enumerated are arranged in a series thus :—

Justin's Christianity

Orthodox Judaism	Judæo-Christianity					Idolothytic Christianity	Pagan-ism
I.	II.	III.	IV.	V.	VI.	VII.	VIII.

it is obvious that they form a gradational series from orthodox Judaism, on the extreme left, to Paganism, whether philosophic or popular, on the extreme right; and it will further be observed that, while Justin's conception of Christianity is very broad, he rigorously excludes two classes of persons who, in his time, called themselves Christians; namely, those who insist on circumcision and other observances of the Law on the part of Gentile converts : that is to say, the strict Judæo-Christians (II.); and, on the other hand, those who assert the lawfulness of eating meat offered to idols—whether they are Gnostic or not (VII.). These last I have called " idolothytic " Christians, because I cannot devise a better name, not because it is strictly defensible etymologically.

At the present moment, I do not suppose there is an English missionary in any heathen land who would trouble himself whether the materials of his dinner had been previously offered to idols or not. On the other hand, I suppose there is no Protestant sect within the pale of orthodoxy, to say nothing of the Roman and Greek Churches, which would hesitate to declare the practice of circumcision and the observance of the Jewish Sabbath and dietary rules shockingly heretical.

Modern Christianity has, in fact, not only shifted far to the right of Justin's position, but it is of much narrower compass.

	Justin		
	Judæo-	*Modern*	*Pagan-*
	Christianity	*Christianity*	*ism*
Judaism			
I.	II. III. IV. V.	VI. VII.	VIII.

For, though it includes VII., and even, in saint and relic worship, cuts a " monstrous cantle " out of paganism, it excludes, not only all Judæo-Christians, but all who doubt that such are heretics. Ever since the thirteenth century, the Inquisition would have cheerfully burned, and in Spain did abundantly burn, all persons who came under the categories II., III., IV., V. And the wolf would play the same havoc now, if it could only get its blood-stained jaws free from the muzzle imposed by the secular arm.

Further, there is not a Protestant body except the

Unitarian which would not declare Justin himself a heretic, on account of his doctrine of the inferior godship of the Logos; while I am very much afraid that, in strict logic, Dr. Wace would be under the necessity, so painful to him, of calling him an "infidel," on the same and on other grounds.

Now let us turn to our other authority. If there is any result of critical investigations of the sources of Christianity which is certain,[1] it is that Paul of Tarsus wrote the Epistle to the Galatians somewhere between the years 55 and 60 A.D., that is to say, roughly, twenty or five-and-twenty years after the Crucifixion. If this is so, the Epistle to the Galatians is one of the oldest, if not the very oldest, of extant documentary evidences of the state of the primitive Church. And, be it observed, if it is Paul's writing, it unquestionably furnishes us with the evidence of a participator in the transactions narrated. With the exception of two or three of the other Pauline Epistles, there is not one solitary book in the New Testament of the authorship and authority of which we have such good evidence.

And what is the state of things we find disclosed? A bitter quarrel, in his account of which Paul by no means minces matters, or hesitates to hurl defiant sarcasms against those who were "reputed to be pillars": James, "the brother of the Lord," Peter, the rock on whom Jesus is said to have built his Church, and John, "the beloved disciple." And no deference toward "the rock" withholds Paul from charging Peter to his face with "dissimulation."

The subject of the hot dispute was simply this. Were Gentile converts bound to obey the Law or not? Paul answered in the negative; and, acting upon his opinion, he had created at Antioch (and elsewhere) a specifically "Christian" community, the sole qualifications for admission into which were the confession

---

[1] I guard myself against being supposed to affirm that even the four cardinal Epistles of Paul may not have been seriously tampered with. See note 1, p. 181 above.

of the belief that Jesus was the Messiah, and baptism upon that confession. In the Epistle in question, Paul puts this—his " gospel," as he calls it—in its most extreme form. Not only does he deny the necessity of conformity with the Law, but he declares such conformity to have a negative value. " Behold, I, Paul, say unto you, that if ye receive circumcision, Christ will profit you nothing " (Galatians v. 2). He calls the legal observances " beggarly rudiments," and anathematises every one who preaches to the Galatians any other gospel than his own. That is to say, by direct consequence, he anathematises the Nazarenes of Jerusalem, whose zeal for the Law is testified by James in a passage of the Acts cited further on. In the first Epistle to the Corinthians, dealing with the question of eating meat offered to idols, it is clear that Paul himself thinks it a matter of indifference; but he advises that it should not be done, for the sake of the weaker brethren. On the other hand, the Nazarenes of Jerusalem most strenuously opposed Paul's " gospel," insisting on every convert becoming a regular Jewish proselyte, and consequently on his observance of the whole Law; and this party was led by James and Peter and John (Galatians ii. 9). Paul does not suggest that the question of principle was settled by the discussion referred to in Galatians. All he says is, that it ended in the practical agreement that he and Barnabas should do as they had been doing, in respect to the Gentiles; while James and Peter and John should deal in their own fashion with Jewish converts. Afterwards, he complains bitterly of Peter, because, when on a visit to Antioch, he at first inclined to Paul's view and ate with the Gentile converts; but when " certain came from James," " drew back, and separated himself, fearing them that were of the circumcision. And the rest of the Jews dissembled likewise with him; insomuch that even Barnabas was carried away with their dissimulation " (Galatians ii. 12–13).

There is but one conclusion to be drawn from Paul's account of this famous dispute, the settlement of which determined the fortunes of the nascent religion. It is that the disciples at Jerusalem, headed by " James, the Lord's brother," and by the leading apostles, Peter and John, were strict Jews, who had objected to admit any converts into their body unless these, either by birth or by becoming proselytes, were also strict Jews. In fact, the sole difference between James and Peter and John, with the body of the disciples whom they led, and the Jews by whom they were surrounded, and with whom they, for many years, shared the religious observances of the Temple, was that they believed that the Messiah, whom the leaders of the nation yet looked for, had already come in the person of Jesus of Nazareth.

The Acts of the Apostles is hardly a very trustworthy history; it is certainly of later date than the Pauline Epistles, supposing them to be genuine. And the writer's version of the conference of which Paul gives so graphic a description, if that is correct, is unmistakably coloured with all the art of a reconciler, anxious to cover up a scandal. But it is none the less instructive on this account. The judgment of the " council " delivered by James is that the Gentile converts shall merely " abstain from things sacrificed to idols, and from blood and from things strangled, and from fornication." But notwithstanding the accommodation in which the writer of the Acts would have us believe, the Jerusalem Church held to its endeavour to retain the observance of the Law. Long after the conference, some time after the writing of the Epistles to the Galatians and Corinthians, and immediately after the despatch of that to the Romans, Paul makes his last visit to Jerusalem, and presents himself to James and all the elders. And this is what the Acts tells us of the interview :—

And they said unto him, Thou seest, brother, how many thousands [or myriads] there are among the Jews of them which have believed; and they are all zealous for the law;

and they have been informed concerning thee, that thou teachest all the Jews, which are among the Gentiles to forsake Moses, telling them not to circumcise their children, neither to walk after the customs.   (Acts xxi. 20, 21.)

They therefore request that he should perform a certain public religious act in the Temple, in order that

all shall know that there is no truth in the things whereof they have been informed concerning thee; but that thou thyself walkest orderly, keeping the law (*ibid.* 24).[1]

How far Paul could do what he is here requested to do, and which the writer of the Acts goes on to say he did, with a clear conscience, if he wrote the Epistles to the Galatians and Corinthians, I may leave any candid reader of these Epistles to decide.   The point to which I wish to direct attention is the declaration that the Jerusalem Church, led by the brother of Jesus and by his personal disciples and friends, twenty years and more after his death, consisted of strict and zealous Jews.

Tertullus, the orator, caring very little about the internal dissensions of the followers of Jesus, speaks of Paul as a " ringleader of the sect of the Nazarenes " (Acts xxiv. 5), which must have affected James much in the same way as it would have moved the Archbishop of Canterbury, in George Fox's day, to hear the latter called a " ringleader of the sect of Anglicans." In fact, " Nazarene " was, as is well known, the distinctive appellation applied to Jesus; his immediate followers were known as Nazarenes; while the congregation of the disciples, and, later, of converts at Jerusalem—the Jerusalem Church—was emphatically the " sect of the Nazarenes," no more, in itself, to be regarded as anything outside Judaism than the sect of the Sadducees, or that of the Essenes.[2]   In fact,

[1] [Paul, in fact, is required to commit in Jerusalem, an act of the same character as that which he brands as " dissimulation " on the part of Peter in Antioch.]

[2] All this was quite clearly pointed out by Ritschl nearly forty years ago. See *Die Entstehung der alt-katholischen Kirche* (1850), p. 108.

the tenets of both the Sadducees and the Essenes diverged much more widely from the Pharisaic standard of orthodoxy than Nazarenism did.

Let us consider the position of affairs now (A.D. 50–60) in relation to that which obtained in Justin's time, a century later. It is plain that the Nazarenes—presided over by James, " the brother of the Lord," and comprising within their body all the twelve Apostles—belonged to Justin's second category of " Jews who observe the Law, believe Jesus to be the Christ, but who insist on the observance of the Law by Gentile converts," up till the time at which the controversy reported by Paul arose. They then, according to Paul, simply allowed him to form his congregations of non-legal Gentile converts at Antioch and elsewhere; and it would seem that it was to these converts, who would come under Justin's fifth category, that the title of " Christian " was first applied. If any of these Christians had acted upon the more than half-permission given by Paul, and had eaten meats offered to idols, they would have belonged to Justin's seventh category.

Hence it appears that, if Justin's opinion, which was probably that of the Church generally in the middle of the second century, was correct, James and Peter and John and their followers could not be saved; neither could Paul, if he carried into practice his views as to the indifference of eating meats offered to idols. Or, to put the matter another way, the centre of gravity of orthodoxy, which is at the extreme right of the series in the nineteenth century, was at the extreme left, just before the middle of the first century, when the " sect of the Nazarenes " constituted the whole Church founded by Jesus and the Apostles; while in the time of Justin it lay midway between the two. It is therefore a profound mistake to imagine that the Judæo-Christians (Nazarenes and Ebionites) of later times were heretical outgrowths from a primitive universalist " Christianity." On the contrary, the universalist " Christianity " is an outgrowth from the primitive, purely Jewish, Nazarenism; which, gradually eliminating all the ceremonial and dietary parts of the Jewish law, has thrust aside its parent, and all the intermediate stages of its development, into the position of damnable heresies.

Such being the case, we are in a position to form a safe judgment of the limits within which the teaching of Jesus of Nazareth must have been confined. Ecclesiastical authority would have us believe that the words which are given at the end of the first Gospel, " Go ye, therefore, and make disciples of all the nations, baptizing them in the name of the Father and of the Son and of the Holy Ghost," are part of the last commands of Jesus, issued at the moment of his parting with the eleven. If so, Peter and John must have heard these words; they are too plain to be misunderstood; and the occasion is too solemn for them ever to be forgotten. Yet the Acts tells us that Peter needed a vision to enable him so much as to baptize Cornelius; and Paul, in the Galatians, knows nothing of words which would have completely borne him out as against those who, though they heard, must be supposed to have either forgotten or ignored them. On the other hand, Peter and John, who are supposed to have heard the " Sermon on the Mount," know nothing of the saying that Jesus had not come to destroy the Law, but that every jot and tittle of the Law must be fulfilled, which surely would have been pretty good evidence for their view of the question.

We are sometimes told that the personal friends and daily companions of Jesus remained zealous Jews and opposed Paul's innovations, because they were hard of heart and dull of comprehension. This hypothesis is hardly in accordance with the concomitant faith of those who adopt it in the miraculous insight and superhuman sagacity of their Master; nor do I see any way of getting it to harmonise with the orthodox postulate; namely, that Matthew was the author of the first Gospel and John of the fourth.

If that is so, then, most assuredly, Matthew was no dullard; and as for the fourth Gospel—a theosophic romance of the first order—it could have been written by none but a man of remarkable literary capacity, who had drunk deep of Alexandrian philosophy. Moreover, the doctrine of the writer of the fourth Gospel is more remote from that of the " sect of the Nazarenes " than is that of Paul himself. I am quite aware that orthodox critics have been capable of maintaining that John, the Nazarene, who was probably well past fifty years of age when he is supposed to have written the most thoroughly Judaising book in the New Testament—the Apocalypse—in the roughest of Greek, underwent an astounding metamorphosis of both doctrine and style by the time he reached the ripe age of ninety or so, and provided the world with a history in which the acutest critic cannot [always] make out where the speeches of Jesus end and the text of the narrative begins; while that narrative is utterly irreconcilable, in regard to matters of fact, with that of his fellow-Apostle, Matthew.

The end of the whole matter is this :—The " sect of the Nazarenes," the brother and the immediate followers of Jesus, commissioned by him as apostles, and those who were taught by them up to the year 50 A.D., were not " Christians " in the sense in which that term has been understood ever since its asserted origin at Antioch, but Jews—strict orthodox Jews—whose belief in the Messiahship of Jesus never led to their exclusion from the Temple services, nor would have shut them out from the wide embrace of Judaism.[1] The open proclamation of their special view about the Messiah was doubtless offensive to the Pharisees, just as rampant Low Churchism is offensive to bigoted High Churchism in our own country; or as

[1] " If every one was baptized as soon as he acknowledged Jesus to be the Messiah, the first Christians can have been aware of no other essential differences from the Jews."— Zeller, *Vorträge* (1865), p. 26.

any kind of dissent is offensive to fervid religionists of all creeds. To the Sadducees, no doubt, the political danger of any Messianic movement was serious; and they would have been glad to put down Nazarenism, lest it should end in useless rebellion against their Roman masters, like that other Galilean movement headed by Judas a generation earlier. Galilee was always a hotbed of seditious enthusiasm against the rule of Rome; and high priest and procurator alike had need to keep a sharp eye upon natives of that district. On the whole, however, the Nazarenes were but little troubled for the first twenty years of their existence; and the undying hatred of the Jews against those later converts, whom they regarded as apostates and fautors of a sham Judaism, was awakened by Paul. From their point of view, he was a mere renegade Jew, opposed alike to orthodox Judaism and to orthodox Nazarenism; and whose teachings threatened Judaism with destruction. And from their point of view they were quite right. In the course of a century, Pauline influences had a large share in driving primitive Nazarenism from being the very heart of the new faith into the position of scouted error; and the spirit of Paul's doctrine continued its work of driving Christianity farther and farther away from Judaism, until " meats offered to idols " might be eaten without scruple, while the Nazarene methods of observing even the Sabbath, or the Passover, were branded with the mark of Judaising heresy.

But if the primitive Nazarenes of whom the Acts speaks were orthodox Jews, what sort of probability can there be that Jesus was anything else? How can he have founded the universal religion which was not heard of till twenty years after his death?[1] That

---

[1] Dr. Harnack, in the lately-published second edition of his *Dogmengeschichte*, says (p. 39), " Jesus Christ brought forward no new doctrine "; and again, (p. 65), " It is not difficult to set against every portion of the utterances of Jesus an observation which deprives him of originality." See also Zusatz 4, on the same page.

Jesus possessed, in a rare degree, the gift of attaching men to his person and to his fortunes; that he was the author of many a striking saying, and the advocate of equity, of love, and of humility; that he may have disregarded the subtleties of the bigots for legal observance, and appealed rather to those noble conceptions of religion which constituted the pith and kernel of the teaching of the great prophets of his nation seven hundred years earlier; and that, in the last scenes of his career, he may have embodied the ideal sufferer of Isaiah, may be, as I think it is, extremely probable.   But all this involves not a step beyond the borders of orthodox Judaism.   Again, who is to say whether Jesus proclaimed himself the veritable Messiah, expected by his nation since the appearance of the pseudo-prophetic work of Daniel, a century and a half before his time; or whether the enthusiasm of his followers gradually forced him to assume that position?

But one thing is quite certain : if that belief in the speedy second coming of the Messiah which was shared by all parties in the primitive Church, whether Nazarene or Pauline; which Jesus is made to prophesy, over and over again, in the Synoptic Gospels; and which dominated the life of Christians during the first century after the Crucifixion;—if he believed and taught that, then assuredly he was under an illusion, and he is responsible for that which the mere effluxion of time has demonstrated to be a prodigious error.

AGNOSTICISM AND CHRISTIANITY

Nemo ergo ex me scire quærat, quod me nescire scio, nisi forte ut nescire discat.—AUGUSTINUS, *De Civ. Dei,* xii. 7.

THE people who call themselves "Agnostics" have been charged with doing so because they have not the courage to declare themselves "Infidels." It has been insinuated that they have adopted a new name in order to escape the unpleasantness which attaches to their proper denomination. To this wholly erroneous imputation, I have replied by showing that the term "Agnostic" did, as a matter of fact, arise in a manner which negatives it; and my statement has not been, and cannot be, refuted. Moreover, speaking for myself, and without impugning the right of any other person to use the term in another sense, I further say that Agnosticism is not properly described as a "negative" creed, nor indeed as a creed of any kind, except in so far as it expresses absolute faith in the validity of a principle, which is as much ethical as intellectual. This principle may be stated in various ways, but they all amount to this : that it is wrong for a man to say that he is certain of the objective truth of any proposition unless he can produce evidence which logically justifies that certainty. This is what Agnosticism asserts; and, in my opinion, it is all that is essential to Agnosticism. That which Agnostics deny, and repudiate as immoral, is the contrary doctrine, that there are propositions which men ought to believe, without logically satisfactory evidence; and that reprobation ought to attach to the profession of disbelief in such inadequately supported propositions. The justification of the Agnostic principle lies in the success which follows upon its application, whether in the field of natural, or in that of civil, history; and in the fact that, so far as these topics are concerned, no sane man thinks of denying its validity.

Still speaking for myself, I add, that though Agnosticism is not, and cannot be, a creed, except in so far as its general principle is concerned; yet that the application of that principle results in the denial of, or the suspension of judgment concerning, a number of propositions respecting which our contemporary ecclesiastical " gnostics " profess entire certainty. And, in so far as these ecclesiastical persons can be justified in their old-established custom (which many nowadays think more honoured in the breach than the observance) of using opprobrious names to those who differ from them, I fully admit their right to call me and those who think with me " Infidels "; all I have ventured to urge is that they must not expect us to speak of ourselves by that title.

The extent of the region of the uncertain, the number of the problems the investigation of which ends in a verdict of not proven, will vary according to the knowledge and the intellectual habits of the individual Agnostic. I do not very much care to speak of anything as " unknowable." [1] What I am sure about is that there are many topics about which I know nothing; and which, so far as I can see, are out of reach of my faculties. But whether these things are knowable by any one else is exactly one of those matters which is beyond my knowledge, though I may have a tolerably strong opinion as to the probabilities of the case. Relatively to myself, I am quite sure that the region of uncertainty—the nebulous country in which words play the part of realities—is far more extensive than I could wish. Materialism and Idealism; Theism and Atheism; the doctrine of the soul and its mortality or immortality—appear in the history of philosophy like the shades of Scandinavian heroes, eternally slaying one

---

[1] I confess that, long ago, I once or twice made this mistake; even to the waste of a capital " U." 1893.

another and eternally coming to life again in a meta-physical " Nifelheim." It is getting on for twenty-five centuries, at least, since mankind began seriously to give their minds to these topics. Generation after generation, philosophy has been doomed to roll the stone uphill; and, just as all the world swore it was at the top, down it has rolled to the bottom again. All this is written in innumerable books; and he who will toil through them will discover that the stone is just where it was when the work began. Hume saw this; Kant saw it; since their time, more and more eyes have been cleansed of the films which prevented them from seeing it; until now the weight and number of those who refuse to be the prey of verbal mystifications have begun to tell in practical life.

It was inevitable that a conflict should arise between Agnosticism and Theology; or, rather, I ought to say, between Agnosticism and Ecclesiasticism. For Theology, the science, is one thing; and Ecclesiasticism, the championship of a foregone conclusion [1] as to the truth of a particular form of Theology, is another. With scientific Theology, Agnosticism has no quarrel. On the contrary, the Agnostic, knowing too well the influence of prejudice and idiosyncrasy, even on those who desire most earnestly to be impartial, can wish for nothing more urgently than that the scientific theologian should not only be at perfect liberty to thresh out the matter in his own fashion; but that he should, if he can, find flaws in the Agnostic position; and, even if demonstration is not to be had, that he should put, in their full force, the grounds of the conclusions he thinks probable. The scientific theologian admits the Agnostic principle, however widely his results may differ from those reached by the majority of Agnostics.

But, as between Agnosticism and Ecclesiasticism, or, as our neighbours across the Channel call it,

---

[1] " Let us maintain, before we have proved. This seeming paradox is the secret of happiness " (Dr. Newman : Tract 85, p. 85).

Clericalism, there can be neither peace nor truce. The Cleric asserts that it is morally wrong not to believe certain propositions, whatever the results of a strict scientific investigation of the evidence of these propositions. He tells us " that religious error is, in itself, of an immoral nature." [1] He declares that he has prejudged certain conclusions, and looks upon those who show cause for arrest of judgment as emissaries of Satan. It necessarily follows that, for him, the attainment of faith, not the ascertainment of truth, is the highest aim of mental life. And, on careful analysis of the nature of this faith, it will too often be found to be, not the mystic process of unity with the divine, understood by the religious enthusiast; but that which the candid simplicity of a Sunday scholar once defined it to be. " Faith," said this unconscious plagiarist of Tertullian, " is the power of saying you believe things which are incredible."

Now I, and many other Agnostics, believe that faith, in this sense, is an abomination; and though we do not indulge in the luxury of self-righteousness so far as to call those who are not of our way of thinking hard names, we do feel that the disagreement between ourselves and those who hold this doctrine is even more moral than intellectual. It is desirable there should be an end of any mistakes on this topic. If our clerical opponents were clearly aware of the real state of the case, there would be an end of the curious delusion, which often appears between the lines of their writings, that those whom they are so fond of calling " Infidels " are people who not only ought to be, but in their hearts are, ashamed of themselves. It would be discourteous to do more than hint the antipodal opposition of this pleasant dream of theirs to facts.

The clerics and their lay allies commonly tell us that if we refuse to admit that there is good ground for expressing definite convictions about certain

[1] Dr. Newman, *Essay on Development*, p. 357.

topics, the bonds of human society will dissolve and mankind lapse into savagery. There are several answers to this assertion. One is that the bonds of human society were formed without the aid of their theology; and, in the opinion of not a few competent judges, have been weakened rather than strengthened by a good deal of it. Greek science, Greek art, the ethics of old Israel, the social organisation of old Rome, contrived to come into being without the help of any one who believed in a single distinctive article of the simplest of the Christian creeds. The science, the art, the jurisprudence, the chief political and social theories, of the modern world have grown out of those of Greece and Rome—not by favour of, but in the teeth of, the fundamental teachings of early Christianity, to which science, art, and any serious occupation with the things of this world were alike despicable.

Again, all that is best in the ethics of the modern world, in so far as it has not grown out of Greek thought, or Barbarian manhood, is the direct development of the ethics of old Israel. There is no code of legislation, ancient or modern, at once so just and so merciful, so tender to the weak and poor, as the Jewish law; and, if the Gospels are to be trusted, Jesus of Nazareth himself declared that he taught nothing but that which lay implicitly, or explicitly, in the religious and ethical system of his people.

And the scribe said unto him, Of a truth, Teacher, thou hast well said that he is one; and there is none other but he, and to love him with all the heart, and with all the understanding, and with all the strength, and to love his neighbour as himself, is much more than all whole burnt offerings and sacrifices. (Mark xii. 32, 33.)

Here is the briefest of summaries of the teaching of the prophets of Israel of the eighth century; does the Teacher, whose doctrine is thus set forth in his presence, repudiate the exposition? Nay; we are told, on the contrary, that Jesus saw that he " answered discreetly," and replied, " Thou art not far from the kingdom of God."

So that I think that even if the creeds, from the so-called " Apostles' " to the so-called " Athanasian," were swept into oblivion; and even if the human race should arrive at the conclusion that whether a bishop washes a cup or leaves it unwashed is not a matter of the least consequence, it will get on very well. The causes which have led to the development of morality in mankind, which have guided or impelled us all the way from the savage to the civilised state, will not cease to operate because a number of ecclesiastical hypotheses turn out to be baseless. And even if the absurd notion that morality is more the child of speculation than of practical necessity and inherited instinct had any foundation; if all the world is going to thieve, murder, and otherwise misconduct itself as soon as it discovers that certain portions of ancient history are mythical; what is the relevance of such arguments to any one who holds by the Agnostic principle?

Surely, the attempt to cast out Beelzebub by the aid of Beelzebub is a hopeful procedure as compared to that of preserving morality by the aid of immorality. For I suppose it is admitted that an Agnostic may be perfectly sincere, may be competent, and may have studied the question at issue with as much care as his clerical opponents. But, if the Agnostic really believes what he says, the " dreadful consequence " argufier (consistently, I admit, with his own principles) virtually asks him to abstain from telling the truth, or to say what he believes to be untrue, because of the supposed injurious consequences to morality. " Beloved brethren, that we may be spotlessly moral, before all things let us lie," is the sum total of many an exhortation addressed to the " Infidel." Now, as I have already pointed out, we cannot oblige our exhorters. We leave the practical application of the convenient doctrines of " Reserve " and " Nonnatural interpretation " to those who invented them.

I trust that I have now made amends for any ambiguity, or want of fulness, in my previous exposition of that which I hold to be the essence of the Agnostic doctrine. Henceforward, I might hope to hear no more of the assertion that we are necessarily Materialists, Idealists, Atheists, Theists, or any other *ists*, if experience had led me to think that the proved falsity of a statement was any guarantee against its repetition. And those who appreciate the nature of our position will see, at once, that when Ecclesiasticism declares that we ought to believe this, that, and the other, and are very wicked if we don't, it is impossible for us to give any answer but this : We have not the slightest objection to believe anything you like, if you will give us good grounds for belief; but if you cannot we must respectfully refuse, even if that refusal should wreck morality and insure our own damnation several times over. We are quite content to leave that to the decision of the future. The course of the past has impressed us with the firm conviction that no good ever comes of falsehood, and we feel warranted in refusing even to experiment in that direction.

In the course of the present discussion it has been asserted that the " Sermon on the Mount " and the " Lord's Prayer " furnish a summary and condensed view of the essentials of the teaching of Jesus of Nazareth, set forth by himself. Now this supposed *Summa* of Nazarene theology distinctly affirms the existence of a spiritual world, of a heaven, and of a hell of fire; it teaches the Fatherhood of God and the malignity of the Devil; it declares the superintending providence of the former and our need of deliverance from the machinations of the latter; it affirms the fact of demoniac possession and the power of casting out devils by the faithful. And from these premises the conclusion is drawn that those Agnostics who deny that there is any evidence of such a character as to justify certainty, respecting the existence and the nature of the spiritual world, contradict the express declarations of Jesus. I have replied to this argumentation by showing that there is strong reason to doubt the historical accuracy of the attribution to Jesus of either the " Sermon on the Mount " or the " Lord's Prayer " ; and, therefore, that the conclusion in question is not warranted, at any rate, on the grounds set forth.

But, whether the Gospels contain trustworthy statements about this and other alleged historical facts or not, it is quite certain that from them, taken together with the other books of the New Testament, we may collect a pretty complete exposition of that theory of the spiritual world which was held by both Nazarenes and Christians ; and which was undoubtedly supposed by them to be fully sanctioned by Jesus, though it is just as clear that they did not imagine it contained any revelation by him of something heretofore unknown. If the pneumatological doctrine which pervades the whole New Testament is nowhere systematically stated, it is everywhere assumed. The writers of the Gospels and of the Acts take it for granted, as a matter of common knowledge ; and it is easy to gather from these sources a series of propositions, which only need arrangement to form a complete system.

In this system, Man is considered to be a duality formed of a spiritual element, the soul ; and a corporeal [1] element, the body. And this duality is repeated in the Universe, which consists of a corporeal world embraced and interpenetrated by a spiritual world. The former consists of the earth, as its principal and central constituent, with the subsidiary sun, planets, and stars. Above the earth is the air, and below is the watery abyss. Whether the heaven,

---

[1] It is by no means to be assumed that " spiritual " and " corporeal " are exact equivalents of " immaterial " and " material " in the minds of ancient speculators on these topics. The " spiritual body " of the risen dead (1 Cor. xv.) is not the " natural " " flesh and blood " body. Paul does not teach the resurrection of the body in the ordinary sense of the word " body " ; a fact, often overlooked, but pregnant with many consequences.

which is conceived to be above the air, and the hell in, or below, the subterranean deeps, are to be taken as corporeal or incorporeal is not clear. However this may be, the heaven and the air, the earth and the abyss, are peopled by innumerable beings analogous in nature to the spiritual element in man, and these spirits are of two kinds, good and bad. The chief of the good spirits, infinitely superior to all the others, and their creator, as well as the creator of the corporeal world and of the bad spirits, is God. His residence is heaven, where he is surrounded by the ordered hosts of good spirits; his angels, or messengers, and the executors of his will throughout the universe.

On the other hand, the chief of the bad spirits is Satan, *the* devil *par excellence.* He and his company of demons are free to roam through all parts of the universe, except the heaven. These bad spirits are far superior to man in power and subtlety; and their whole energies are devoted to bringing physical and moral evils upon him, and to thwarting, so far as their power goes, the benevolent intentions of the Supreme Being. In fact, the souls and bodies of men form both the theatre and the prize of an incessant warfare between the good and the evil spirits—the powers of light and the powers of darkness. By leading Eve astray, Satan brought sin and death upon mankind. As the gods of the heathen, the demons are the founders and maintainers of idolatry; as the " powers of the air " they afflict mankind with pestilence and famine; as " unclean spirits " they cause disease of mind and body.

The significance of the appearance of Jesus, in the capacity of the Messiah, or Christ, is the reversal of the satanic work by putting an end to both sin and death. He announces that the kingdom of God is at hand, when the " Prince of this world " shall be finally " cast out " (John xii. 31) from the cosmos, as Jesus, during his earthly career, cast him out from individuals. Then will Satan and all his devilry,

along with the wicked whom they have seduced to
their destruction, be hurled into the abyss of unquench-
able fire—there to endure continual torture, without
a hope of winning pardon from the merciful God, their
Father; or of moving the glorified Messiah to one
more act of pitiful intercession; or even of interrupting, by a momentary sympathy with their
wretchedness, the harmonious psalmody of their
brother angels and men, eternally lapped in bliss
unspeakable.

The straitest Protestant, who refuses to admit the
existence of any source of divine truth, except the
Bible, will not deny that every point of the pneumatological theory here set forth has ample scriptural
warranty. The Gospels, the Acts, the Epistles, and
the Apocalypse assert the existence of the devil, of
his demons and of hell, as plainly as they do that of
God and his angels and heaven. It is plain that the
Messianic and the Satanic conceptions of the writers
of these books are the obverse and the reverse of the
same intellectual coinage. If we turn from Scripture
to the traditions of the Fathers and the confessions
of the Churches, it will appear that, in this one particular at any rate, time has brought about no important deviation from primitive belief. From Justin
onwards, it may often be a fair question whether God,
or the devil, occupies a larger share of the attention
of the Fathers. It is the devil who instigates the
Roman authorities to persecute; the gods and god-
desses of paganism are devils, and idolatry itself is
an invention of Satan; if a saint falls away from
grace, it is by the seduction of the demon; if heresy
arises, the devil has suggested it; and some of the
Fathers [1] go so far as to challenge the pagans to a
sort of exorcising match, by way of testing the truth

---

[1] Tertullian (*Apolog. adv. Gentes,* cap. xxiii.) thus challenges
the Roman authorities : let them bring a possessed person
into the presence of a Christian before their tribunal; and if
the demon does not confess himself to be such, on the order
of the Christian, let the Christian be executed out of hand.

of Christianity. Mediæval Christianity is at one with patristic on this head. The masses, the clergy, the theologians, and the philosophers alike, live and move and have their being in a world full of demons, in which sorcery and possession are everyday occurrences. Nor did the Reformation make any difference. Whatever else Luther assailed, he left the traditional demonology untouched; nor could any one have entertained a more hearty and uncompromising belief in the devil than he and, at a later period, the Calvinistic fanatics of New England did. Finally, in these last years of the nineteenth century the demonological hypotheses of the first century are, explicitly or implicitly, held and occasionally acted upon by the immense majority of Christians of all confessions.

Only here and there has the progress of scientific thought, outside the ecclesiastical world, so far affected Christians that they and their teachers fight shy of the demonology of their creed. They are fain to conceal their real disbelief in one half of Christian doctrine by judicious silence about it; or by flight to those refuges for the logically destitute, accommodation or allegory. But the faithful who fly to allegory in order to escape absurdity resemble nothing so much as the sheep in the fable who—to save their lives—jumped into the pit. The allegory pit is too commodious, is ready to swallow up so much more than one wants to put into it. If the story of the Temptation is an allegory; if the early recognition of Jesus as the Son of God by the demons is an allegory; if the plain declaration of the writer of the first Epistle of John (iii. 8), " To this end was the Son of God manifested, that He might destroy the works of the devil," is allegorical, then the Pauline version of the Fall may be allegorical, and still more the words of consecration of the Eucharist, or the promise of the Second Coming; in fact, there is not a dogma of ecclesiastical Christianity the scriptural basis of which may not be whittled away by a similar process.

As to accommodation, let any honest man who can

read the New Testament ask himself whether Jesus and his immediate friends and disciples can be dishonoured more grossly than by the supposition that they said and did that which is attributed to them; while, in reality, they disbelieved in Satan and his demons, in possession, and in exorcism?[1]

An eminent theologian has justly observed that we have no right to look at the propositions of the Christian faith with one eye open and the other shut. (Tract 85, p. 29.)   It really is not permissible to see, with one eye, that Jesus is affirmed to declare the personality and the Fatherhood of God, his loving providence and his accessibility to prayer; and to shut the other to the no less definite teaching ascribed to Jesus, in regard to the personality and the misanthropy of the devil, his malignant watchfulness, and his subjection to exorcistic formulæ and rites. Jesus is made to say that the devil " was a murderer from the beginning " (John viii. 44) by the same authority as that upon which we depend for his asserted declaration that " God is a spirit " (John iv. 24).

To those who admit the authority of the famous Vincentian dictum that the doctrine which has been held " always, everywhere, and by all " is to be received as authoritative, the demonology must possess a higher sanction than any other Christian dogma, except, perhaps, those of the Resurrection and of the Messiahship of Jesus; for it would be difficult to name any other points of doctrine on which the Nazarene does not differ from the Christian, and the different historical stages and contemporary subdivisions of Christianity from one another.   And, if the demonology is accepted, there can be no reason for rejecting all those miracles in which demons play a part.   The Gadarene story fits into the general scheme of Christianity; and the evidence for " Legion " and their doings is just as good as any

---

[1] See the expression of orthodox opinion upon the " accommodation " subterfuge already cited above, pp. 147 and 148.

other in the New Testament for the doctrine which the story illustrates.

It was with the purpose of bringing this great fact into prominence; of getting people to open both their eyes when they look at Ecclesiasticism; that I devoted so much space to that miraculous story which happens to be one of the best types of its class. And I could not wish for a better justification of the course I have adopted, than the fact that my heroically consistent adversary has declared his implicit belief in the Gadarene story and (by necessary consequence) in the Christian demonology as a whole. It must be obvious by this time that, if the account of the spiritual world given in the New Testament, professedly on the authority of Jesus, is true, then the demonological half of that account must be just as true as the other half. And, therefore, those who question the demonology, or try to explain it away, deny the truth of what Jesus said, and are, in ecclesiastical terminology, " Infidels " just as much as those who deny the spirituality of God. This is as plain as anything can well be, and the dilemma for my opponent was either to assert that the Gadarene pig-bedevilment actually occurred, or to write himself down an " Infidel." As was to be expected, he chose the former alternative; and I may express my great satisfaction at finding that there is one spot of common ground on which both he and I stand. So far as I can judge, we are agreed to state one of the broad issues between the consequences of agnostic principles (as I draw them), and the consequences of ecclesiastical dogmatism (as he accepts it), as follows.

Ecclesiasticism says: The demonology of the Gospels is an essential part of that account of that spiritual world, the truth of which it declares to be certified by Jesus.

Agnosticism (*me judice*) says: There is no good evidence of the existence of a demoniac spiritual world, and much reason for doubting it.

Hereupon the ecclesiastic may observe: Your

doubt means that you disbelieve Jesus; therefore you are an " Infidel " instead of an " Agnostic." To which the Agnostic may reply : No; for two reasons : first, because your evidence that Jesus said what you say he said is worth very little; and secondly, because a man may be an Agnostic, in the sense of admitting he has no positive knowledge, and yet consider that he has more or less probable ground for accepting any given hypothesis about the spiritual world. Just as a man may frankly declare that he has no means of knowing whether the planets generally are inhabited or not, and yet may think one of the two possible hypotheses more likely than the other, so he may admit that he has no means of knowing anything about the spiritual world, and yet may think one or other of the current views on the subject, to some extent, probable.

The second answer is so obviously valid that it needs no discussion. I draw attention to it simply in justice to those Agnostics who may attach greater value than I do to any sort of pneumatological speculations; and not because I wish to escape the responsibility of declaring that, whether Jesus sanctioned the demonological part of Christianity or not, I unhesitatingly reject it. The first answer, on the other hand, opens up the whole question of the claim of the biblical and other sources, from which hypotheses concerning the spiritual world are derived, to be regarded as unimpeachable historical evidence as to matters of fact.

Now, in respect of the trustworthiness of the Gospel narratives, I was anxious to get rid of the common assumption that the determination of the authorship and of the dates of these works is a matter of fundamental importance. That assumption is based upon the notion that what contemporary witnesses say must be true, or, at least, has always a *prima facie* claim to be so regarded; so that if the writers of any of the Gospels were contemporaries of the events (and still more if they were in the position of eye-witnesses), the miracles they narrate must be historically true, and, consequently, the demonology which they involve must be accepted. But the story of the " Translation of the blessed martyrs Marcellinus and Petrus," and the other considerations (to which endless additions might have been made from the Fathers and the mediæval writers) set forth in a preceding essay, yield, in my judgment, satisfactory proof that, where the miraculous is concerned, neither considerable intellectual ability, nor undoubted honesty, nor knowledge of the world, nor proved faithfulness as civil historians, nor profound piety, on the part of eye-witnesses and contemporaries, affords any guarantee of the objective truth of their statements, when we know that a firm belief in the miraculous was ingrained in their minds, and was the presupposition of their observations and reasonings.

Therefore, although it be, as I believe, demonstrable that we have no real knowledge of the authorship, or of the date of composition, of the Gospels, as they have come down to us, and that nothing better than more or less probable guesses can be arrived at on that subject, I have not cared to expend any space on the question. It will be admitted, I suppose, that the authors of the works attributed to Matthew, Mark, Luke, and John, whoever they may be, are personages whose capacity and judgment in the narration of ordinary events are not quite so well certified as those of Eginhard; and we have seen what the value of Eginhard's evidence is when the miraculous is in question.

I have been careful to explain that the arguments which I have used in the course of this discussion are not new; that they are historical, and have nothing to do with what is commonly called science; and that they are all, to the best of my belief, to be found in the works of theologians of repute.

The position which I have taken up, that the evidence in favour of such miracles as those recorded by Eginhard, and consequently of mediæval demonology, is quite as good as that in favour of such miracles as the Gadarene, and consequently of Nazarene demonology, is none of my discovery. Its strength was, wittingly or unwittingly, suggested, a century and a half ago, by a theological scholar of eminence; and it has been, if not exactly occupied, yet so fortified with bastions and redoubts by a living ecclesiastical Vauban, that, in my judgment, it has been rendered impregnable. In the early part of the last century, the ecclesiastical mind in this country was much exercised by the question, not exactly of miracles, the occurrence of which in biblical times was axiomatic, but by the problem : When did miracles cease? Anglican divines were quite sure that no miracles had happened in their day, nor for some time past; they were equally sure that they happened sixteen or seventeen centuries earlier. And it was a vital question for them to determine at what point of time, between this *terminus a quo* and that *terminus ad quem*, miracles came to an end.

The Anglicans and the Romanists agreed in the assumption that the possession of the gift of miracle-working was *prima facie* evidence of the soundness of the faith of the miracle-workers. The supposition that miraculous powers might be wielded by heretics (though it might be supported by high authority) led to consequences too frightful to be entertained by people who were busied in building their dogmatic house on the sands of early Church history. If, as the Romanists maintained, an unbroken series of genuine miracles adorned the records of their Church throughout the whole of its existence, no Anglican could lightly venture to accuse them of doctrinal corruption. Hence, the Anglicans, who indulged in such accusations, were bound to prove the modern, the mediæval Roman, and the later Patristic, miracles false; and to shut off the wonder-working power from the Church at the exact point of time when Anglican doctrine ceased and Roman doctrine began. With a little adjustment—a squeeze here and a pull there—

the Christianity of the first three or four centuries might be made to fit, or seem to fit, pretty well into the Anglican scheme. So the miracles, from Justin say to Jerome, might be recognised; while in later times, the Church having become " corrupt "—that is to say, having pursued one and the same line of development further than was pleasing to Anglicans— its alleged miracles must needs be shams and impostures.

Under these circumstances, it may be imagined that the establishment of a scientific frontier between the earlier realm of supposed fact and the later of asserted delusion had its difficulties; and torrents of theological special pleading about the subject flowed from clerical pens; until that learned and acute Anglican divine, Conyers Middleton, in his *Free Inquiry*, tore the sophistical web they had laboriously woven to pieces, and demonstrated that the miracles of the patristic age, early and late, must stand or fall together, inasmuch as the evidence for the later is just as good as the evidence for the earlier wonders. If the one set are certified by contemporaneous witnesses of high repute, so are the other; and in point of probability there is not a pin to choose between the two. That is the solid and irrefragable result of Middleton's contribution to the subject. But the Free Inquirer's freedom had its limits; and he draws a sharp line of demarcation between the patristic and the New Testament miracles—on the professed ground that the accounts of the latter, being inspired, are out of the reach of criticism.

A century later, the question was taken up by another divine, Middleton's equal in learning and acuteness, and far his superior in subtlety and dialectic skill; who, though an Anglican, scorned the name of Protestant; and, while yet a Churchman, made it his business to parade, with infinite skill, the utter hollowness of the arguments of those of his brother Churchmen who dreamed that they could be both Anglicans and Protestants. The argument of the *Essay on the*

Miracles recorded in the Ecclesiastical History of the Early Ages,[1] by the present [1889] Roman Cardinal, but then Anglican Doctor, John Henry Newman, is compendiously stated by himself in the following passage :—

If the miracles of Church history cannot be defended by the arguments of Leslie, Lyttelton, Paley, or Douglas, how many of the Scripture miracles satisfy their conditions? (P. cvii.)

And, although the answer is not given in so many words, little doubt is left on the mind of the reader that in the mind of the writer it is : None. In fact, this conclusion is one which cannot be resisted, if the argument in favour of the Scripture miracles is based upon that which laymen, whether lawyers, or men of science, or historians, or ordinary men of affairs, call evidence. But there is something really impressive in the magnificent contempt with which, at times, Dr. Newman sweeps aside alike those who offer and those who demand such evidence.

Some infidel authors advise us to accept no miracles which would not have a verdict in their favour in a court of justice; that is, they employ against Scripture a weapon which Protestants would confine to attacks upon the Church; as if moral and religious questions required legal proof, and evidence were the test of truth [2] (p. cvii).

" As if evidence were the test of truth ! "—although the truth in question is the occurrence, or the non-occurrence, of certain phenomena at a certain time and in a certain place. This sudden revelation of

[1] I quote the first edition (1843). A second edition appeared in 1870. Tract 85 of the *Tracts for the Times* should be read with this *Essay*. If I were called upon to compile a Primer of " Infidelity," I think I should save myself trouble by making a selection from these works, and from the *Essay on Development* by the same author.

[2] Yet, when it suits his purpose, as in the Introduction to the *Essay on Development*, Dr. Newman can demand strict evidence in religious questions as sharply as any " infidel author "; and he can even profess to yield to its force (*Essay on Miracles*, 1870; note, p. 391).

the great gulf fixed between the ecclesiastical and the scientific mind is enough to take away the breath of any one unfamiliar with the clerical organon. As if, one may retort, the assumption that miracles may, or have, served a moral or a religious end, in any way alters the fact that they profess to be historical events, things that actually happened; and, as such, must needs be exactly those subjects about which evidence is appropriate and legal proofs (which are such merely because they afford adequate evidence) may be justly demanded. The Gadarene miracle either happened, or it did not. Whether the Gadarene " question " is moral or religious, or not, has nothing to do with the fact that it is a purely historical question whether the demons said what they are declared to have said, and the devil-possessed pigs did, or did not, rush over the heights bounding the Lake of Gennesaret on a certain day of a certain year, after A.D. 26 and before A.D. 36; for, vague and uncertain as New Testament chronology is, I suppose it may be assumed that the event in question, if it happened at all, took place during the procuratorship of Pilate. If that is not a matter about which evidence ought to be required, and not only legal, but strict scientific, proof demanded by sane men who are asked to believe the story—what is? Is a reasonable being to be seriously asked to credit statements which, to put the case gently, are not exactly probable, and on the acceptance or rejection of which his whole view of life may depend, without asking for as much " legal " proof as would send an alleged pickpocket to gaol, or as would suffice to prove the validity of a disputed will?

" Infidel authors " (if, as I am assured, I may answer for them) will decline to waste time on mere darkenings of counsel of this sort; but to those Anglicans who accept his premises, Dr. Newman is a truly formidable antagonist. What, indeed, are they to reply when he puts the very pertinent question :—

whether persons who not merely question, but prejudge the Ecclesiastical miracles on the ground of their want of resemblance, whatever that be, to those contained in Scripture—as if the Almighty could not do in the Christian Church what He had not already done at the time of its foundation, or under the Mosaic Covenant—whether such reasoners are not siding with the sceptic,

and

whether it is not a happy inconsistency by which they continue to believe the Scriptures while they reject the Church [1] (p. liii).

Again, I invite Anglican orthodoxy to consider this passage :—

the narrative of the combats of St. Antony with evil spirits, is a development rather than a contradiction of revelation, viz. of such texts as speak of Satan being cast out by prayer and fasting. To be shocked, then, at the miracles of Ecclesiastical history, or to ridicule them for their strangeness, is no part of a scriptural philosophy (pp. liii–liv).

Further on, Dr. Newman declares that it has been admitted

that a distinct line can be drawn in point of character and circumstance between the miracles of Scripture and of Church history; but this is by no means the case (p. lv). . . . specimens are not wanting in the history of the Church, of miracles as awful in their character and as momentous in their effects as those which are recorded in Scripture. The fire interrupting the rebuilding of the Jewish Temple, and the death of Arius, are instances, in Ecclesiastical history, of such solemn events. On the other hand, difficult instances in the Scripture history are such as these : the serpent in Eden, the Ark, Jacob's vision for the multiplication of his cattle, the speaking of Balaam's ass, the axe swimming at Elisha's word, the miracle on the swine, and various instances of prayers or prophecies, in which, as in that of Noah's blessing and curse, words which seem the result of private feeling are expressly or virtually ascribed to a Divine suggestion (p. lvi).

Who is to gainsay our ecclesiastical authority here? " Infidel authors " might be accused of a wish to ridicule the Scripture miracles by putting them on a

---

[1] Compare Tract 85, p. 110: " I am persuaded that were men but consistent who oppose the Church doctrines as being unscriptural, they would vindicate the Jews for rejecting the Gospel."

level with the remarkable story about the fire which
stopped the rebuilding of the Temple, or that about
the death of Arius—but Dr. Newman is above suspicion. The pity is that his list of what he delicately
terms " difficult " instances is so short. Why omit
the manufacture of Eve out of Adam's rib, on the
strict historical accuracy of which the chief argument
of the defenders of an iniquitous portion of our present
marriage law depends? Why leave out the account
of the " Bene Elohim " and their gallantries, on which
a large part of the worst practices of the mediæval
inquisitors into witchcraft was based? Why forget
the angel who wrestled with Jacob, and, as the account
suggests, somewhat overstepped the bounds of fair
play at the end of the struggle? Surely, we must
agree with Dr. Newman that, if all these camels have
gone down, it savours of affectation to strain at such
gnats as the sudden ailment of Arius in the midst of
his deadly, if prayerful,[1] enemies; and the fiery
explosion which stopped the Julian building operations. Though the *words* of the " Conclusion " of the
Essay on Miracles may, perhaps, be quoted against
me, I may express my satisfaction at finding myself
in substantial accordance with a theologian above all
suspicion of heterodoxy. With all my heart, I can
declare my belief that there is just as good reason for
believing in the miraculous slaying of the man who fell
short of the Athanasian power of affirming con-

---

[1] According to Dr. Newman, " This prayer [that of Bishop
Alexander, who begged God to ' take Arius away '] is said to
have been offered about 3 P.M. on the Saturday; that same
evening Arius was in the great square of Constantine, when he
was suddenly seized with indisposition " (p. clxx). The
" infidel " Gibbon seems to have dared to suggest that " an
option between poison and miracle " is presented by this
case; and, it must be admitted, that, if the Bishop had been
within the reach of a modern police magistrate, things might
have gone hardly with him. Modern " Infidels," possessed
of a slight knowledge of chemistry, are not unlikely, with no
less audacity, to suggest an " option between firedamp and
miracle " in seeking for the cause of the fiery outburst at
Jerusalem.

tradictories, with respect to the nature of the God-head, as there is for believing in the stories of the serpent and the ark told in Genesis, the speaking of Balaam's ass in Numbers, or the floating of the axe, at Elisha's order, in the Second Book of Kings.

It is one of the peculiarities of a really sound argument that it is susceptible of the fullest development; and that it sometimes leads to conclusions unexpected by those who employ it. To my mind, it is impossible to refuse to follow Dr. Newman when he extends his reasoning from the miracles of the patristic and mediæval ages backward in time as far as miracles are recorded. But if the rules of logic are valid, I feel compelled to extend the argument forwards to the alleged Roman miracles of the present day, which Dr. Newman might not have admitted, but which Cardinal Newman may hardly reject. Beyond question, there is as good, or perhaps better, evidence of the miracles worked by our Lady of Lourdes as there is for the floating of Elisha's axe or the speaking of Balaam's ass. But we must go still further; there is a modern system of thaumaturgy and demonology which is just as well certified as the ancient.[1] Veracious, excellent, sometimes learned

---

[1] A writer in a spiritualist journal takes me roundly to task for venturing to doubt the historical and literal truth of the Gadarene story. The following passage in his letter is worth quotation : " Now to the materialistic and scientific mind, to the uninitiated in spiritual verities, certainly this story of the Gadarene or Gergesene swine presents insurmountable difficulties; it seems grotesque and nonsensical. To the experienced, trained, and cultivated Spiritualist this miracle is, as I am prepared to show, one of the most instructive, the most profoundly useful, and the most beneficent which Jesus ever wrought in the whole course of His pilgrimage of redemption on earth." Just so. And the first page of this same journal presents the following advertisement, among others of the same kidney :—

" To WEALTHY SPIRITUALISTS.—A Lady Medium of tried power wishes to meet with an elderly gentleman who would be willing to give her a comfortable home and maintenance in Exchange for her Spiritualistic services, as her guides consider

and acute persons, even philosophers of no mean pretensions, testify to the " levitation " of bodies much heavier than Elisha's axe; to the existence of " spirits " who, to the mere tactile sense, have been indistinguishable from flesh and blood; and, occasionally, have wrestled with all the vigour of Jacob's opponent; yet, further, to the speech, in the language of raps, of spiritual beings, whose discourses, in point of coherence and value, are far inferior to that of Balaam's humble but sagacious steed. I have not the smallest doubt that if these were persecuting times there is many a worthy " spiritualist " who would cheerfully go to the stake in support of his pneumatological faith, and furnish evidence, after Paley's own heart, in proof of the truth of his doctrines. Not a few modern divines, doubtless struck by the impossibility of refusing the spiritualist evidence, if the ecclesiastical evidence is accepted, and deprived of any *a priori* objection by their implicit belief in Christian Demonology, show themselves ready to take poor Sludge seriously, and to believe that he is possessed by other devils than those of need, greed, and vainglory.

Under these circumstances, it was to be expected, though it is none the less interesting to note the fact, that the arguments of the latest school of " spiritualists " present a wonderful family likeness to those which adorn the subtle disquisitions of the advocate of ecclesiastical miracles of forty years ago. It is unfortunate for the " spiritualists " that, over and over again, celebrated and trusted media, who really, in some respects, call to mind the Montanist [1] and

---

her health is too delicate for public sittings : London preferred. —Address ' Mary,' Office of *Light*."

Are we going back to the days of the Judges, when wealthy Micah set up his private ephod, teraphim, and Levite?

[1] Consider Tertullian's " sister " (*hodie apud nos*), who conversed with angels, saw and heard mysteries, knew men's thoughts, and prescribed medicine for their bodies (*De Anima.* cap. 9). Tertullian tells us that this woman saw the soul as corporeal, and described its colour and shape. The " infidel " will probably be unable to refrain from insulting the memory

Gnostic seers of the second century, are either proved in courts of law to be fraudulent impostors; or, in sheer weariness, as it would seem, of the honest dupes who swear by them, spontaneously confess their long-continued iniquities, as the Fox women did the other day in New York.[1]   But whenever a catastrophe of this kind takes place, the believers are no wise dismayed by it.   They freely admit that not only the media, but the spirits whom they summon, are sadly apt to lose sight of the elementary principles of right and wrong; and they triumphantly ask : How does the occurrence of occasional impostures disprove the genuine manifestations (that is to say, all those which have not yet been proved to be impostures or delusions)?   And in this they unconsciously plagiarise from the churchman, who just as freely admits that many ecclesiastical miracles may have been forged; and asks, with calm contempt, not only of legal proofs, but of common-sense probability : Why does it follow that none are to be supposed genuine?   I must say, however, that the spiritualists, so far as I know, do not venture to outrage right reason so boldly as the ecclesiastics.   They do not sneer at " evidence "; nor repudiate the requirement of legal proofs.   In fact, there can be no doubt that the spiritualists produce better evidence for their manifestations than can be shown either for the miraculous death of Arius, or for the Invention of the Cross.[2]

of the ecstatic saint by the remark that Tertullian's known views about the corporeality of the soul may have had something to do with the remarkable perceptive powers of the Montanist medium, in whose revelations of the spiritual world he took such profound interest.

[1] See the New York *World* for Sunday, 21st October, 1888; and the *Report of the Seybert Commission*, Philadelphia, 1887.

[2] Dr. Newman's observation that the miraculous multiplication of the pieces of the true cross (with which " the whole world is filled," according to Cyril of Jerusalem; and of which some say there are enough extant to build a man-of-war) is no more wonderful than that of the loaves and fishes, is one that I do not see my way to contradict. See *Essay on Miracles*, 2d ed. p. 163.

From the " levitation " of the axe at one end of a period of near three thousand years to the " levitation " of Sludge & Co. at the other end, there is a complete continuity of the miraculous, with every gradation from the childish to the stupendous, from the gratification of a caprice to the illustration of sublime truth. There is no drawing a line in the series that might be set out of plausibly attested cases of spiritual intervention. If one is true, all may be true; if one is false, all may be false.

This is, to my mind, the inevitable result of that method of reasoning which is applied to the confutation of Protestantism, with so much success, by one of the acutest and subtlest disputants who have ever championed Ecclesiasticism—and one cannot put his claims to acuteness and subtlety higher.

. . . the Christianity of history is not Protestantism. If ever there were a safe truth it is this. . . . " To be deep in history is to cease to be a Protestant." [1]

I have not a shadow of doubt that these anti-Protestant epigrams are profoundly true. But I have as little that, in the same sense, the " Christianity of history is not " Romanism; and that to be deeper in history is to cease to be a Romanist. The reasons which compel my doubts about the compatibility of the Roman doctrine, or any other form of Catholicism, with history, arise out of exactly the same line of argument as that adopted by Dr. Newman in the famous essay which I have just cited. If with one hand Dr. Newman has destroyed Protestantism, he has annihilated Romanism with the other; and the total result of his ambidextral efforts is to shake Christianity to its foundations. Nor was any one better aware that this must be the inevitable result of his arguments—if the world should refuse to accept Roman doctrines and Roman miracles—than the writer of Tract 85.

[1] *An Essay on the Development of Christian Doctrine*, by J. H. Newman, D.D., pp. 7 and 8. (1878.)

Dr. Newman made his choice, and passed over to the Roman Church half a century ago. Some of those who were essentially in harmony with his views preceded, and many followed him. But many remained; and, as the quondam Puseyite and present Ritualistic party, they are continuing that work of sapping and mining the Protestantism of the Anglican Church which he and his friends so ably commenced. At the present time, they have no little claim to be considered victorious all along the line. I am old enough to recollect the small beginnings of the Tractarian party; and I am amazed when I consider the present position of their heirs. Their little leaven has leavened, if not the whole, yet a very large lump of the Anglican Church; which is now pretty much of a preparatory school for Papistry. So that it really behoves Englishmen (who, as I have been informed by high authority, are all legally members of the State Church, if they profess to belong to no other sect) to wake up to what that powerful organisation is about, and whither it is tending. On this point, the writings of Dr. Newman, while he still remained within the Anglican fold, are a vast store of the best and the most authoritative information. His doctrines on Ecclesiastical miracles and on Development are the corner-stones of the Tractarian fabric. He believed that his arguments led either Romeward, or to what ecclesiastics call "Infidelity," and I call Agnosticism. I believe that he was quite right in this conviction; but while he chooses the one alternative, I choose the other; as he rejects Protestantism on the ground of its incompatibility with history, so, *a fortiori*, I conceive that Romanism ought to be rejected; and that an impartial consideration of the evidence must refuse the authority of Jesus to anything more than the Nazarenism of James and Peter and John. And let it not be supposed that this is a mere "Infidel" perversion of the facts. No one has more openly and clearly admitted the possibility that they may be fairly interpreted in this way than Dr. Newman. If, he says, there are texts which seem to show that Jesus contemplated the evangelisation of the heathen :

. . . Did not the Apostles hear our Lord? and what was *their* impression from what they heard? Is it not certain that the Apostles did not gather this truth from His teaching? (Tract 85, p. 63.)

He said, " Preach the Gospel to every creature." These words *need* have only meant " Bring all men to Christianity through Judaism." Make them Jews, that they may enjoy Christ's privileges, which are lodged in Judaism; teach them those rites and ceremonies, circumcision and the like, which hitherto have been dead ordinances, and now are living : and so the Apostles seem to have understood them (*ibid.* p. 65).

So far as Nazarenism differentiated itself from contemporary orthodox Judaism, it seems to have tended towards a revival of the ethical and religious spirit of the prophetic age, accompanied by the belief in Jesus as the Messiah, and by various accretions which had grown round Judaism subsequently to the exile. To these belong the doctrines of the Resurrection, of the Last Judgment, of Heaven and Hell; of the hierarchy of good angels; of Satan and the hierarchy of evil spirits. And there is very strong ground for believing that all these doctrines, at least in the shapes in which they were held by the post-exilic Jews, were derived from Persian and Babylonian [1] sources, and are essentially of heathen origin.

How far Jesus positively sanctioned all these indrainings of circumjacent Paganism into Judaism; how far any one has a right to declare that the refusal to accept one or other of these doctrines, as ascertained verities, comes to the same thing as contradicting Jesus, it appears to me not easy to say. But it is hardly less difficult to conceive that he could have distinctly negatived any of them; and, more

---

[1] Dr. Newman faces this question with his customary ability. " Now, I own, I am not at all solicitous to deny that this doctrine of an apostate Angel and his hosts was gained from Babylon : it might still be Divine nevertheless. God who made the prophet's ass speak, and thereby instructed the prophet, might instruct His Church by means of heathen Babylon " (Tract 85, p. 83). There seems to be no end to the apologetic burden that Balaam's ass can carry.

especially, that demonology which has been accepted by the Christian Churches, in every age and under all their mutual antagonisms. But I repeat my conviction that, whether Jesus sanctioned the demonology of his time and nation or not, it is doomed. The future of Christianity, as a dogmatic system, and apart from the old Israelitish ethics which it has appropriated and developed, lies in the answer which mankind will eventually give to the question, whether they are prepared to believe such stories as the Gadarene and the pneumatological hypotheses which go with it, or not. My belief is they will decline to do anything of the sort, whenever and wherever their minds have been disciplined by science. And that discipline must, and will, at once follow and lead the footsteps of advancing civilisation.

The preceding pages were written before I became acquainted with the contents of the May number of the *Nineteenth Century*, wherein I discover many things which are decidedly not to my advantage. It would appear that " evasion " is my chief resource, "incapacity for strict argument " and " rottenness of ratiocination " my main mental characteristics, and that it is " barely credible " that a statement which I profess to make of my own knowledge is true. All which things I notice, merely to illustrate the great truth, forced on me by long experience, that it is only from those who enjoy the blessing of a firm hold of the Christian faith that such manifestations of meekness, patience, and charity are to be expected.

I had imagined that no one who had read my preceding papers could entertain a doubt as to my position in respect of the main issue, as it has been stated and restated by my opponent :

an Agnosticism which knows nothing of the relation of man to God must not only refuse belief to our Lord's most undoubted teaching, but must deny the reality of the spiritual convictions in which He lived.[1]

---

[1] *Nineteenth Century*, May 1889 (p. 701).

That is said to be " the simple question which is at issue between us," and the three testimonies to that teaching and those convictions selected are the " Sermon on the Mount," the " Lord's Prayer," and the Story of the Passion.

My answer, reduced to its briefest form, has been : In the first place, the evidence is such that the exact nature of the teachings and the convictions of Jesus is extremely uncertain; so that what ecclesiastics are pleased to call a denial of them may be nothing of the kind. And, in the second place, if Jesus taught the demonological system involved in the Gadarene story —if a belief in that system formed a part of the spiritual convictions in which he lived and died—then I, for my part, unhesitatingly refuse belief in that teaching, and deny the reality of those spiritual convictions. And I go further, and add that, exactly in so far as it can be proved that Jesus sanctioned the essentially pagan demonological theories current among the Jews of his age, exactly in so far, for me, will his authority in any matter touching the spiritual world be weakened.

With respect to the first half of my answer, I have pointed out that the " Sermon on the Mount," as given in the first Gospel, is, in the opinion of the best critics, a " mosaic work " of materials derived from different sources, and I do not understand that this statement is challenged. The only other Gospel—the third— which contains something like it, makes, not only the discourse, but the circumstances under which it was delivered, very different. Now, it is one thing to say that there was something real at the bottom of the two discourses—which is quite possible; and another to affirm that we have any right to say what that something was, or to fix upon any particular phrase and declare it to be a genuine utterance. Those who pursue theology as a science, and bring to the study an adequate knowledge of the ways of ancient historians, will find no difficulty in providing illustrations of my meaning. I may supply one which has come within range of my own limited vision.

In Josephus's *History of the Wars of the Jews* (chap. xix.),that writer reports a speech which he says Herod made at the opening of a war with the Arabians. It is in the first person, and would naturally be supposed by the reader to be intended for a true version of what Herod said.   In the *Antiquities*, written some seventeen years later, the same writer gives another report, also in the first person, of Herod's speech on the same occasion.   This second oration is twice as long as the first, and though the general tenor of the two speeches is pretty much the same, there is hardly any verbal identity, and a good deal of matter is introduced into the one which is absent from the other.   Josephus prides himself on his accuracy; people whose fathers might have heard Herod's oration were his contemporaries; and yet his historical sense is so curiously undeveloped that he can, quite innocently, perpetrate an obvious literary fabrication; for one of the two accounts must be incorrect.   Now, if I am asked whether I believe that Herod made some particular statement on this occasion; whether, for example, he uttered the pious aphorism, "Where God is, there is both multitude and courage," which is given in the *Antiquities*, but not in the *Wars*, I am compelled to say I do not know.   One of the two reports must be erroneous, possibly both are : at any rate, I cannot tell how much of either is true.   And, if some fervent admirer of the Idumean should build up a theory of Herod's piety upon Josephus's evidence that he propounded the aphorism, is it a " mere evasion " to say, in reply, that the evidence that he did utter it is worthless?

It appears again that, adopting the tactics of Conachar when brought face to face with Hal o' the Wynd, I have been trying to get my simple-minded adversary to follow me on a wild-goose chase through the early history of Christianity, in the hope of escaping impending defeat on the main issue.   But I may be permitted to point out that there is an alternative hypothesis which equally fits the facts;

and that, after all, there may have been method in the madness of my supposed panic.

For suppose it to be established that Gentile Christianity was a totally different thing from the Nazarenism of Jesus and his immediate disciples; suppose it to be demonstrable that, as early as the sixth decade of our era at least, there were violent divergencies of opinion among the followers of Jesus; suppose it to be hardly doubtful that the Gospels and the Acts took their present shapes under the influence of those divergencies; suppose that their authors, and those through whose hands they passed, had notions of historical veracity not more eccentric than those which Josephus occasionally displays : surely the chances that the Gospels are altogether trustworthy records of the teaching of Jesus become very slender. And, since the whole of the case of the other side is based on the supposition that they are accurate records (especially of speeches, about which ancient historians are so curiously loose), I really do venture to submit that this part of my argument bears very seriously on the main issue; and, as ratiocination, is sound to the core.

Again, when I passed by the topic of the speeches of Jesus on the Cross, it appears that I could have had no other motive than the dictates of my native evasiveness. An ecclesiastical dignitary may have respectable reasons for declining a fencing match " in sight of Gethsemane and Calvary "; but an ecclesiastical " Infidel " ! Never. It is obviously impossible that, in the belief that " the greater includes the less," I, having declared the Gospel evidence in general, as to the sayings of Jesus, to be of questionable value, thought it needless to select for illustration of my views those particular instances which were likely to be most offensive to persons of another way of thinking. But any supposition that may have been entertained that the old familiar tones of the ecclesiastical wardrum will tempt me to engage in such needless discussion had better be renounced. I shall do nothing of the kind. Let it suffice that I ask my readers to turn to the twenty-third chapter of Luke (Revised Version), verse thirty-four, and he will find in the margin

Some ancient authorities omit : And Jesus said, " Father, forgive them, for they know not what they do."

So that, even as late as the fourth century, there were ancient authorities, indeed some of the most ancient and weightiest, who either did not know of this utterance, so often quoted as characteristic of Jesus, or did not believe it had been uttered.

Many years ago, I received an anonymous letter, which abused me heartily for my want of moral courage in not speaking out. I thought that one of the oddest charges an anonymous letter-writer could bring. But I am not sure that the plentiful sowing of the pages of the article with which I am dealing with accusations of evasion may not seem odder to those who consider that the main strength of the answers with which I have been favoured (in this review and elsewhere) is devoted, not to anything in the text of my first paper, but to a note which occurs at p. 144. In this I say :

Dr. Wace tells us : " It may be asked how far we can rely on the accounts we possess of our Lord's teaching on these subjects." And he seems to think the question appropriately answered by the assertion that it " ought to be regarded as settled by M. Renan's practical surrender of the adverse case."

I requested Dr. Wace to point out the passages of M. Renan's works in which, as he affirms, this " practical surrender " (not merely as to the age and authorship of the Gospels, be it observed, but as to their historical value) is made, and he has been so good as to do so. Now let us consider the parts of Dr. Wace's citation from Renan which are relevant to the issue :—

The author of this Gospel [Luke] is certainly the same as the author of the Acts of the Apostles. Now the author of the Acts seems to be a companion of St. Paul—a character which accords completely with St. Luke. I know that more than one objection may be opposed to this reasoning : but one thing, at all events, is beyond doubt, namely, that the author of the third Gospel and of the Acts is a man who belonged to the second apostolic generation; and this suffices for our purpose.

This is a curious " practical surrender of the adverse case."   M. Renan thinks that there is no doubt that the author of the third Gospel is the author of the Acts—a conclusion in which I suppose critics generally agree.   He goes on to remark that this person *seems* to be a companion of St. Paul, and adds that Luke was a companion of St. Paul.   Then, somewhat needlessly, M. Renan points out that there is more than one objection to jumping from such data as these to the conclusion that " Luke " is the writer of the third Gospel.   And, finally, M. Renan is content to reduce that which is " beyond doubt " to the fact that the author of the two books is a man of the second apostolic generation.   Well, it seems to me that I could agree with all that M. Renan considers " beyond doubt " here, without surrendering anything, either " practically " or theoretically.

Dr. Wace (*Nineteenth Century*, March, p. 363) states that he derives the above citation from the preface to the 15th edition of the *Vie de Jésus*.   My copy of *Les Évangiles*, dated 1877, contains a list of Renan's " Œuvres Complètes," at the head of which I find *Vie de Jésus*, 15ᵉ édition.   It is, therefore, a later work than the edition of the *Vie de Jésus* which Dr. Wace quotes.   Now *Les Évangiles*, as its name implies, treats fully of the questions respecting the date and authorship of the Gospels; and any one who desired, not merely to use M. Renan's expressions for controversial purposes, but to give a fair account of his views in their full significance, would, I think, refer to the later source.

If this course had been taken, Dr. Wace might have found some as decided expressions of opinion, in favour of Luke's authorship of the third Gospel, as he has discovered in *The Apostles.* I mention this circumstance because I desire to point out that, taking even the strongest of Renan's statements, I am still at a loss to see how it justifies that large-sounding phrase, " practical surrender of the adverse case." For, on p. 438 of *Les Évangiles,* Renan speaks of the way in which Luke's " excellent intentions " have led him to torture history in the Acts ; he declares Luke to be the founder of that "eternal fiction which is called ecclesiastical history " ; and on the preceding page he talks of the " myth " of the Ascension—with its " *mise en scène voulue.*" At p. 435, I find " *Luc, ou l'auteur quel qu'il soit du troisième Évangile* " ; at p. 280, the accounts of the Passion, the death and the resurrection of Jesus, are said to be " *peu historiques* " ; at p. 283, " *La valeur historique du troisième Évangile est sûrement moindre que celles des deux premiers.*" A Pyrrhic sort of victory for orthodoxy, this " surrender " ! And, all the while, the scientific student of theology knows that, the more reason there may be to believe that Luke was the companion of Paul, the more doubtful becomes his credibility, if he really wrote the Acts. For, in that case, he could not fail to have been acquainted with Paul's account of the Jerusalem conference, and he must have consciously misrepresented it.

We may next turn to the essential part of Dr. Wace's citation (*Nineteenth Century,* p. 365) touching the first Gospel :—

St. Matthew evidently deserves peculiar confidence for the discourses. Here are the " oracles "—the very notes taken while the memory of the instruction of Jesus was living and definite.

M. Renan here expresses the very general opinion as to the existence of a collection of " logia," having a different origin from the text in which they are embedded, in Matthew. " Notes " are somewhat suggestive of a shorthand writer, but the suggestion is unintentional, for M. Renan assumes that these " notes " were taken, not at the time of the delivery of the " logia," but subsequently, while (as he assumes) the memory of them was living and definite; so that, in this very citation, M. Renan leaves open the question of the general historical value of the first Gospel; while it is obvious that the accuracy of " notes " taken, not at the time of delivery, but from memory, is a matter about which more than one opinion may be fairly held. Moreover, Renan expressly calls attention to the difficulty of distinguishing the authentic " logia " from later additions of the same kind (*Les Évangiles*, p. 201). The fact is, there is no contradiction here to that opinion about the first Gospel which is expressed in *Les Évangiles* (p. 175).

The text of the so-called Matthew supposes the pre-existence of that of Mark, and does little more than complete it. He completes it in two fashions—first, by the insertion of those long discourses which gave their chief value to the Hebrew Gospels; then by adding traditions of a more modern formation, results of successive developments of the legend, and to which the Christian consciousness already attached infinite value.

M. Renan goes on to suggest that besides " Mark," " Pseudo-Matthew " used an Aramaic version of the Gospel, originally set forth in that dialect. Finally, as to the second Gospel (*Nineteenth Century*, p. 365):—

He [Mark] is full of minute observations, proceeding, beyond doubt, from an eye-witness. There is nothing to conflict with the supposition that this eye-witness . . . was the Apostle Peter himself, as Papias has it.

Let us consider this citation by the light of *Les Évangiles* :—

This work, although composed after the death of Peter, was, in a sense, the work of Peter; it represents the way in which Peter was accustomed to relate the life of Jesus (p. 116).

M. Renan goes on to say that, as an historical document, the Gospel of Mark has a great superiority (p. 116); but Mark has a motive for omitting the discourses, and he attaches a " puerile importance " to miracles (p. 117). The Gospel of Mark is less a legend, than a biography written with credulity (p. 118). It would be rash to say that Mark has not been interpolated and retouched (p. 120).

If any one thinks that I have not been warranted in drawing a sharp distinction between " scientific theologians " and " counsels for creeds "; or that my warning against the too-ready acceptance of certain declarations as to the state of biblical criticism was needless; or that my anxiety as to the sense of the word " practical " was superfluous; let him compare the statement that M. Renan has made a " practical surrender of the adverse case " with the facts just set forth. For what is the adverse case? The question, as Dr. Wace puts it, is: " It may be asked, How far can we rely on the accounts we possess of our Lord's teaching on these subjects? " It will be obvious that M. Renan's statements amount to an adverse answer—to a " practical " denial that any great reliance can be placed on these accounts. He does not believe that Matthew, the Apostle, wrote the first Gospel; he does not profess to know who is responsible for the collection of " logia," or how many of them are authentic; though he calls the second Gospel the most historical, he points out that it is written with credulity, and may have been interpolated and retouched; and as to the author, " quel qu'il soit," of the third Gospel, who is to " rely on the accounts " of a writer who deserves the cavalier treatment which " Luke " meets with at M. Renan's hands?

I repeat what I have already more than once said, that the question of the age and the authorship of the Gospels has not, in my judgment, the importance which is so commonly assigned to it; for the simple reason that the reports, even of eye-witnesses, would not suffice to justify belief in a large and essential part of their contents; on the contrary, these reports would discredit the witnesses. The Gadarene miracle, for example, is so extremely improbable that the fact of its being reported by three, even independent, authorities could not justify belief in it, unless we had the clearest evidence as to their capacity as observers and as interpreters of their observations. But it is evident that the three authorities are not independent; that they have simply adopted a legend, of which there were two versions; and instead of their proving its truth, it suggests their superstitious credulity: so that if " Matthew," " Mark," and " Luke " are really responsible for the Gospels, it is not the better for the Gadarene story, but the worse for them.

A wonderful amount of controversial capital has been made out of my assertion in the note to which I have referred, as an *obiter dictum* of no consequence to my argument, that if Renan's work [1] were non-extant the main results of biblical criticism, as set forth in the works of Strauss, Baur, Reuss, and Volkmar, for example, would not be sensibly affected. I thought I had explained it satisfactorily already, but it seems that my explanation has only exhibited still more of my native perversity, so I ask for one more chance.

In the course of the historical development of any branch of science, what is universally observed is this: that the men who make epochs, and are the real architects of the fabric of exact knowledge, are those who introduce fruitful ideas or methods. As a rule, the man who does this pushes his idea, or his method, too far; or, if he does not, his school is sure to do so; and those who follow have to reduce his work to its proper value, and assign it its place in the whole. Not unfrequently they, in their turn, overdo the critical process, and in trying to eliminate error throw away truth.

Thus, as I said, Linnæus, Buffon, Cuvier, Lamarck, really " set forth the results " of a developing science, although they often heartily contradict one another. Notwithstanding this circumstance, modern classificatory method and nomenclature have largely grown out of the work of Linnæus: the modern conception

[1] I trust it may not be supposed that I undervalue M. Renan's labours, or intended to speak slightingly of them.

of biology as a science, and of its relation to clima-
tology, geography, and geology, is as largely rooted
in the results of the labours of Buffon; comparative
anatomy and palæontology owe a vast debt to Cuvier's
results; while invertebrate zoology and the revival of
the idea of evolution are intimately dependent on the
results of the work of Lamarck. In other words, the
main results of biology up to the early years of this
century are to be found in, or spring out of, the works
of these men.

So, if I mistake not, Strauss, if he did not originate
the idea of taking the mythopœic faculty into account
in the development of the Gospel narratives, and
though he may have exaggerated the influence of that
faculty, obliged scientific theology, hereafter, to take
that element into serious consideration; so Baur, in
giving prominence to the cardinal fact of the divergence
of the Nazarene and Pauline tendencies in the primitive Church; so Reuss, in setting a marvellous example of the cool and dispassionate application of the
principles of scientific criticism over the whole field of
Scripture; so Volkmar, in his clear and forcible statement of the Nazarene limitations of Jesus, contributed
results of permanent value in scientific theology.   I
took these names as they occurred to me.   Undoubtedly, I might have advantageously added to
them; perhaps I might have made a better selection.
But it really is absurd to try to make out that I did
not know that these writers widely disagree; and I
believe that no scientific theologian will deny that,
in principle, what I have said is perfectly correct.
Ecclesiastical advocates, of course, cannot be expected
to take this view of the matter.   To them, these mere
seekers after truth, in so far as their results are
unfavourable to the creed the clerics have to support,
are more or less " Infidels," or favourers of " infidelity "; and the only thing they care to see, or
probably can see, is the fact that in a great many
matters the truth-seekers differ from one another, and
therefore can easily be exhibited to the public as if

they did nothing else; as if any one who referred to their having, each and all, contributed his share to the results of theological science was merely showing his ignorance; and as if a charge of inconsistency could be based on the fact that he himself often disagrees with what they say. I have never lent a shadow of foundation to the assumption that I am a follower of either Strauss, or Baur, or Reuss, or Volkmar, or Renan; my debt to these eminent men—so far my superiors in theological knowledge—is, indeed, great; yet it is not for their opinions, but for those I have been able to form for myself, by their help.

In *Agnosticism: a Rejoinder*, I have referred to the difficulties under which those professors of the science of theology whose tenure of their posts depends on the results of their investigations must labour; and, in a note, I add :—

Imagine that all our chairs of Astronomy had been founded in the fourteenth century, and that their incumbents were bound to sign Ptolemaic articles. In that case, with every respect for the efforts of persons thus hampered to attain and expound the truth, I think men of common sense would go elsewhere to learn astronomy.

I did not write this paragraph without a knowledge that its sense would be open to the kind of perversion which it has suffered; but, if that was clear, the necessity for the statement was still clearer. It is my deliberate opinion: I reiterate it; and I say that, in my judgment, it is extremely inexpedient that any subject which calls itself a science should be entrusted to teachers who are debarred from freely following out scientific methods to their legitimate conclusions, whatever those conclusions may be. If I may borrow a phrase paraded at the Church Congress, I think it "ought to be unpleasant" for any man of science to find himself in the position of such a teacher.

Human nature is not altered by seating it in a professional chair, even of theology. I have very little doubt that if, in the year 1859, the tenure of my office had depended upon my adherence to the doctrines of Cuvier, the objections to them set forth in the *Origin of Species* would have had a halo of gravity about them that, being free to teach what I pleased, I failed to discover. And, in making that statement, it does not appear to me that I am confessing that I should have been debarred by " selfish interests " from making candid inquiry, or that I should have been biassed by "sordid motives." I hope that even such a fragment of moral sense as may remain in an ecclesiastical " infidel " might have got me through the difficulty; but it would be unworthy to deny, or disguise, the fact that a very serious difficulty must have been created for me by the nature of my tenure. And let it be observed that the temptation, in my case, would have been far slighter than in that of a professor of theology; whatever biological doctrine I had repudiated, nobody I cared for would have thought the worse of me for so doing. No scientific journals would have howled me down, as the religious newspapers howled down my too-honest friend, the late Bishop of Natal; nor would my colleagues of the Royal Society have turned their backs upon me, as his episcopal colleagues boycotted him.

I say these facts are obvious, and that it is wholesome and needful that they should be stated. It is in the interests of theology, if it be a science, and it is in the interests of those teachers of theology who desire to be something better than counsel for creeds, that it should be taken to heart. The seeker after theological truth, and that only, will no more suppose that I have insulted him than the prisoner who works in fetters will try to pick a quarrel with me if I suggest that he would get on better if the fetters were knocked off; unless indeed, as it is said does happen in the course of long captivities, that the victim at length ceases to feel the weight of his chains, or even takes to hugging them as if they were honourable ornaments.

ORDER FORM

GREAT BOOKS IN PHILOSOPHY PAPERBACK SERIES

ETHICS

Aristotle—*The Nicomachean Ethics*	$8.95
Marcus Aurelius—*Meditations*	5.95
Jeremy Bentham—*The Principles of Morals and Legislation*	8.95
Epictetus—*Enchiridion*	3.95
Immanuel Kant—*Fundamental Principles of the Metaphysic of Morals*	4.95
John Stuart Mill—*Utilitarianism*	4.95
George Edward Moore—*Principia Ethica*	8.95
Friedrich Nietzsche—*Beyond Good and Evil*	8.95
Bertrand Russell On Ethics, Sex, and Marriage (edited by Al Seckel)	17.95
Benedict de Spinoza—*Ethics* and *The Improvement of the Understanding*	9.95

SOCIAL AND POLITICAL PHILOSOPHY

Aristotle—*The Politics*	7.95
The Basic Bakunin: Writings, 1869–1871 (translated and edited by Robert M. Cutler)	10.95
Edmund Burke—*Reflections on the Revolution in France*	7.95
John Dewey—*Freedom and Culture*	10.95
G. W. F. Hegel—*The Philosophy of History*	9.95
Thomas Hobbes—*The Leviathan*	7.95
Sidney Hook—*Paradoxes of Freedom*	9.95
Sidney Hook—*Reason, Social Myths, and Democracy*	11.95
John Locke—*Second Treatise on Civil Government*	4.95
Niccolo Machiavelli—*The Prince*	4.95
Karl Marx/Frederick Engels—*The Economic and Philosophic Manuscripts of 1844* and *The Communist Manifesto*	6.95
John Stuart Mill—*Considerations on Representative Government*	6.95
John Stuart Mill—*On Liberty*	4.95
John Stuart Mill—*On Socialism*	7.95

John Stuart Mill—*The Subjection of Women* 4.95
Thomas Paine—*Rights of Man* 7.95
Plato—*The Republic* 9.95
Plato on Homosexuality: Lysis, Phaedrus, and *Symposium* 6.95
Jean-Jacques Rousseau—*The Social Contract* 5.95
Mary Wollstonecraft—*A Vindication of the Rights of Women* 6.95

METAPHYSICS/EPISTEMOLOGY

Aristotle—*De Anima* 6.95
Aristotle—*The Metaphysics* 9.95
George Berkeley—*Three Dialogues Between Hylas and
   Philonous* 4.95
René Descartes—*Discourse on Method* and *The Meditations* 6.95
John Dewey—*How We Think* 10.95
Sidney Hook—*The Quest for Being* 11.95
David Hume—*An Enquiry Concerning Human Understanding* 4.95
David Hume—*Treatise of Human Nature* 9.95
William James—*Pragmatism* 7.95
Immanuel Kant—*Critique of Pure Reason* 9.95
Plato—*The Euthyphro, Apology, Crito,* and *Phaedo* 5.95
Bertrand Russell—*The Problems of Philosophy* 8.95
Sextus Empiricus—*Outlines of Pyrrhonism* 8.95

PHILOSOPHY OF RELIGION

Ludwig Feuerbach—*The Essence of Christianity* 7.95
David Hume—*Dialogues Concerning Natural Religion* 4.95
John Locke—*A Letter Concerning Toleration* 3.95
Thomas Paine—*The Age of Reason* 13.95
Bertrand Russell On God and Religion (edited by Al Seckel) 17.95

SPECIAL—For your library . . . the entire collection of 48 "Great Books in Philosophy" and 7 "Great Minds" available at a savings of more than 15%. Only $330.00 for the "Great Books" and $62.00 for the "Great Minds" (plus $12.00 postage and handling). Please indicate "Great Books/Great Minds—Complete Set" on your order form.

The books listed can be obtained from your book dealer or directly from Prometheus Books. Please indicate the appropriate titles. Remittance must accompany all orders from individuals. Please include $3.50 postage and handling for the first book and $1.75 for each additional title (maximum $12.00, NYS residents please add applicable sales tax). Books will be shipped fourth-class book post. **Prices subject to change without notice.**

Send to _____
(Please type or print clearly)

Address _____

City _____ State _____ Zip _____

Amount enclosed _____

Charge my ☐ **VISA** ☐ **MasterCard**

Account # ⬚⬚⬚⬚⬚⬚⬚⬚⬚⬚⬚⬚⬚⬚⬚⬚⬚⬚

Exp. Date _____/_____ Tel.# _____

Signature _____

Prometheus Books Editorial Offices
700 E. Amherst St., Buffalo, New York 14215

Distribution Facilities
59 John Glenn Drive, Amherst, New York 14228

Phone Orders call toll free: (800) 421-0351
FAX: (716) 691-0137
Please allow 3-6 weeks for delivery